The *Long Enduring* ROAD TO SUCCESS

Published by: Good Vibes Records & Music Ltd
Registered Office: Philwise Limited, Ferndale Ave, Chertsey, Surrey KT16 9RB
Website: www.goodvibesonline.co.uk
Email: gvrm@email.com

The Long Enduring Road to Success

First published in Great Britain 2015

Joyce Rennie-Pascall: Editorial and Creative Design Management
Alex Pascall Esq: O.B.E: Sub-Editor
Graphic Designer: Loulita Gill
Cover Illustration: AllyDay Creative Projects Ltd

Printed & Bound in Great Britain by SSMedia Ltd

CIP: Catalogue Record for this book from the British Library, London, UK
ISBN: 978-0-9935312-0-0

The Long Enduring ROAD TO SUCCESS

Valentino A Jones

GOOD VIBES RECORDS & MUSIC Ltd

Men who are honest are not afraid
of consequences.

MARCUS GARVEY

Dedication

This book is dedicated
to the Estate Labourers of the 1950's.
Those who preceded them;
and those who followed after.

Our singers, composers and musicians
Must be encouraged
To sing the song of struggle,
Resistance to degradation,
Resistance to our humiliation,
Resistance to the eradication
Of all our values
That would keep us going as a country.
Our actors and sculptors and painters
And writers and poets
Must be made to know that
We appreciate them,
That in fact it is their work
That put starch in our back bone.

MAYA ANGELOU

Foreword

Valentino Jones' "Long Enduring Road to Success" is an exceptionally entertaining literary exercise. Firstly, it is uncompromisingly grounded in the realities of the Grenadian social, economic, religious, physical, intellectual and cultural landscape.

The discerning, perceptive, able and aware reader has no problem in allowing himself\herself to accompany the protagonist, Doc, on that journey towards self-actualization.

Secondly, the varying themes of slavery, greed, one-upmanship, love, poverty, struggle, companionship and eventual success in the face of adversity, encourage one to identify with the challenges of the characters.

Finally, one can only admire Velma's (Doc's girlfriend and future wife) decisiveness; her temerity and her goal-driver resolve to maintain her feminine purity, even when it seemed so easy to succumb to the fallible, and indeed, foibles of youthfulness.

Brilliant! This story is firmly entrenched in the Grenadian psyche.

Clyde A. Belfon

Language Arts Lecturer/Writer
Teacher Education Department
T.A. Marryshow Community College
Grenada.

Contents

The road ahead is piled high
with difficulties.
We must meet these difficulties
and crush them.

CHARLES DICKENS

Book One

The Rocky Boys

- I -

Doc, Ghost, Cold Coucou Face and Mud Mask, collectively known as the Rocky Boys, met on the first day of their summer holidays at the old Ticket Gate of the Telescope horse racing track, situated at the top of the hill that overlooked La Baye – the Grenville town and harbour. (The inhabitants of the parish preferred this old French colonial name to the English colonial name of Grenville) – some currents running stronger than blood, clashing incessantly like the waves of history that had pushed the town there, allowing coral straits for the schooners to berth and provide some supplies for the east of the island, export Grenadian produce or help empty the island of its able-bodied population, who would go away to help the imperial and other developing countries build their dreams.

The sea rolled like Ms. Stella's currant rolls, bursting their salty champagne tears all the way from Africa, and further afield, to the Caribbean – sweetening less and less the island's sugarcane fields, its farm lands, the life of yard boys. When the easterlies were strong, the Atlantic Ocean's dress would be adorned with white frills for miles, salting the air and the land, fertilising Grenada with one of the richest soils in the world and its ordinary people with little money for their hopes to live on.

Ten minutes away from Grenville, Telescope is a small village to the east of the island of Grenada, in the parish of Saint Andrew with a population of less than a hundred people. The villagers lived generally in small, wooden, two bedroom houses – common to the 1900's generation; they lived like one large family. Their board houses had wooden shingles on their sides and were pinned to the hem of the mud road or hanging like a bell at the end of the spider web footpaths that snaked their way through former plantation lands; the once dispossessed possessed great deal of land, the lands their ancestors were enslaved to.

In front of the houses were little flower gardens with roses, anthurium lilies, queen of flowers and fern fencing. At their sides and back would be fruit trees: guava, coconut, mango, a gospo tree, an orange or some other citrus. Somewhere on their smallholdings there would be a little kitchen garden where ground provision would be cultivated, and plantain, bluggoe and different species of banana grown.

It was not uncommon to find the boli tree or saffron, and many other medicinal herbs around. But there was only so much one could grow on his small plot, so different families would specialise in certain products and everyone would live off the free supplies of nature from the estates.

The yard fowls would sleep high up in one of the trees in the yard at nights, protected from the hunting eyes of the mongoose, rats or manicou, or the unholy hands that might seek to wring their necks into purgatory at a devil hour in the night to make a stolen pot. They would roam freely in the day, the rooster marshalling his harem and fertilising them as he pleased in broad daylight, where youthful eyes could spy. King Rooster would knife down the cockerels, youthful, solitary upstarts who dared to challenge his power in his colonial domains. These young challengers would have to kill their father's power over them or stalk his reign or travel from his place that might have been home, to plant their seeds in another land. Their mothers would not cackle a word, for their natural bonding was cut once a chick had grown into his or her own.

Never challenge Mother Hen with her young brood; she would freeze your life in you with the alarm bells in her throat. She would screech the hell out of you, whether you be Goliath or goose, lifting her porcupine feathers of defence and the butchering knife in her accelerating pecking beak, defending her offspring by land and air.

The families in Telescope were generally large in number: five, eight, nine, ten, as the fertility of the groins would brood on grounds that knew no contraceptive, except abstinence, withdrawal, or the ladies' herbs which turned some inexperienced or overzealous mothers into humus, manure, that would nourish other mothers' dreams of a controlled family or a desired pregnancy.

Large families were common in the islands. Numbers and hunger too, for the small kitchen gardens that hemmed the houses could never produce enough food or wealth to fully sustain manhood, womanhood, much less family and the pleasure of racing a horse through the length of Telescope. The lack of money made you feel poor, think poor, see poor, be poor, not just in spirit but in the very essence of your being that would draw the very flavours out of your life, if it were possible.

The poor would come to Telescope horse racing track, from near and far, to gamble with the wealthy; gamble their hard earned cash from the fields on a horse that was neither theirs nor their fathers'. They enjoyed the sweetness of a molasses moment, the illusion of instant galloping victory; the delusion that they were on par with the wealthy – for a season – or that they would surprise their wives and children at home, returning rich enough to buy a new bed or so.

When they returned to their modest homes rich with their losses and a wealth of experience, the boli whips of their wives' tongues awaited them to tread the mills of muscles that carved their backs and arms and buttocks and thighs, just like the season of canes. The race horses sighed smoke at the poor man's dreams of fools' gold, as horse owners jockeyed home wealthier, taking back the cash they had paid out their hard working island labourers.

Wives waited at home to knead the dough of their men's failures and senseless pleasures at the betting in the salty winds of the Atlantic Ocean, their eyes cutting with a salty miserable glare.

If their men won, well it was party time. He was the luckiest man in the world and another child might be conceived to eat out future possible victories.

The Ticket Gate at the Telescope race track was a cool place for the Rocky Boys to meet and knit their films of life; it was a symbol of activity, success, power, harmony, where the wealthy and the poor would meet for the cane flower of a season of horse racing – one side asserting, flaunting its power and influence; the other its desires and dreams that would pass in the smoke of a moment and settling like cooked ground provision at the depressed bottom of a meatless sangcoach. The Rocky Boys called the Gate their Forum, their European culture trotting, trampling in their veins. But they were torn between two continents, no three, their culture knitted together with the vines of Time! They had stripped their name from a film they had seen and hung it on the tapestry of their lives.

The Forum was their usual meeting place, their Rome in Grenada of the 1950's, where they would ole talk and ting: shoot Jazz, tease people, chat up the girls that passed by, plan mischief and feel time go by. This was the day they were waiting for: the end of Term. But it was more than that; it was the end of school for them and hello to life and adulthood, because their parents could not afford to pay their Secondary Education; and they had not worked hard enough for the limited scholarships available.

The Rocky Boys had attended different religious primary/ elementary schools in the area – R.C. Anglican, Methodist, which had given them an oil down of colonial and religious education. Now they were free but not independent; graduated but not men; work-worthy but unemployed; rich in dreams and poor in means. They were like their mother's half-cooked homemade bread in a drum-pan oven behind the house on a Saturday evening, under which the coals of life had gone out before its time or over which the coconut shell and husk breathed no flame, before the bread was properly cooked or had taken colour.

Ready or not for life, the end of school was, for them, a time to celebrate and kill time, the air around them throbbing with life: the cock solei, the sea gulls, the albatross, the griff, the black bird, the soursop bird, the ground doves, the parrot laughing at man's try at life without much visible opportunities. The roosters chimed his manhood; the Rocky Boys felt theirs missing out on life.

The annual racing Season was over and the school of life was only now beginning in earnest; the only thing was that the Rocky Boys were oblivious to it, in any case, not in that way; not in the way adults or their parents saw life with its struggles to coin enough money for their needs. The Telescope roads were reverting to their old pock marked state and boredom settled on the hems of their lives like the suck stones in Paradise River nearby.

Time dripped and disappeared behind the curtains of each day as the sea's champagne in the sands on Telescope Beach. The nicely redone dirt roads to the Telescope racetrack were as long lasting as the two days of the horse racing season. Both Grenada's wealthy and lower class had passed on them, one mobile the other on foot. They had enjoyed the races with their friends and placed the bets of their lives. When that was out of the way and the rain season came in again, the roads would flood with the memories of a dry season pouring with new children, and their fathers not at home, looking for work.

Waters flowed on the roads like little rivers, with estuaries spreading out like cobwebs in different directions and seriously competing with the Great River, Paradise River. If you were going to Grenville, you would have to skip over the pools or be a long jumper to escape the dirty water. That was not all, you would have to wait until you get to Miss Phillipas' Shop, where Telescope Road joined Canal Road, before you could clean your feet, especially between your ten commandments, and then put on your nicely polished leather or canvas shoes that lasted you a lifetime, and might be handed down to someone else.

The Forum itself was jammed against a coconut tree. Across the road from where it was standing were idle estate lands overflowing with thick black sage bush, lime trees, guava trees, cashew with their red and yellow fruits and nuts, plus a whole variety of mangoes in various stages of maturity, spreading out their tentacles that were laden with tempting succulent fruits, begging to be had by cascading stomachs.

This was Telescope, a tightly knit community on the east of the island with less than one hundred houses, where everybody knew everybody and any adult would cut your tail if they found you doing something wrong. Were you foolish enough to report them to your parents, you would get a surprise of your life, for you would get a second un-consoling licking and a third from yourself too, for not seeing your parents licking coming. La Baye, Grenville Town, would hear you bawling for your life.

"De jail door close and dat's what we was waiting for," said Mud Mask with a broad grin.

Ghost said, "School finish for us, and we free. We is we own man now and no damn teacher could tell us what to do."

Their concept of manhood was premature, twisted by their young age. Parents never really seemed to educate you as to what manhood or womanhood really was. That part of their lives was almost a virgin estate. One learnt a lot by imitation.

"Boy, we mussen laugh too quick, you know. We finish school, but we doh have nothing to do," said Doc thoughtfully.

"How you mean we doh have nothing to do?" Mud Mask asked.

"We doh have nothing to do and dat's dat."

"So wha' we doing here is nothing then?"

They burst out in a strong belly laugh, except Doc; he had strong reservations as his parents did not like idleness. His mother said idleness was the Devil's workshop; she would not stand for it. She believed in taking what you get till better came along, for a little was better than nothing at all; half a loaf was better than none. That "little" or "half a loaf" was a nasty slave master that kept you still stationed on your small plots of hope, hoping for a better day hemmed in by the metal sea.

Life felt like those crab traps set neatly by the sea shore to harvest the blue and grey lives of those hairy crustaceans, before they were transformed into culinary works of art that left tongues and teeth wanting more. Money flowed, if you had the means to see and exploit business opportunities.

If Doc had his way, he would not have left school, not because he hated home or anything like that; but because he was held by the nostalgic net of school days or that un-tarrying desire to hold on childishly to something you liked or loved or something that loved you stronger than the desire to break loose and depart. Sometimes parting could feel like death coming; but staying did not necessarily mean there was life there either. It was just something to do, something to keep you going, a dream that would make something of you, something for your parents to look at and feel proud in the end, thank God, just like the picture that hung on the partition in the hall: 'God bless this house'; for in a kind of way a child was a house many mothers framed into a picture from their wombs and never really let go, even long after the umbilical cord was cut.

Mothers would dress up that house, not because they had nothing else to do, it just came naturally to them, love, love of family. Their love was magnanimous sometimes and they would lend their boys to help their neighbours do their field work and get the same service in return. They sowed their children into neighbours' lives, hoping to find bread on the water after many days. They knitted their lives together like their white doilies starched on the mahogany centre table in the hall or on top the mahogany safe keeping guard outside the partition of their bedroom.

Sometimes their love grew hungry and stifled you with kindness or order, setting what work was girl-work, boy-work and man-work. They were the queen of flowers in the home: strong and fragile, eternal and transient, love and terror, fragrant and bilious, negotiator and terminator. Mother was empire. She shaped you like the creases on her brow, bathed your soul with her ever watchful eyes and words. She hemmed your straying feet with the yard to clean every morning of the fallen leaves, the fowl shit to put in the manure, the kitchen garden, the steps to scrub, the wood for the fire. She shaped you into a man without your knowing it, under the absent working eyes of your father, whose role was to bring the flour home for mammy to cook into little delicious and delightful miracles.

Doc would have liked to remain in school and let a pupil teacher become him or go to secondary school and become something else, something better, a head teacher maybe. His Teacher, the Assistant Master, said that "they" – Doc's parents – should try and send him off to secondary school; but Mr. Secondary School left him berthed at the docks of Telescope, waiting at the Ticket Gate for sailors to man his future or just for the right wind. What if he should make his own wind?

Many of his school teachers were kind people and very helpful to their students, especially Mr. Anderson, the Assistant Head. He was a very good teacher. He had a lot of brains. Even the drops of sweat from his head were beads of knowledge, sensitive to the way they flowed down the ravines of his life and into theirs; none of those pearls of water had the same shape; none of them had exactly the same smell, the same size, the same colour of his ever advancing age. Some days flowed Limacol, others garlic, saffron, hot Grenadian cocoa tea, cinnamon, bay leaf, ripe bananas, fried plantains and breadfruit with salt fish souse and smoked herring.

Some days, they just mixed together like callaloo soup in Grenadian spicy incense that tunnelled through the nostrils of God. Teacher Anderson's words were like waters of life they spoke about in the St. Andrew's Methodist School (SAMS) he had attended. His words stood out like chains of clear water in the crayfish canes, sweetening their green lives. He was sensitive and understanding to pupils' needs but the lack of money was the real problem for Doc and the Rocky Boys – those blasted coins that kept rolling down Telescope hill like gingerbreads, away from them and into the dark bushes of the idle estate lands.

The lack of money was as a warship in the harbour of the working class man's life, protecting his lack of education – that education that was like a bamboo kite flying too high up in the sky and for which he did not have the money to buy the number nine thread from a store in Grenville, La Baye. Secondary education was free for those who could pay for it. It was not equal. It was not even at the fingertip of the ordinary working class colonial, to help engineer the growth and development of the colony.

Even thinking about going to secondary school on tip toe was not free; it cost you something: some joy, some gravel of bile in the mouth, some acid from the stomach, every time – every time you saw one a dem passing in school uniform, marching away from you, away from your reach, like one a dem sails that went to Trinidad from Grenville pregnant with Grenada's provisions and coming back with lovely merchandise we could not produce here or work hard to afford. Only people of substance were able to send their children to the secondary schools in Grenville, some in town, wid boarding house by Ms. Martineau and others. For the girls, Convent and Anglican Girl Schools; for the boys, Grammar School and others.

Some people, like the Briggs' in Paraclete, never bothered about money, mainly because they had it; they were born into it; they made it grow and it grew on them; it gave them name, power, influence and opportunities; they could call the tune and the poor would dance; but for the Rocky Boys, whose parents lacked it, it put a strain on them. It could make them mean and stressful; it shortened the hem of their tempers; an impatient hand would fly more easily or be extended with a pot spoon, a whip... to a child's body. When the heat of the dry season rose and steamed and hunger tightened its belt on the lid of the stomach, parents' tongues might have a go at each other for the mishaps, negligence, apparent lack of concern....... because the flatulence of need had to be let out to ease the pain, the strain, the pressure. There was nothing romantic in poverty for them. They often had to forego basic needs like food and extra clothing.

None of the boys' parents were able to afford the fees for Mr. Secondary School, even if they wanted them to continue with their studies, for the winds of fortune had neither blown in their direction nor emancipated them. Sometimes a fortunate wind would blow but not for long enough or with enough money. It was so with their parents and their parents before them. History was unwilling to change its uniform to ordinary clothes. Thus, like it or not, academic schooling was over for the Rocky Boys. Done. Gone. They had heard the last ring of the bell, for them. They were forced by the situation in which they were born to keep to the straight and narrow paths of poverty, still hoping that the wind of fortune would one day blow in their direction and wheel them out of the colonial straight jacket life that History had imposed upon them.

The lack of money cashed in on their will and attitude to a fulfilled life as well. It put a FULL STOP to their educational aspirations, bursting their dreams like the sea foam on La Baye's Atlantic tide that once beached their ancestors there. It prevented the majority of children, not much older, or indeed different from the Rocky Boys, from proceeding beyond the Ultimate Standard Seven of Elementary school's Royal Reader education – the few exceptions would get into the Scholarship class – but that was the exception. The Boys sat down and drank their fill from the empty cups of their temporary freedom. The dust of idleness settled on them. There was a lot of ole talk and bravado. Well, what de hell... They all shouted in unison their Mantra:

Rocky Boys from Rocky Lane; when *springtime comes*; we *will be back again!*

They had copied the lines from a Western film, starred by Alan 'Rocky' Lane, their American hero. The liquor of his memory in them, they felt good, tough, full of life, and invincible, like a dream. They were infused by his film. They had to keep going back to its bottle for more identity. Life filmed them through the camera eyes of the villagers, who watched their future wasting away like fallen water lemons on the ground and could die like the oral tradition, with the fall of every illiterate ancestor who failed to pass on their oral literature to the next generation.

They did not yet realise that the future was not only a dream but, a dream the success of which you had to plan for, sacrifice for and for which one must be prepared to die. At the time, the only lessons the Rocky Boys seemed to be able to draw from the Western was a name, some words and some strong feelings. Their name gave them identity, a foreign identity, an American ID, an American Dream that couldn't quite yet find a cradle, a real actuation on the Grenadian landscape, except in the landscape of the mind. It was as if History could only teach them to take on foreign identity, a conqueror's identity rather than the knowledge that the life and identity of the seed are in the seed.

Time went by and Doc wondered what his ancestors would say about them: the first waves of Africans who knew their African history and culture, and their descendants, who might have heard the stories of their people from Ancient Egypt becoming the first "STATE" in History, when Pharaoh Naimer united the two parts of Ancient Egypt and set up a dynastic period some 7000 years ago. Doc also heard that they had built Pyramids, and even changed the course of the River Nile. He often heard these stories from a man who had fought in World War II and had been to Egypt. World War II had made that man a different individual. War taught him that the Black man, the coloured man, the colonial man, the White man, the Yellow man, the colonised man... all had worth, courage and responsibility in the face of the Nazi bullets and bombs, in the defence of empire; but more so, the ideals of freedom, love, good, existence, life...

Strongholds of slavery and the debilitating colonial education were bombed in his mind, shrapnel in the library museum of his memory, where he alone could enter, where he alone could let you see and feel through the film of his words, flavoured by his forked tongue – bitter-sweet.

He had come back to Grenada a different man, resurrected from the open sarcophagi of World War II; looking fresh, smelling stale; feeling exhausted and a new man out of the travailing wombs of Time. He preached the gospel of African civilisation to a people who were taught in colonial primary and secondary schools that their ancestors had no history or culture and that to have culture was to become English/British or French or Spanish or Italian or German. You had to be a conqueror and of the conquerors to have culture and education; but the horrible war trenches of Europe, Africa, Asia and the Middle East taught him differently: the Dark Continent was not in Africa; it was in man, fallen man, the beast-man sitting in palaces on thrones and other places of power, drinking the dark blood pudding of Sugarcanes.

Doc also had an Uncle in the War that used to write and tell them many similar stories of a great Africa that included Egypt of the pyramids. He believed those stories and had wanted to study History: African History, his history from his people's perspective; but that was not to be at that time in this part of the British Empire, for Britannia still ruled the waves... Britannia still ruled the seas, especially the seas of History that hid volumes of truth in corals and other chests of the seas in the Triangular Trade between Europe, Africa and the New World. Africa passed between the pages of a bloody history of lies and half truths – a blend too distasteful for any tongue! But what? The sea never stops churning its salty pages, for life goes on: a merciless sun, tempered clouds, wind, storms and raining revolutions. Castaways of life are born with hope, only they must find it.

The Rocky Boys went over to Miss Ethel's land and 'raided' her mangoes, plums, tangerines and mandarins. Then they sat down under the colourful flamboyant tree, and feasted on another person's labour. Life. When they finished, they straightened their innocent Beep-bop caps with the peaks pointed straight and revealing their mantra: 'Rocky Boys from Rocky Lane'. They rode out on the ponies of their feet.

Weeks came and went with the same old film reeling like the sugarcane chains on River Antoine Estate further North. Doc's father, who was a builder, had hoped in vain that Doc would voluntarily follow in his footsteps, by coming to be an apprentice under him. Nothing doing. One morning he took a turn in Doc's tail and said to him, "Tomorrow you comin wid me to learn trade. A big little boy like you, you leave school an you not doin' anything useful wid youself. You jus dey playing de dam fool wid yuh friends, calling you-all self: 'Rocky Boys from Rocky Lane'. Life is not a dream you know. If you doh make up you bed is rock you go sleep on! If a man doh work he kyan eat. Dat is *Bible*. Dat not good enough at all. School done; life start. Ah picking up some lumber from de lumber yard to-day for Mr. David' house.

You comin wid me tomorrow. As yuh mother does say: 'Idle hands is de devil workshop'. Ah doh want no devil in me house. Ah prefer a son, my son."

Doc walked around in their outside kitchen like a cornered crab in a lard pan. He then went outside. He knew what his father said made sense. Their dog jumped up and licked him, as if in agreement. Then he made a turn under the cocoa, passing under the golden apple tree. Their dog escorted him. They went and checked out Ghost at his home. When he told him about learning a trade, Ghost wanted to come too. Doc told him his father would agree to let him come too. Bright and early Tuesday morning they took up Doc's father's tools and went down to Ford, where the job to build Mr. David's house was to start. They made their way, not with any great zeal, down the pock road with the hope of becoming apprentices to the building trade. Building a house in those days was no easy matter. Mr. David was able to do it because he had recently returned from working in Aruba, as did many other Grenadians who now invested in houses, lands, buses and other business ventures. You had to leave Grenada, as the ole people said, to make man or to make woman.

Mr. David was a middle aged man, who had married a beautiful, young, vigorous wife, as many middle aged and elderly men did at the time, and still do. Women saw their future with a man for it was a man's world of sorts; hers was to bear and raise children under the Crown. Many women became housewives; but house-wife meant multiple tasks really, for they tended the garden as well, sold provisions from the land, made goodies for sale and kept the home together. Mothers were everything and tried their hands at almost everything. When need be, she was both mother and father.

Doc wanted to become a mason; Ghost thought of being a mason too – but all the same, he wasn't too sure. They were like two bodies with one soul. As long as Doc dey, Ghost dey too, holding a slack end tight. They were wearing their Beep-bop caps – Rocky Boys from Rocky Lane, the Western distilled in their blood. On the job, they tried to look serious. Tom was the senior worker who checked on them. They started with small jobs: fetching water, carrying various tools to the workmen when they requested them, and mixing concrete 3:1 – 3 buckets of sand to 1 bucket of cement. They broke stones, bent and straightened nails; made juice, bought cakes at Ms. Phillipa's shop for the men. Doc's Dad had bought a tape measure and a trowel for him and showed him how to use them. Ghost got a tape too and a hammer. They tackled the same tasks every day, their muscles and their attitudes being shaped for service. The job grew on them like whelks on the rocky sea shore: they started dreaming that one day they would set up as partners in the building business.

Four or five weeks passed and they were beginning to love their jobs more and more. They started to feel comfortable as manhood seasoned their minds and muscles. They started to smell like men and sometimes their tongues drifted into big people talk. One morning, things were not as brisk. There wasn't much to do because the carpenters were preparing the boxing for casting the beams, so Doc and Ghost were just holding on here and there waiting for the beams to be completed, and the casting to start. They had an early lunch, and while relaxing on the grass nearby Mrs. David glided by and went into the shower enclosure situated behind the house to have a cool down. She was a beautiful, energetic, young woman, more like Mr. David's daughter than his wife. Ghost made a joke about them, speculating whether Mr. David could handle her, because she looked so young for him! Doc giggled. The talk was sweet and the gossip cheap: "I wonder if he could hold it down?" Doc jested. "She is like a little frisky mare." They giggled some more, eventually bursting into some serious belly laughs, and louder jesting about the couple, as the thread of their discussions unreeled and degenerated. They spoke about the way she moved as smooth as silk cotton in the breeze; the way she flashed her eyes and swung the music of her hips; her physical blossoming qualities, and finally speculating about her amorous disposition.

They did not know the old proverb "bush have ears" or if they did, they cast care to the winds. They were not aware that all this time Mr. David was listening to them carrying on. He was a short stocky man with a bull's courage, a roundish stomach, like the casks of rum at River Antoine Estate. He had short stubby arms that could bend a cutlass without ruffling the breeze. His index fingers had tufts of hair. His head was partly bald like a compo and the remaining hair started greying like the receding sea-island cotton on Carriacou. Normally, he had an affable to serious face: friendly at one moment and serious the next – that fickle tide of emotion made one feel uncertain as a young fishing boat between the two tides outside the safety of La Baye's fishing reefs.

He was listening behind a nutmeg tree at the back of the house, a little distance from the boys. When the boy's bantering dripped across the matted eves of his hairy ears, his heart chucked at the cage of his chest; his jugular thundered in his head and lightening rage fired the dykes in his eyes. His legs hoisted him to a singular mission: crush the source of the not too flattering remarks of himself and the small talk regarding his wife. The instant adrenaline of jealous rage made him grow in stature in no time. His rage pounced upon them, like a chicken hawk would the chickens in Doc's backyard in Telescope, his talons seizing both Ghost and Doc by their collars, banishing them from his castle in the making and his marital domain.

You could smell the myristica of his anger as he turned their early siesta cold. A man had to be boss in he own home, on his own property. No apprentice, be he son of the builder or not, go come in mih damn yard and insult me like that! Ah work too hard in Aruba for mih money. Ah put up wid enough racial insults over dere to have to be insulted in dis manner to spend mih money in mih own country on dis young, good-for-noting generation. He screamed furiously: "Aron! George! Get outa mih yard! Ah say to get outa mih yard! Get outa me yard, right away! You little good-for-nothing vagabonds!"

They were lucky that he did not take them by the skin of their necks, as cats their kittens. The tsunami of his emotions choked other words in the bay of his throat, saliva oozing from the rim of his mouth. The other workmen stopped working and wondered what the commotion was all about. The truth eventually stuttered, stumbled out of the doorway of his lips. Discovering the facts of the matter, Alpheus the head mason began to laugh, followed by the carpenters and labourers. More jesting and small talk ensued here and there on the site. The full, yellow, nutmeg pods split open showing the red teeth of the mace and fell to the ground – nutmeg pod one way; nutmeg another. The house, Ah have to finish de house. Ah have to finish mih house for me and my wife sake. Dese boys must go.

Doc's father thought that Mr. David should have reported the matter to him before doing anything. He was in charge of the work and any firing should have come through him. The 303 was his to shoot. That was how tings get done in construction in Grenada. You kyan put a man in charge of you work and den just come an do what you want on de wuk after, firing he workers. Every ting go turn ole mass. The captain ha to be in charge of 'e ship, uddawise is mutiny an all fall down. Order is orderly; and correct is right.

Doc's Dad felt overthrown both by his employer and his son, and his son's friends. He felt a bit disarmed because he needed the work while the little Aruba construction boom lasted; he could not let his pride make him walk out on the job. Trouble don't set up like rain; but when the rain comes, you ha to know not only whey you go shelter, but how you go shelter and for how long. After all, Doc was his son; but work was scarce. The truth was that quietly and privately, Doc's dad, as well as other workers, had spoken about the difference between the ages of Mr. David and the 'Temptress', as some of the workmen branded her under their jealous breaths.

Mr. David, his serene feathers ruffled, spoke very little after his exchanges with Doc's father. He went upstairs his old house on the heels of his wife, squaring his shoulders, muttering to her sweet things, sour things, sweet things that turned sour sop under his breath. He stayed out of sight for a good while, the old house rocking with emotions. He wanted his new house to finish on time; he had got a good price to get it built. What dey think? She marry im for he money? Does love have age? Dey juss jealous mih. A man not suppose to covet anodda man wife. Dey looking for trouble.

When Mr. David returned, his military chest high in the air, his arms wrestling the air, nose up, the men started reflecting and criticizing in general the behaviour of young people these days. Comedy had to come in and save the day. "Dese chilren today lack respect an' manners," said Mr. Williams, with a smile. "Dey doh seem to appreciate wha' people trying to do for them." This was followed by a string of other moralizing statements by some of the older men. Mr. David left soon after and a small understanding smile played on the men's faces.

"Dese young people doh care for God or man," opined Larius.

"But you know, she ain' easy neider. She *is* look hard to handle," said another. "What she comin and bathe dere for, everyday, just before de sun hit e peak at midday? Da ooman go gee im trouble. Ah see dat aready. Dem things does have death in it.

- II -

Recovering from Mr. David's rough handling, Doc and Ghost glazed the whole episode as a big joke and laughed all the way down to the stand pipe at the end of Ford road, where they straightened themselves and adjusted their images on life's screen. They fixed up their Beep-bop caps, pushed their hands deep into their pockets and sailed down the road into Grenville. Underneath the cloak of joviality, the sun of his father's glare burned into his skin and heart. Doc made a false start. His father could have passed on his trade to him: from father to son; from blood to blood.

Arriving in La Baye, Doc and his friend went to their favourite café, which was near the entrance to the market. They sat on the tall stools and ordered rock cakes and milk from the little money they had gleaned from their apprenticeship. In those days, you did not really get paid for apprenticeship; just as the planters had done to the African forced labourers they called "slaves", after the official abolition of English slavery. Apprentice. What is there to "learn" in digging trenches, filling holes, straightening nails, filling buckets with sand, cement, gravel and water and mixing them all together nicely, like children *coucou tè* or calalloo soup and then bringing that grey porridge for the masons to pour into pillar boxes or on a decking, like plates of food for a household?

What apprenticeship has to do with buying cakes and other foodstuff in the shop for the seasoned workers? Where is the apprenticeship in that, if not learning to serve the elders or to obey orders or learning to get seasoned on the job, for a job, for life? Why one shouldn't be properly paid for labour done? Isn't the labourer worthy of his higher, as the priest said? Since ah small ah learn to dig tings in the garden: yams, tannias, sweet potatoes dat we en makin sugar wid yet, dasheen, eddoes, crab. Why do we have to pay the fares of apprenticeship, to learn to do what we already know?

"Is like if we kyann grow up at all," Doc said.

"We big but we not man yet," Ghost responded.

"Wha' make we diffrent? Is just age!"

"Mammy does tell me ah playin man and how ah not a man yet."

"Boy, no matter how ole we get, we still we parents' chilren. Da is wha' mine always sayin', anyway............."

"Mine no different. She does say de same ting."

"Is like we mother and dem ha' the same mind – one mind joined together like cobwebs across a garden path in Telescope."

"You can say dat again."

"Boy we go ha to leave home one day. Een ha' no other way."

"You right. We go ha' to leave home to make man, like everybody else."

"Daddy does tell me if I is a man ah must go an turn mih own key."

"Wha' you tink we mother go say when we reach home, boy?"

"Ah doh know. But ah sure de news of what we did today might reach home before us."

Ghost teased a few girls as they passed by in La Baye: "Long mouth", "Mango lung" and "Goat foot". They limed around Seppy's shop at the corner of Victoria Street; passed in Hutchinson's shop, while he was outside gossiping with Mr. McLaren; then they went into Bata's Shoe Shop and greeted the owner – a youthful "Paramount", as they used to call him. Time came to go home, and to avoid the scorching sun, they passed on the bay, walking through the Anglican School yard.

They made their slow journey along the track that passed through the bushes, guava, limes, black sage shrubs, on the way to their little hut – the old Ticket Gate at Telescope. When they arrived there, they scoped out things. Afterwards, they went home, but there was nothing to eat in either of their homes. They shared a very common bond, like the two crossing sweepers: "...to each other they were bound by Poverty's strong ties!" Whatever they had they shared, equally. They were great friends, bosom pals. The day ebbed away as they drifted again onto the estate lands in Telescope, where they ate guavas and mangoes. A growing young man had to eat.

Ghost climbed a coconut tree and cut down a grapp of jelly nuts, which was a usual thing to do. Village culture at the time allowed one to take food from another person's land for one's personal needs. They devoured the bunch and the tide of hunger lost its swell. Lazily, they laid down between the sweet brooms on the grass, gazing up at the sky's canopy, as if seeking answers to their situation. No easy answers came, if there were to be, it would probably take another decade or so to find them. They yawed, kicking ideas around on the beaten racetracks in their minds. What to do next? Ghost suggested that they go down to Maracaibo and raid the Paradise boys' crab traps. Doc thought it better to tackle the boys at the back of Johnson's place, in the middle of Canal Road.

"Boy, ah doh know. Ah doh feel like getting up yet," Ghost said.

"Come on man; we have to make a move; it getting late!" Doc urged.

"Whey we going first?" asked Ghost, belching and repeating the fruits he had just eaten, while rubbing his belly playfully.

They went to Maracaibo, raided some of the crab traps they found, looking out all the time to see if the owners of the traps would filter through thin air and catch them from behind, from their sides or just head on. Some traps had crabs and others not. They tied up the crabs they found with vines found and went home with them to make a pot for dinner and the rest some fast cash from people like Ms. Stella, the village crab-back maker, or to exchange them for some other product.

At the Forum, months came and went and the zest with which the Rocky Boys had greeted their release from the "school jail" was now a thing of the past. Doc wondered whether it was a good thing – the way time was passing them by. Their parents chided them regularly for wasting their time and their lives:

"Boy, fine some work to do before something do you."

"If crab ain walk e wun get fat."

"Go an' learn a trade."

"No work; no food."

"De way you make up yuh bed, da is how you go lie down in it."

"De Devil ha' work for idle hands to do."

"How a tree fall, is so e go lie."

Their lives became a litany of proverbs and sayings and tellings.

Doc remembered the time when his grandmother would spread a bag under the mango tree in her yard and read for him on Sundays. One of her favourite stories was about a girl named Cathleen. "Cathleen," she would read, "prepare the table for dinner then we will have to go to St. Petersburg to ask the Czar to pardon your father......................."

Stories often came from far, from abroad, just like colonial education was shipped from the Mother Country, well packaged, clean, great and Royal – unable to help them to meaningful jobs at the time, or to be self-employed.

Primary Education was rationed to them, tight-fitting for colonial island subjects. At the end, your parents and family and village would tell you that you ha' to learn a trade, like if your education was Nansi Story. "Boy, why you doh go and learn a trade?" It was like if 'trade' was *the* key to life, *the* key to development, *the* key to the house that you did not yet build, and education, well... Not enough education – primary school education left you unprepared both for work and for life. You felt in-between, like the vulnerable crayfish that just changed their exoskeleton in the Paradise River. It was easy to catch them, as their gundies could not pinch you.

Doc loved to hear his grandmother read and he particularly liked the story of Cathleen. It stirred up things inside him that words could not harness, to give them shape, to give them texture, taste and smell. It made him feel good and his eyes dreamy and glassy, like his dad's, when his rum factory was fired up in his Christmas veins. He was sharing the story of Cathleen with the Boys, with the same ease, when Ms. Stella, one of their well respected villagers came up and criticized them for wasting the best part of their lives. They listened to her at first and then Ghost spirited in, "Let us go and spin we top an ting. We go have enough time for dat kine a talk later."

"No. Let's listen to wha' Ms. Stella ha' to say," said Doc, pushing back the tugs of procrastination. They got down from the top of the Forum, while Ms. Stella continued preaching to them about the importance of education. Surely she must have known that they could not get a secondary education, because no money; no school. No school; no education. The arithmetic was clear.

They did not yet realise that education was more than the schooling they got from within the walls of the church schools or the public schools. Education was life itself and life was a school without walls, well, at least not the walls you could touch with your hands; its walls were different, transparent, philosophical, built in different ways and with different materials, to last.

Dem walls dey, you feel dem in you soul, in you mind, under your skin. It had classes too, where the merit was genes, status, money, colour..... When you see dem walls of life dey, education not enough to get the leopard out of you and put it into their lion's whelp. You can feel the wall inside of you keeping you out a dem education there. Dem kina life experience dey, dem centuries old walls like Fort Frederick and Fort George – started by one and continued by another; it hard to mash dem up. But one day, real education go chisel down dem words dat build dose walls so high that it left your mounted parts exposed to the elements of man's malicious benevolence. Education is a collage of the bric-a-brac of human existence. It can fool you long enough to kill you ignorant. Sometimes you have to re-educate your education to find your life and its meaning in the Forums that encircle it.

"We is African people," Ms Stella continued, "brought here durin' slavery. De Masters, a lotta dem wretches and dem, never teach us to read and write deir language; but dose slaves and dem wanted to learn. Dey wuz not beast. Maybe one day you might learn dat our ancestors used to write before dey came here to build de British Empire from our blood, sweat and tears. If only you all de know... Dey coulda die to learn to read and write. Dey woulda like to have what you wasting here today: time and education. Doh waste you time sitting around doin nothing! Honour dem by getting something to do to improve you'selves. Get a trade! Take a correspondence course! Get into local talent and thing!"

Ghost said to her, "We tried de trade ting but e doh like us."

"How you mean trade doh like you? Who livin', you own trade?" Ms Stella challenged him.

Doc slipped in quickly, "We doh mine workin', but e doh ha' work for us."

"Ah know tings tight," she replied, "but de days of slavery done dead and gone." Ms. Stella added: "Doh enslave all-yuh self to idleness in this Ticket Gate. Da is de worse shackles of all – staying at a gateway that leads nowhere."

"I not no slave, Ms. Stella," Doc defended.

"Me neider," Ghost chorused.

Ms Stella challenged them: "Den do something before something do you. If you-all look hard enough, Ah sure you-all go fine something worthwhile to do. Big dreams start small sometimes, with the right gestures. De most hardest things to see sometimes is what is in front you nose. You all doh have a dream?"

"Whaz de point of dreaming, when dere's no strength to climb de coconut tree to get the water nut?" Ghost asked. "No money to go to school..........."

She looked them hard in the eye and fired through them, "Wha come first: the chicken or the egg, book or common sense? In horse riding, who is de jockey, the horse or man?"

The ground felt light under them, like giggles. They riddled there, not too sure of her drift. Their stomachs stirred with the smell of her delicious crab-backs. She shook her head pitifully at them, bent down, took up her locally made whist basket of crab-backs, and, with the same speed she came, she left them there, smoke fizzling out of their Western ears and the smell of food filling their stomachs.

She made her way to Grenville town on foot to sell her culinary creations to whoever would buy. Her cooking delighted many; she never came back with an unsold crab-back. She left the Rocky Boys standing there rubbing theirs idle hands, like dreams not yet awake to be born into dumplings. Doc's dog left their yard, stirred by the crab-backs, wondering why one did not take a chance and fall out of her basket.

One morning, not long after Ms. Stella's lecture, Ms. Catherine met Doc by the Forum with his friends. She was an elderly widow and the local seamstress. She was struggling to carry her bucket of water home from the village stand pipe. In those days, pipe borne water in village homes was a dream. It was customary at the time for the younger people to help the older ones with their load, when they met them on the road or if they met you on the road; so on seeing her, Doc helped her carry the water to her house. As he was leaving, Ms. Catherine's face dawned and she invested an idea on him. She told him about a job, a yard boy's job with her sister in Paraclete.

"I told her about you," Ms. Catherine said, smiling warmly, her glasses resting on her nose. "Would you like to go and see her about it?" she asked in a squeaky voice.

"Well, ah in ha' nutting doin' now. Ah doh mind givin' it a try. How ah go get dere?"

"You go go by bus son," she said in a friendly voice. "My sister son have a bus. You go travel wid 'im. If you take de job, you go live in my sister house."

"Ah go ha' to talk to Mammy first to see wha' dey say."

"Of course. Ah go talk to your parents too; dat's how to do it and is a big decision, leavin' home."

Doc was a little concerned about being away from his family and friends. It was one thing to find work; it was another thing to live in your workplace. He sat and pondered on the offer, even though he trusted Ms. Catherine's judgment, for she was a kind and loving member of the neighbourhood and the neighbourhood was family. Ms. Catherine was a short, quiet widow of about sixty. She lived alone after her husband's passing. Her house was situated between those of Doc and Ghost's parents. She was an affable, lovable person. She often walked quietly, with an unsteady, withered gait. Sometimes she stumbled along, the result of her fondness for a glass of River Antoine Rum that fired up her slow, aging factory of muscles or kept her nights warm. She greeted everyone with smiling luminous eyes, especially after a glass or two of her favourite spirited beverage were distilled into her soul.

A coconut tree stood in the middle of her yard. Surrounding the house was her kitchen garden of peas, okra, sweet potatoes and so on, and a large chinee plum tree. Being the only seamstress in the neighbourhood, she made clothes for boys, girls and some of the older women. She had also sewed for Doc and Ghost, when they were much younger. Telescope inhabitants lived like a tribe. Everyone looked out for one other and it was a common thing for a neighbour to ask another for some salt, sugar, a stick of match, a roast breadfruit or a "piece of fire", and so forth.

If people were unable to pay Ms. Catherine cash for her services, being the type of neighbourhood it was, they would often give her bananas, peas, chicken or whatever, by way of payment. Money was anything of value that you would use to transact a business deal. She was always favourably disposed to Doc, since he was much younger. In fact, it was in her yard that the ceremony for the first cutting of Doc's hair took place.

It was Ms. Catherine who, remembering some of her African traditions, said that the cutting of a boy's hair for the first time had special significance and distinctive rights, which called for a ceremonial celebration. She organized it, informing the members in their small community. She got Hilton to perform the barber's role. Refreshments were provided by all. People brought or gave what they had. In those days, you learned to make do with what you had.

It was a Sunday afternoon. Doc was about five or six and still wearing his long baby plaits. He was not a Samson or a Nazarite; there was just the belief that a boy's hair should not be cut too soon, especially before they spoke. There was the belief or fear that if his hair was cut before five or six years old, he could go dumb. In any case, his lovely plaited hair was no more manageable for his mother.

Doc came and sat on a stool that was placed under the coconut tree. The oldest man spoke with him and they brought a calabash of water for him to wash his hands and a piece of cloth to wipe them. Afterwards, Doc was given a large homemade bun to which he held on very tightly. Then another older man came and sprinkled some water on his head, while the barber poised with his scissors and comb, ready to set to action. But before he could start on Doc's head, someone played music on a banjo; others African drums, a quatro that spoke payol, the mouth organ, the Grenada cocoa lute, shack-shacks, the conch shell, tambou bamboo and anything that could make pleasant sounds.

While they played, they sang a tune laced with some African words, Patois and Creole English, spiced only in the Grenadine Isles. As soon as the singing was over, a little joy was spread around. Then Hilton wriggled in with his metal pincers and comb; but Doc held on for dear life to his plaits, with his free hand. To cut his plaits was to cut his life. They were his umbilical cord to his early childhood; he did not want to move on; he was not ready to move on; he was sad to lose his plaits, until Ms. Catherine coaxed him nicely and he yielded.

Hilton chinksed away at Doc's hair until most of it was gone, except for a little muff at the top; he did not want to give him a clean head. The sides and back were cut very low. He gave him a nice sharp roungs. When he was finished, Hilton placed a mirror in front of Doc, who suddenly pulled back, as if he had seen a ghost in the mirror. He wondered who was that creature looking back at him, mimicking his every move, gesture and grimace. The onlookers laughed, gathering around him and congratulating and kissing him, telling him how nice and new he looked. His grandmother called him saga boy. They hugged him and encouraged him to eat his bun.

The men had a 'little thing': some rum and water. The women and children had juice, except Ms. Catherine, who had her spirits fired up to the skies above, like the men, to rain down her eloquence with the softness of clouds. Doc was given the first cup of juice and they all laughed as he sank his teeth in his bun. Everyone had a bun as well, but Doc's bun was the biggest of them all. They sang some more and danced. Doc looked on, taking it all in. It was a memorable day, painted indelibly on the canvas of his childhood memory. This special ceremony had bonded him to Ms. Catherine, and as he grew older, his bond with her and their community was recorded on a film in his mental archive. His love and respect for the older people grew.

After the discussion with Ms. Stella regarding their wasting of their time and life, Doc thought he would do something to improve himself, so when Ms. Catherine told him about the job, he did not mind giving it a try. It was an opportunity for another jumpstart, an occasion to sort out this "chicken and egg" business.

"Yard boy work ain' ha no future in it," Doc's mom said to him. "Dat kinda work is like housewife work in a way: een ha no thanks, no promotion. You go ha to do any and everything."

"It better dan doin nothing, mammy" Doc put in.

"As long as you know that. If you di work hard enough in Primary for the scholarship, you woulda be in secondary now..."

"Well Ah din make it for the scholarship but Ah din drop outa school like some."

"True. Dat was good. You think you have belly for this yard boy job?"

"I dunno. I'll do my best."

"De apprentice mason work wid yuh father… You go and put you mouth in big people business... Behave you self up dey. Doh dutty we name in Paraclete. A good name is better than riches. Ah have nine of you, plus you father ...."

"Ah go be good, mammy."

"You had better," she said starting to hum a tune. "And when you get pay, send de money home for me to hold it for you."

"Yes mammy."

"You startin' to work but you in turn man yet."

When Doc told Ms. Catherine he would take the yard boy job, she knew deep down that that was not the job for him; she saw it as a stepping stone, a kind of a crank start with his economic life and future, a place to stand up in the world, a beginning – only a beginning. She was sitting on the steps of her house, when he came to tell her he was taking the job.

"You go get the bus by my sister's house in Paradise," she said to Doc. "She house is just a stone throw from Paradise Bridge. You know de Suez Canal?"

"Ah know de Suez Canal."

"Well as you come out de short cut, just keep walkin' towards de end of de bridge and you go see de house on de right hand side of de bridge, on the way to Pearls Airport. Is a wall house."

"Ah know it," Doc replied. "It have three plum tree in de yard."

"Dat's it. Ask for Mary and Martha. You know dem. Dey come here to spend time wid me. You see dem many times aready; they are my nieces."

"Ah know dem. One ah dem give me sweets one day," Doc added.

He knew them very well. He wanted to say something about Mary, for The Rocky Boys had a nickname for her, because of her stylish manner of walking. The Boys called her 'the model'. He thought she was nice and secretly referred to her as: "Mary, Mary, quite contrary." As he recalled these thoughts, he stifled a laugh, remembering how contrary she made him feel every time he looked at her passing by the Ticket Gate of his memory.

"You go take de bus by deir house," she continued. "It does pass dere every day from town. My brother-in-law own it. De number is H239, called 'Our Favourite'. You mussa seen it passin' on de Canal Road." Doc said he knew the bus.

"When you get to de house, tell de servant who you are and what you come for."

"Yes Ms. Catherine," he replied nodding his head. "Ok, bye Ms. Catherine."

"God bless you," she said quietly. Without looking at him in the face, she patted him softly on the shoulders and said with a serious voice: "Make us proud, son. Go on son. Be good." She waved him on. As he walked away, she got up from the steps and went into her house.

"Make us proud, son," she said to herself, like a prayer. He felt the warning note in her voice as much as she saw the restlessness of youth in his adventurous veins and muscles. She knew her sister had a daughter, about his age, and the last thing one would want is youthful fires burning in the wrong places, that would be seen all the way to Telescope. The mischief of early fatherhood or motherhood was like damning a river at the wrong place and time.

- III -

The day came for Doc to leave. He packed his 'jola' with his sling-shot and other personal belongings, for being a yard boy meant you had to be in the person's yard - you had to live in or stay close by; but Paraclete was too far to foot it every day God made, going and coming. He hugged his mom.

"Be a good boy now."

"Yes Mammy."

"Ah don't want no bad news coming to me 'bout you."

"No mammy."

"A good name is better dan riches. Ah raise you up to be a good boy, well man. You gettin big now, wid dem lickle wiskers around you mout and dem feathers under your chinny chin chin dey."

Doc smiled proudly, straightening up a bit. His mother's observations added about a foot and a half to his five feet five.

"And don't forget to save you money and send it for me."

"No Mammy."

"No what? What you mean by 'no'?"

"Ah mean ah go sen it or bring it when ah could come, Mammy."

"Dat's my boy. Ah know ah could bank on you." Doc said goodbye to his four brothers and three sisters; he was the third born. Dad had gone to the garden early and Mother would say goodbye for him. Doc's jola saddled his left shoulder, weighing it down a bit. Everyone at home had long faces when he was leaving.

Mammy's eyes flooded like the tender Red Sea, as her son's umbilical cord was being cut anew, this time from within her: the soul. The bursting of her waters doused his soul. He hit the dirt road with his one pair of genuine leather shoes, whose heels had learnt the contours of his gait and its top, the waves of his curling feet. The day felt new, although it was afternoon.

Doc passed by his friends, The Rocky Boys, to check them out and to say bye, but consolation was not there, for he was leaving the Telescope Ranch, one less cowhand with which to play ranch (cowboy and bow-bow), fighting the cattle rustlers and the Wild Indians with sling-shots and homemade wooden toy guns: pistols, rifles, shotguns.

As the natural head of the group, Doc's departure was like leaving the flock shepherd-less; but if the matured cocoa bean never left the pods of Telescope Estate, there would be no cocoa tea, no chocolate, no cocoa butter. They would rot right there on the tree, if a rat did not emancipate them in time with their teeth, sucking their juices out of their silky coat and letting them fall like hail to the ground, where they would sprout with new life for another generation of farm labourers to clean, nurture and harvest in tasks, measured with ten foot poles, squared.

Ghost had no smile on his face at the parting news from Doc. In fact, they were both very stoical about it. They embraced and Ghost gave him a friendly tap on the shoulder. Ghost knew the pain of parting, for his younger sister had died early. His father was never around. Ghost had started to learn tailoring, but not with much spirit. He too had to get out of his pod to make his own cocoa tea.

"Is only for a short time, man," Doc consoled him, rising above his own sadness.

"You know we is we and no weevils can come between us," Ghost added philosophically, his jaw tightening optimistically.

Doc replied, "Ah know. We go catch up man." He tapped Ghost once on the chest and left, remembering Ms. Stella's favourite African proverb: one who has family and friends is richer than one who has money. His youthful heart pumped that old truth through every fibre of his being as he was leaving home: a cruel necessity, but he had to move on and so left he did. He passed through the short-cut in Cocoa Field. On the way, he picked up a few mangoes and greeted some farm labourers cutting their tasks that never seemed to end. One task was measured one forty feet squared. The foreman came around with a ten foot pole to do the measurement. That was a lot of cutting to accomplish in a day, especially for the women.

Mud Mask's mother did task on the Telescope Estate and he had to help her finish her jobs, so that she could collect her pay. She followed from where her parents left off. It was as if time had stood still like the waters of Grand Étang. Task was a slave master and the pay, their driver, little. The masters had changed over time and another Emancipation Act, without Apprenticeship, with fair wages and meaningful education was necessary to take them out of the ordeal in which they lived. Task work and agriculture erased some of Mud Mask's days on the school register and the school slate.

Cash crops sent him to the family garden and market on Fridays and Saturdays. His education slid downhill and his manual muscles went up to the powerful open doors of the estate labour market, till he could find something else to do or learn some trade or emigrate like others to greener pastures overseas, like the 'Mother Country' – that 'Mother Country' that kept taking the islands' children. The reels of life filmed slowly in the isles.

Cold Coucou Face was at his family corn mill when Doc passed to say goodbye. His family owned a corn mill that served the village and surrounding areas. Some people paid in kind (corn) to have their corn milled; it was as good as money, except for the weevil that would come alive in it. Others paid in cash or trusted, promising to pay later. Some would bring meat or eggs or a fowl or fish. Cold Cocou Face was sad as well but he knew that life was like that.

Change came in cycles and seasons, even though things remained the same. There was planting time, weeding and moulding time, harvesting time, feeding the cattle corn stalk time, corn drying time, corn milling time and then all the delicacies that would be made from corn: roast corn, boiled corn, asham or ashum, coucou, fry coucou, kongkey, corn porridge, corn dumpling. It was amazing what the cornfields and corn could mill in the miraculous hands of mammies and grannies.

"Well boy, it's Paraclete time."

"I see dat. I'll keep your coucou warm."

They both laughed at their old joke.

"Ah go be coming from time to time, as time would allow."

"Just doh lose in de bush up dey."

"Grandpa always said: " without bush, without food."

Doc trickled down the shortcut from Telescope Estate to Paradise Road. He passed by the playing area he and other boys from the village had cut out and cleaned from time to time to play cricket and other community games. Actually, it was a part of Telescope Estate lands that the watchman had allowed them to use as a kind of village common. Indeed, he allowed villagers to take things from the estate, like firewood, mangoes, citrus, coconuts, other fruits and victuals, since many of the villagers worked on the estate. He did not muzzle the ox that grinded the corn.

However, some villagers lost the plots of land they had worked under a *métayage* system where the plantation owner gave an estate worker a portion of land to cultivate and develop over a period of time. He was free to sell what he grew on that plot and pay a rent to the landlord. But when those plots were sufficiently developed, the planter or his overseer would reclaim the land and offer another uncultivated plot for development. It was a discouraging system for villagers as they did not have enough time to fully benefit from their hard labour. They were forced to move from these types of holdings, with their wooden houses, sometimes without much notice from the estate owner or overseer. Today they would be there and tomorrow they would be gone, cursing the light out of the day.

Doc soon got to Paradise Bridge from where he was going to cross over to a new life, well new life of sorts. From the Bridge, the house Ms. Catherine spoke to him about was quite visible. When he got there, the bus had not yet arrived. He introduced himself, explaining the reasons for his visit. Meanwhile, they served him a glass of juice and he spent the rest of the time wondering about the big grassy yard. He climbed their huge plum tree with their permission and ate his fill and even put some in his pockets for later.

The evening sun began to slant the shadows of the trees around. It was about half past four when the bus, 'Our Favourite', pulled up in the yard, and a tall, slightly stooping man came out and walked slowly towards the house, holding two parcels in his hands. This was Mr. Rupert, his prospective employer who went into the house and greeted Thelma. "My girl, you looking good yes!" he said to Thelma. She straightened herself, passed her hand across her mouth and took the parcels from Mr. Rupert, grinning sheepishly in the process.

Holding the parcels in her hands, she shouted to the girls, "Martha! Mary! Uncle Rupert come!" On hearing their names, both Martha and Mary lazily, almost reluctantly, descended the stairs into the living room, greeted their Uncle, and introduced Doc.

"This is Doc, your new yard boy."

"So you is the boy," he replied without looking at Doc or shaking his hand.

"Yes sir," Doc replied, eyeing Mr. Rupert suspiciously.

"Your name is not Doc. Is It?"

"Yes", replied Doc somewhat puzzled.

"What is your real name? Doc is your nickname," Mr. Rupert

added. "Now tell me your real name, the one you get when you were baptized."

"Oh ho! Well dat is George, sah."

"Well George or Doc, we go leave just now for Paraclete." There were some rumbling around in the kitchen between Mary, Martha and Thelma while they sorted out parcels to be delivered en route, and others to take home for the cousins, Uncle Rupert's children. That was soon out of the way and they left after 'Our Favourite', jerked shook and backfired, forcing dogs in the area to bark at the commotion. They stopped at intervals to drop off parcels and passengers, mainly shoppers who went to town for groceries to replenish their village shops. They brought back basic items like sugar, flour, matches, candles and so forth.

"Gi me a low here," shouted one gentlemen, as he reached Mount Horn. He was a regular man of some substance, who had a shop downstairs his large house.

"And doh go with me box of bully beef and me two bags of flour and sugar," one passenger said.

"Man what wrong with you this evening, you have woman problem?" enquired Man Man, a compacted, hard-faced-looking man.

Further on, Edwin and his wife got off. Not long after this observation of Man Man, Mr. Rupert and Doc arrived home, and not too soon either, for Doc was sandwiched between two men whose body odour was very offensive to him. The Briggs house was a large one, made partly from concrete and partly from wood. It stood on tall concrete pillars. The greater part of the house was board and on the weather side the board was covered with shingles.

The house itself was built on a steep hill with the front facing the road. The sea was visible in the far, far distance. The back and sides were shaded by nutmeg, cocoa and banana. The bus could not go up the hill so it was parked in the gap on the roadside near the communal standpipe, opposite a tall, blighted mango tree. As soon as Mr. Rupert alighted from the bus his two daughters, Sally-Ann and Clarissa, rushed down the hill to greet him. Mr. Rupert delightedly hugged them and patted their heads by turn.

"Good evening daddy," they greeted him. "What you bring for us?"

"Take up dis basket with you, Sally," handing her the one in his left hand. "Claire, look on the front seat you go see a parcel and paper bag, take them up. Be careful with the paper bag; it have some fry fish in it."

"Yes daddy, I will be careful," replied Clarissa.

He ascended the hill slowly. His shirt was partly out of his trousers. He looked quite spent after a long day behind the wheel. The children walked on either side of him until they entered the house, then they rummaged through the packets expecting their usual afternoon treat: sweets, sugar cake or whatever. Doc followed behind them unacknowledged until they reached the house. After some family formalities, he was then introduced, as an afterthought to Mrs. Briggs.

She was slim, spriggy, and of medium height. Her skin was as pale as a forced ripe golden apple. She wore a thin pair of spectacles with a supportive chain attached. On meeting Doc, she removed it from her eyes and forcing them open, she glared in a firm voice: "I'm Mrs. Briggs. You will report to me." As time went by, the glasses stayed more on her collar bone than on her nose.

"My name is Doc, well George. I come to work Ma'am."

"I know you come to work. I hope you have good manners and respect. I don't like children who don't have manners." She did not shake hands with him either. After this, she went to the pantry and returned with a glass of juice. She sat on her rocking chair and drank it. Having composed and refreshed herself she then turned to Doc and told him to have a seat. He did so, timidly. He was thirsty, but he said nothing.

He sat there patiently holding on to his personal belongs as if for dear life. Mrs. Briggs was unmindful of his apparent unease; she was aware of the social differences and probably played it up. She felt very strong and powerful. Doc felt very weak, almost helpless and of course, he was penniless.

His duties were outlined by Mrs. Briggs in a cool, firm, deliberate manner. "You must sweep the yard first thing every morning and clean the dog mess under the house. After you finish that, wash out their pans and feed them. Then you must sweep the kitchen clean. (She emphasized the word 'clean.') Then come into the house to collect your breakfast, which you would eat in the kitchen. You hear me boy? You understand?"

Doc said he did, and further replied, "Ah hear what you say, Mam," looking her straight in the eye, which made her feel somewhat uncomfortable.

"After breakfast..." she continued tersely, leaning closer to Doc to emphasize the firmness of her presence and her authority and power over him, because Doc continued looking at her in the eye, "After breakfast," she repeated in a high pitched voice, "you will go to the garden. Dotlyn will show you where it is. Can you climb, boy?" To Doc she appeared vague and blank like a spirit; as bloodless as a cloud, a very thin, cotton-looking piece of cloud that would soon disappear against the wide canopy of the breezy Caribbean sky.

"Not big trees Ma'am. Ah fraid ah fall and break me neck."

"You will have to climb, boy. I'm sure you won't fall and break your neck. You will have to bring in the provision and fruits and I would want you to roast breadfruits for me sometimes. Raydon looks after the wood. You can manage that am sure," she said, her voice weakening in authority.

"Well Ma'am, ah go try my best."

"You will have to," she muttered quietly, almost to herself.

When he thought the description of his duties was finished and was about to ask for some food, she added on his slate: "Another thing, before I forget, on Sundays you must bathe the dogs." She finally drank the last of her juice, got off her chair and walked away, leaving him there. He felt tearful. The day was long. He was both hungry and thirsty and he felt that this new environment was very unfriendly to him. Mr. Rupert kept three large hunting dogs. One of them was quite sickly with sores and ticks and smelled like a dung heap. Doc shuddered at the thought of touching it. This was more than he had bargained for.

Mrs. Briggs returned again, this time to inform him that he would be sleeping with two friends of the family - Mr. Troy and Mr. Joseph - who lived on the opposite side of the Brigg's down the hill near where the bus was parked. Doc was disappointed that he was not sleeping in the big house. Not long after, Dothlyn announced dinner. "Dinner ready. De table set already, Ma'am," said she, speaking with a familiar air. She seemed to act as part of the family in an appendix sort of way. Finally, like a passing thought, Mrs. Brigg's asked Doc whether he was hungry. He replied dryly, "Yes."

The setting of the table did not include him. He was given or offered some supper in the same after thought manner, hastily put together by Dothlyn – Dots as they called her. She raked off some here, scraped off some there, creamed off others where possible, until she came up with something in an enamel dish. "Follow me, Doc," she shouted and led the way to the outside kitchen – a separate little building.

At the time, it was common for the kitchen to be separate from the houses, because many persons cooked on a wood fire or with coals but the Briggs's house had a kitchen as part of the main house as well. The outside kitchen had two stools, one chair, a table and a fireplace with three stones. When Doc finished eating, he wanted to go and ask for some more, like Oliver Twist, but he just returned the container, cleaned like a whistle. Then and only then was he formally introduced to the other folks in general, in the kitchen.

Sally-Ann, Mr. Rupert's older daughter, was tall and slim with a high forehead and prominent cheekbones. Her eyes were wide, with a concentrated gaze which she focused on him with an imperious air. She seemed to peer deep into his soul like a chicken hawk. She was about thirteen or fourteen years old and strutted around like the Queen of Sheba. Her younger sister Clarissa was only about ten or eleven. She was dumpy, with loose watery eyes and two long plaits hanging down on each side of her cheeks like rabbit ears.

"Hi Doc," she said, staring almost comically at his worn-out shoes. Dot grinned healthily, revealing a twisted front tooth. She was very attractive and shapely for her sixteen or seventeen years. She was always smiling and was somewhat frisky.

Raydon was a relatively short, broad-chested young man in his mid twenties. He was there to meet Doc as well. "He works for us," Sally-Ann said. She added breathlessly, "He goes to the mountain and pick up de nutmegs. He cuts wood and burn coals." Doc yawned demonstratively, and hoped the point was taken that he was tired and sleepy.

"You will go with Dots. She will show you the house where you would sleep. They're expecting you. Dothlyn you ready?"

"Yes Mersey," she replied. Doc said goodnight, as Dothlyn led the way down the hill to the house not far off.

It was now dark and the fireflies blinked; the frogs croaked; the night insects whistled, orchestrating their nocturnal performances. The owl screeched its way into the long night like a falling star, complementing the performance. Arriving at the house, Doc was introduced to Mr. Troy and Mr. Joseph. "Dis is Doc, well George, the yard boy for de Briggs," Dot said. "Doc, dis is Mr. Troy and Mr. Joseph."

"We've been expecting you," and they invited him in, and offered him a seat. Not long after they showed him into his little room with a wooden sofa.

"My real name is George but everyone call me Doc, so I don't mind if you call me Doc."

"Okay, we will call you Doc. We're not brothers but we've been friends from since school days. The only thing we argue about is scriptures especially "The Great Controversy, but don't mind us," said Troy in an affable voice.

"Whey you come from? Okay, no. I see you tired. We could talk about dat tomorrow," said Joseph. Doc walked through the faint candle-light to his room where he slept until morning. He woke up early, feeling strange in a strange house with strangers. He prayed, brushed his teeth, and then went up the hill at the

Briggs' to begin his first day as a yard boy. A new day and possibly a new life had begun.

Doc was born in and had always experienced scarcity but he'd always been hopeful that one day he would be blessed with plenty. He would have money to build his mother a better home, although he had sprung from, and lived in the ranks of poverty, suffering hardships and privations, he had an honest face and a friendly disposition, which impressed many people. Despite his propensity to help himself to estate fruits to satisfy his hunger, he was the type of youth who would do well if the conditions were different. His otherwise disciplined and organized approach to life increased his standing in the eyes of The Rocky Boys. This discipline and organized approach to things were the values he wanted to bring to his new job.

When Doc got to the Briggs' house, he found the broom leaning up against one of the pillars, idle and silent. First, he swept under the house avoiding the dogs' space. Then he moved them and cleaned the area, removing the dung with shovel and pan, which he dumped between the stool of bananas – natural manure. Afterwards, it was the main yard, which was criss-crossed with many cracks, where little eddies carved out holes in the mud after the rain, as they made their way down the drain to the end of the road. The area was uneven and difficult to sweep. He had to hop here, skip there to avoid getting his feet stuck in the veins in the ground. When Doc finished sweeping, he tackled the rest of his chores methodically, with a feeling of determination.

He had flask-backs of Ford and Mr. David, thinking this time, this time… But he had an open mind and his hopes were high. These kept springing up before him even in his lowly position as a yard boy thinking: yes, even as a yard boy I can do something with my youthful life. He had his feet on the first rung of the economic ladder, but he saw himself not too long now, standing tall at the very top of the ladder. Mrs. Briggs was standing on the veranda looking down at him. She yawned and stretched her fragile looking body, as she kept looking at him. Then she said, "Good morning, Doc."

Doc returned a "Good morning, Mam" and continued diligently with his chores. Clarissa was standing by her side and she said good morning to Doc as well in a childish voice. Raydon came along, greeted his chief Mr. Briggs with a healthy good morning and a smile and then made a sign with his cutlass to Doc saying: "You know you have a funny name. You not a doctor. Ha! Ha! Ha! And we keep calling you Doc." Then he went into the storeroom, got out a bag and ambled around the back of the garden.

Dothlyn came not long afterwards, saw Raydon chopping wood, went up to him and said, "Hi Kicks," grinned and went upstairs under Raydon's watchful lizard eye. Doc had breakfast in the kitchen. After that first morning, he went into the garden with Raydon and Dothlyn, which took them about 20 or 30 minutes walking. When they got there, Raydon climbed the breadfruit tree and picked some breadfruits, while Doc and Dots picked peas, dug potatoes and cut calalloo. They ate mangoes and guavas as time went by.

Afterwards, they sat down in the shade of a mango tree. She told Doc with a semi-comical face that since she was much younger she helped the Briggs in a general way. She said she was an only child who lived opposite Mr. Troy and Joseph and because Mrs. Briggs did not feel well most of the time, she filled in with the domestic chores around the house.

"Is me alone Clarissa wants to comb she hair and make she tea, she is a nice little girl you see. One day, ah hope ah go have a child like 'er," said Dots, beaming. Then she told Doc he was a good worker. Before she finished speaking Raydon came with a large pawpaw and gave her the fruit, which she and Doc ate, while picking peas and okra. After a while she shouted, "Kicks, stop what you doing and come here. Ah want to ask you something." As usual, Raydon never failed to respond to Dots request. He jumped down and sat very close to her.

"What is it?" he asked with a big smile.

"Eh, eh. Ah just wanted you to join us," said Dots. He withdrew a little from her as if to see her better, with his eyes surveying her closely as she reclined now on the trunk of the mango tree. Then their eyes met in a powerful gaze, in a kind of sensual understanding that words were not necessary to explain. Seeing this, Doc took up his bag and strolled down to the stream nearby, washed the dasheen and picked some water cress. Not long afterwards they went home.

Time went by and Doc fulfilled his job, hard, repetitive and menial though it was. He never complained to anyone. He fetched the groceries, bathed and fed the dogs, cleaned and swept with a sense of dutiful responsibility.

One afternoon, not long after lunch, he was relaxing under the canopy of cocoa trees when Mrs. Briggs shouted at him. "Come up here let me talk to you, boy" she said. "From next week you will have to cook dinner."

"I can't cook, Ma'am," Doc replied.

"I'll show you for the first time. It's not difficult."

"Well ah go try."

"You will have to try hard – your hardest. You understand me, boy?"

"Yes, Mam."

"You must also wash down and clean the bus every Sunday and bathe the dogs," she added in a cutting voice. "Use a lot of gospo in the water and when you finish, dry them and put blue on the sores."

"Yes, Ms. Briggs," he said with a lump of anger in his throat, thinking that was advantage. When she go stop exploiting me? He left her sitting on the veranda and went downstairs. He went over and sat in Sally Ann's hammock, which was tied between two cocoa trees, feeling rejected, sad and lonely. Well this job.... it getting too much... too hard... how long ah go put up wid it? Even Sally Ann trying to push me around: "Bring me shoes for me." "Go and pick me some oranges, you, Mr. Doc............"

Doc started teasing her, calling her "River Sally Water," to even things off in his own way. One Sunday afternoon after supper, when she came from swimming and almost caught him in her hammock, standing tall like a gazelle with flashing eyes she said, "I hope you didn't swing in my hammock, you Mr. Doc. I know..." Doc looked through her without replying, completely ignoring her.

She said, "I didn't hear you answer me."

He replied, "Run it again by me nugh."

She repeated herself.

He teased her, "Louder! Ah must be going deaf."

She retorted, a bit irritated, "Am I talking to the cocoa trees? Cocoa trees was in my hammock?"

Trying to calm things down, Doc said, "Keep cool. You going too fast. Ah hear you talkin' as if you didn' see me, so I said nothing. I didn't swing in your precious hammock, River Sally Water. Well, even if I did..?"

She scowled, "Ah tell you already, doh call me River Sally Water!"

Against her will and imperious manner, a relaxed smile played around her face. He teased her some more making uncharacteristic fun out of her indisposition. He had been planning an attack on her for some time, for lately; Sally-Ann developed a sarcastic air towards him and began to grow extra feathers on her emotional wings, especially when talking to Doc. She spoke curtly to him, passed him with her head in the air and if their eyes met, she would cut an eye at him, so he teased her some more. And then, of course, the job.

After all this added work Mrs. Briggs gave him, perhaps to help keep him out of mischief with her girls, who knows if he would hang around here much longer? He therefore decided to see what metal Sally-Ann was made of and what she would do if he played it out to the full. So he continued:

River Sally Water

Sprinkle in the Saucer

Rise Sally rise and

Wipe your weeping eyes

Turn to the East Sally

Turn to the West

Turn to the very one

That you love the best.

She was quite taken aback by his lines. Genuinely surprised, she rushed upstairs and put down her towel, laughing loudly. On her return, she said, opening her big eyes in wonderment, "Where did you learn to do that?"

"I can read and write too."

"Ah din know you could read and write and you walkin' around here talking, well talking and acting like if................"

Doc cut her short saying, "Lie down leh me give you a push."

She dropped into the hammock, still smiling. When she settled down, he gave her a big push. Then smiling to himself (for he got something back on her), he walked down to the gap, went into her parents' bus and sat down.

"Go to the shop and buy me half gallon kerosene and six flash light batteries. Tonight we going and hunt, so cook early," Mr. Briggs said to Doc.

Doc hurried down to Mrs. Agatha's shop and got the 'message'; then he bought a rock cake, sat down on a stool and bit hard into it. While he was sitting there, he saw a twin, big girls, looking at him. Michelle, one of the twins, said to him, "So you the new yard boy workin' at de Briggs?"

"We heard about you," said Marcel, the other sister, "But is the first time we see you. How you do?"

"Ah well, an' most of de time ah does be workin'," Doc replied.

"Alright, you can have some of my cola," Michelle said, offering Doc some of her carbonated beverage in the bottle. He drank some and held on to the bottle.

"Well any-how, we just letting people know about our local concert and talent show that is comin' up soon."

"And what about the dance?" Marcel filled in.

"Well I don't know if he goes to dance," she replied to her sister.

"Still tell him," Marcel nudged.

"Ok I'll tell him," she said to her sister. "And there'll be a dance too, you coming? We invitin' everyone. Briggy Briggs will be there."

Doc smiled when he heard the term 'Briggy Briggs.'

Encouraging him, Michelle said, "You must come, eh? Ent you go come? It go be nice, man."

Doc was quite touched by their sincerity. By now Michelle's cola was almost finished. He offered her the tiny remains but she told him, "You can have it all. You mussa been very thirsty. Hope to see you at the concert and dance. Ok?"

Doc said, "I'll be glad to come. But I don't know your names."

"I'm Michelle," said the slimmer of the two, "and dis is my twin sister, Marcel." She pulled her sister by the sleeve to shake hands with Doc. This done, he finished the drink. Michelle took the bottle from him and headed out the door.

"Whey you all living?"

"We live just after you pass Paraclete River, down in the valley. Ask anyone for Ms. Petrolina's house, everybody know us as 'Mother's Twins'."

"Thank you, Ah ha' to leave now too," Doc said. "Dey waiting for me."

"Well, we go see," said Michelle and they went down in the valley and Doc went up the hill. Weeks later, while Dothlyn was combing Clarissa's hair on a bright starry night, and telling Nansi Stories, she told Doc she knew all about the concert and dance. She added that Raydon was in it and he was practicing to play his guitar and sing a cowboy's song. This did not surprise Doc.

- IV -

Velma lived in a house, which was a stone's throw from the Briggs'. Dothlyn stayed on the right hand side of the road and Velma on the left, heading towards Mont Horne. They were friends. Velma had a freckled face, bright eyes and a high forehead. She also had a graceful walk. Doc and Velma met for the first time one afternoon on the Paraclete Bridge. He was on one of his shopping errands for the Briggs and she was coming home from school. Her hair was combed into two big plaits, in cornrow, and tied in one with a ribbon at the back. She was carrying her school bag, which had wooden handles made with holes through which they could be held.

"Hi Doc," she said as they faced each other. "My name is Velma!" He was not a stranger to her. She had seen him a number of times hurrying along with his shopping. She also gathered from Dothlyn, that he worked at the Briggs'; and as time went by, many nights after her doing her homework she laid on her bed and thought of him, for she liked him from the first time she saw him.

"My name is Doc – well George, but is okay to call me Doc," he replied.

"I know," she said, swinging her bag, full of books. "I know your name and..." Then they stood face to face looking into each others' eyes for a few moments, and for the first time in Velma's life she began to experience a sensation that was new to her. It was different from when the Shear's boy tried to hold her hands and chat her up. It was not the same with Doc.

Meeting Doc and standing there before him, she experienced that utter feeling of weakness of the knees, so that when walking up the hill, and reaching the Hannibalds' gap, where the hill was steepest, she feared she would fall, so she stopped to catch her breath and to ponder on these new feelings.

She felt oppressed and her heart was beating quite painfully. In her mind she felt that there was no need to beat about the bush. It was now certain that she was in love with Doc, and she knew he loved her too. When she was speaking with him, she wanted to throw caution to the wind; she wanted him to kiss her right there on the Bridge, for in her imagination she already felt his lips on hers – she shuddered for in reality she had to control herself and push the thought out of her mind.

Her parents would give her such a beating for behaving like that. She had heard about some parents who made their daughters kneel on a grater, just for talking to boys. She shuddered. But it was a memorable day just to exchange a few words with Doc.

One rainy afternoon, while Doc was under the house with the dogs – the kitchen was too small and he was not generally allowed in the main house – Sally-Ann came dripping wet from head to toe, as if she had just had a dive in Paraclete River. Despite her condition, she came over to talk with him before going upstairs to change. He teased her: "River Sally water".

After the episode with the hammock, she had begun to view him in a new light. She realized that he was not as 'desh' as she had thought he was, so she began to treat him with a certain level of respect, and even with certain amount of fondness. She showed interest in him and was glad to spend time around him when possible.

"Ah saw Velma today – this afternoon, and she asked me if you workin with me – ah mean here with us." Doc smiled nonchalantly.

"What you doing under the house?" She asked in a concerned voice. Then she smiled at him, as if she found the answer in herself, and from her pocket she threw two or three toffees at him, while eyeing him slyly as he caught them.

"We learn a new poem today," she continued. "Ah bet you don't know it."

"Bet me, nugh," he said crouching over a piece of stump under the house, thinking with the rain he wouldn't be able to go down to the bridge to see Velma.

"Go and take off your wet clothes and dry your hair before you catch a cold," Doc suggested. "You go tell me all about the poem afterwards."

Sally-Ann obeyed dutifully. She rushed upstairs.

"Evening, Mersey," she said. Not waiting for a reply, she changed and started drying her hair. Then taking a glass of lemonade, she rushed back under the house to meet Doc, with towel in the other hand drying her hair. Going up to him, she said, "you want to guess the name of the poem?"

"Sally," shouted her mother. "What you doing under the house in this rain?"

"Ah just telling - well asking Doc something," she replied to her mother.

"Who?"

"Doc!" she shouted.

"What something?"

"Ah coming up; ah go tell you."

"Your mother doh like you here with me alone," Doc observed.

"What's the name?" she asked Doc, stooping on the ground, drying her hair.

"Ah doh know. Your mother ......"

"Forget my mother. I want you to tell me the name of the poem," she insisted.

"Ah think you better tell me," he said to her playfully.

"Okay, it's de 'Noble Boy'. Recite it if you know it."

"Why should I say it? I'm not in school. Anyway we did that since in standard three," Doc continued with quiet self confidence.

"Bet you can't now though – you forget it," she said rising from the ground where she was crouching and drying her hair.

"You just want to tease me, ah mean, make fun of me and call me dunce," Doc said testing her.

"No, dats not true. Ah stop all dis stupidness since... Well, I don't want to make fun of you. If you know it, then you can help me; ah mean check me and ting, like dat ah mean you can take me up. Ah have to do it for Recitation next month, when Test come. Ah want to do well in school. Ah want to be a lawyer Doc." She said quietly. Then she went up to Doc and kissed his forehead. He held her and pulled her to him and pressed her against one of the pillars under the house.

"Noooo," she said, pulling away from him, frightened. "No, Doc. No." He released her and they both recomposed themselves.

He said, "Yes, ah know the poem. Is only last year ah leave school you know, ah still remember a lot of things... ah leave school, because........... me mother din have de money..." His voice broke like an egg on the kitchen floor. He was unable to complete the sentence.

"You mean your mother couldn't afford to send you to secondary school because she didn't have the money?" asked Sally-Ann with concerned politeness.

"Yes, something like dat," he replied. "Ah know the poem, okay? I will say some but you must begin. We say it in turns."

"Okay, ah go start," she said wistfully. "You would follow from where I stop. We will try to do as it is done in school."

Sally-Ann: *The woman was old and feeble and grey,*

And bent with the chill of winter's day

The street was wet with the recent snow,

And the woman's feet were weary and slow!

Doc: *She stood at the crossing and waited long, Alone uncared for amid the throng*

Sally-Ann*:* *Then came the boys like a flock of sheep,*
hail and snow piled white and deep.

Doc: *None offered a helping hand to her, so meek,*
so timid afraid to stir.

Sally-Ann *(in high spirits):*
Along came one of the merry troop,
The gayest boy in all the group
He paused beside her and whispered low,
I'll help you across if you wish to go.

Doc *(nervous and uncertain):*
He guided the trembling feet along,
Proud that his own was firm and strong

Both*:* *Then back again to his friends he went,*
His young heart happy and well content
"She is somebody's mother, boys you know,
Though she is poor and old and slow

Sally-Ann*:* *I hope some fellow will lend a hand to my*
Mother you understand,
if ere she's slow and old and grey.

Doc stands with her for the final stanza*:*
And somebody's mother bowed low her head
In her home that night and the prayer she said, was:
"God be kind to that noble boy,
Who is somebody's son and pride and joy."

Sally-Ann thanked him, looking up at him with a mixture of pride and surprise. Her mother called her again. “I have to go, Doc. Dey wonderin’ about me upstairs.” She took up her towel and rushed upstairs. Doc, now alone, had enjoyed her company. He loved her contagious ambition and in some way wanted to be like her, especially in the pursuit of knowledge but…

He went up to the kitchen to prepare supper and serve it. He was praised for his improving culinary skills. When he went “home” that night, he found Mr. Joseph and Mr. Troy deep in argument about a book called “The Great Controversy” and Luther’s struggle to reform the teachings of the Catholic Church. It was argued that Luther’s struggle led to a serious confrontation with the established Catholic teachings, and caused many people to die during the struggle for Reform. Certain statements surprised Doc, like the rich who seemed to favour the established church, especially the great and learned men. They were more superior to those of Luther and his supporters, who were in the majority of poorer and unlearned individuals.

Doc thought: well, there is only one God and that He is for everyone, irrespective of whether they be rich or poor; but he soon took his mind off their heated discussions and went and laid down on the sofa; he was too tired to follow their discussion which escalated into shouting at each other at times. His mind drifted to Velma and his growing feelings for her. Sleep evaded him and so he got up and went outside.

The moon was as bright as day; he decided to walk up the road in the direction of Velma’s house, perchance he would see her, get to stroll with her in the silvery moonlight. They would walk hand in hand, whispering beautiful words to each other. But all this was wishful thinking, because were she to run away with him and be found out, she would be severely disciplined for talking to a boy in the night, in the moonlight.

Her parents would want her to finish her schooling, find a good job and marry a man that would help her make something meaningful of her life. They would be concerned about the wild oats of youthful pleasure sown on the hard bed of the soft moonlight. Doc returned to his sofa after his walk, and he drifted off into sleep.

At last the day of the concert came and expectations were running high. It was a Saturday afternoon. Many people arrived early to secure the best position near the stage to get a good view. Others milled around on the grounds outside, awaiting the commencement of the performances. Many of the performers were already in the changing room. Michelle came in and made it straight to where Doc was sitting. "How you do?" she enquired.

"Ah dey," Doc replied.

"Ah glad too see you. The concert go start in a short while. I go check wid you later. Marcel outside," she said to him, patting him on his shoulder.

She was about to leave when Doc said, "you looking very nice, ah mean beautiful. Ah know ah go enjoy your singing and ting." She went into the changing room. Meanwhile, the Hall became packed; many people were standing around. The master of ceremony, a short shiny face man, did the introduction. He welcomed the audience and thanked them for their patronage.

He expressed gratitude to those who made financial contributions to the event, those who lent tables and chairs or helped in other ways, including donations.

"Without your kind assistance," he stressed, "this event this afternoon would not be possible." He wiped the sweat off his face with a handkerchief and returned it into his back pocket. First came the local talent competition. This was mostly made up of the young, who sang and played the mouth organ, the cocoa lute and some others made music on the comb covered with silver paper gathered from empty cigarette boxes.

The concert had a good kick-off and the performances were exciting. Two children recited poetry: one did "The Village Blacksmith," and the other "The two Crossing Sweepers." They received standing ovations. As a whole, the audience showed much appreciation by responding with fervour and enthusiasm. Following the poems, the actors and actresses staged a play: "The Runaway Slave!" It recounted the story of Nat Turner who led a revolt against slavery somewhere in North America. Although they finally caught and hung him, his followers were very proud of him because, in some places, the revolt led to the improvement of their living conditions. After the play came some singing. Michelle came onstage to do a duet with a young man called Winston, who looked at her very passionately and adoringly. Doc didn't like him because of the way he adored Michelle. Then they did a duet and sang a piece: something about Rags to Riches:

I rather go from rags to riches, If only you'd say that you will care,

And though my pockets will be empty, I will be a millionaire...

Though my clothes be torn and tattered, Yet in my heart I'll be a king,

For its only love that matters: its everything.

So open your arms and open your door, For every treasure you are hoping for,

Hold me, and kiss me and say *you are mine ever more*

Must I forever be a beggar, Whose golden dreams cannot come true

Or must I go from rags to riches, It's up to you..... to y-o-u-u-u.

Then, looking straight into Michelle's eyes while holding her hands, he repeated the last two lines: *Must I forever*......................

The reaction of the audience almost brought the roof down. The crowd applauded wildly; they stood up, clapped their hands, stamped while two young women threw their handkerchiefs at the young man. The men shouted out Michelle's name and some women put their kerchiefs to their eyes. It was a magnificent performance hailed with cries of "*Encore*!" They did the last verse again, and then he and Michelle held each other very closely while they smiled and waved to the audience.

Then it was Kicks', turn; his real name was Raydon. He was dressed up in an American dream, straight from the film strips of Hollywood: he was an un-filmed Black Grenadian cowboy, wearing the complete outfit with a Roy Rogers hat, shirt and pants. The hat had a string and the pants a cord tied around it. All he lacked was a horse. His six stringed guitar rode him in onstage where he holstered the audience's attention, saddled his cowboy song and his fingers galloped across the canyons and strings of the American plains in Grenada. His notes pierced the evening with his:

"O lay heeeeeeeeeeee,

O lay he lay he la-layheeeeee"

He went on olayheeing and laying while the audience applauded heartily, shouting both his name and nickname. He ended with a dynamic flourishing "twang" on his guitar and proceeded off stage. Dothlyn was in high spirits, touched by his singing. During the intermission Kicks went and sat near to her. She looked him over with quiet and proud satisfaction, as friends came to shake his hand. They said things like: "Well done boy," and "You good you know."

The intermission was short, because they were somewhat behind with their programme. People were knitted together here and there in small groups, eating, drinking and making merry; old talk was never in short supply. Michelle brought Doc some ice-cream and Marcel gave him popcorn. Providence was looking after him.

"You enjoyin it?" Michelle asked.

"Yes," Doc responded.

She added, "I saw Velma lookin' at you when we was talking. You know her?"

"Well," he said, surprised, "Ah meet her coming from school sometimes."

Michelle put her hands around him, and she held him close. He liked her adult, floral smell, which came to him as she hugged him; Doc wished that that hug would never end; but things come to an end, sometimes. The intermission ended and the MC reminded them that the final part of the evening event would be the dance.

People danced to the music of the famous "Silver Star Serenaders," a band from the capital, St. George. He, Doc, thought that the musicians looked foreign and acted and spoke like foreigners, but they were all from town and were a little different in some ways from country people. Doc had never seen people dance closely before, so when the Serenaders pitched up the calypso 'Jean and Dinah' and people drifted onto the floor and started moving their waists so rapidly, he was amazed.

He saw the Briggs family at the far corner of the Hall; they sat together around a table by themselves. Mr. Briggs, vague as usual, was well dressed in a long sleeve white shirt and flannel pants. Sally-Ann too was dressed up, looking like a Christmas tree. She was looking healthy and very tall, conducting herself like a proper young lady. She was wearing little heels and a long dress. Her eyes met Doc's. Clarissa hailed him with: "Hi Doc!" She too was looking pretty like a little doll. Doc didn't want to be around his employers, so when Mr. Troy and Joseph came and asked him to go and buy them some sweet drinks, he was relieved to run the errand.

When he went back into the main Hall he saw Velma with her parents. She favoured him with one of her very wholesome smiles, not long after she came and sat close to him. "I've been looking around for you," she said quickly surveying his face. "Where have you been? You were here from the start?" she spoke in a soft honeyed voice, with affection written all over her face; but she felt cheated by not meeting him before, and even more so, when she had heard that he was in the company of Michelle – that big girl who is not even his companion; she frowned.

"I heard you were with Michelle," Velma tested him. Doc explained to her how he met the twins, how Michelle had shared her drink with him and through them he got to know about the concert.

"Is that all? Ah mean with Michelle?" Velma enquired.

"Yes, she has been kind an' friendly. Ah dunno many people in Paraclete," Doc confessed.

"Okay, okay," Velma said. "I knew you were coming."

Surprised, Doc enquired, "How? Who told you? Sally-Ann? Dothlyn?"

"No, Mr. Joseph, he knows ...."

"What he knows?" No reply.

Instead, she said with that steady gaze of hers: "We go dance?" Doc didn't pursue the question about Mr. Joseph any further. "We go dance eh," she insisted. The truth is neither of them knew how to dance.

"I've never been to a dance before," Doc said. "Ah can't dance really."

"Me neither but we can try." They both began dancing, awkwardly at first, their emotions and attraction to each other not helping. Doc remembered and shared an African proverb used by Mr. Jacko, an old man from Telescope, which said: 'If you can talk, you can sing; and if you can walk, you can dance'. He and Velma looked at the moves of the older dancers and decided to imitate them. Doc took her left hand in his and put his right arm on her back, when they did so, emotions ignited their youthful bodies.

As they danced, his right hand slipped down to her waist. They danced to the middle of the crowd on the dance floor to hide from telescopic eyes and screen the awkwardness of their moves; toes winced, knee caps touched, eyes twinkled, lips smiled, palms clamped together; and their hearts beat their own staccatos; their sails tilted this way and that, in the bobbing, swirling, human tide. Every calypso note of the band blew colours into the air; every beat of the drummer a rumour in the soul. Laughs were felt and the noise of the revelry grew as loud as intimate silence in the public eye.

Although she did not see them, Velma felt the glare of her mother's eyes and the heat of her father's gaze, for the dance was too big for her; the tide too strong in the human throng. The sea was deep and the waves wild and wide, and the current strong, in the music of the throng. She could not see them, her parents; but she could feel their control tugging in her school girl's mind and her inner eyes knew they were somewhere looking out for her, peering at her through a neighbour's orbits. Her face lifted up to Doc's and he bent down and stole a kiss. It was a thrilling kiss. Is he the one that would be mine forever? The music stopped like a wave in the sand and the crowd parted. Her mother saw them and came towards her.

"Who is dis young man?" she asked her daughter. "Who is he parents?"

"He name is Doc. He workin' wid de Briggs," she replied. The band was taking a short break before the next song.

"I see. Well is time we go now," she said to Velma. "We have to go now."

"Good night Doc," Velma said to him smiling.

"Night, Velma," Doc replied, as she and her family left the hall.

Sally-Ann was looking on with a mischievous smile on her face. Marcel joined Doc with a glass of juice and Kicks and Dothlyn came towards him as well, as the band struck up another calypso. It was hot and jumpy, and there were no holes barred. The music flowed in a pulsating rhythm and carried them off into a musical frenzy, except for Doc who stayed on the shore of the human sea.

They twirled, bent, spun around in spectacular personal performances; they swung their hips, twisted themselves from Africa to the Caribbean, with a touch of the West African fertility dances, rotating and gyrating with alarming alacrity. Doc stood on the side staring at the rapidity of their movements, his head keeping the rhythm. He thought their waists were operating by electric strings.

Doc disliked the way "Rags to Riches" twirled and twisted and gyrated with Michelle. Worst of all for Doc, she seemed to be enjoying it, for there was a permanent smile curled around her mouth. Dothlyn and Kicks were also enjoying themselves, dancing so close; there was no place for breeze to pass. Her eyes met Doc's; she was smiling from ear to ear, like Brer Anansi.

The final piece for the night was a slow – a piece called "Vaya con Dios" which reminded him of his dance with Velma earlier on. Marcel came and held on to his arm for a short time and then led him onto the dance floor. He held her very tight, but not as close and personal as with Velma.

Halfway through the song Marcel's boyfriend came with his young sister. Marcel went over to dance with her boyfriend and Doc danced with the sister. Rags to Riches danced with Michelle. With the new waltz, he held on to her as if she belonged to him. He had his arms wrapped tightly around her waist and his face was on hers dreamily. After the song, there was a look of exhaustion and pleasure on people's faces. It was late at night or early in the morning, it was time for Doc to go and so he did.

After the concert, life with the Briggs continued with its routine: sweeping, cleaning, cooking, bathing dogs, doing groceries, trips to and from the garden and any other chore that his employer felt to throw at him. How long would he be able to put up with that life that was not a life at all? Sally-Ann was fairly regular at hand and she was amiable towards Doc but his mind was wavering.

He was thinking of making a move, but he was not too sure about the timing and what course of action he would take. Changing job was on the cards; but what other job could he do, finished with school and unskilled? Indecision led to inaction and a sort of festering in his mind, in his spirit, so for a few weeks after the concert he said nothing, nothing about his plans to anyone including Sally-Ann. She of course came from time to time for his assistance with her poetry.

"Take me up; take me up," she would say and Doc would do so willingly. From Julius Caesar to Romeo and Juliet, to the Village Blacksmith and many more, he was there. Unable to go to secondary school, the crumbs of secondary education filtered through to him under the house, as he coached her. Life it seemed was dealing him unfair cards, with gentle spears that javelined him to Rome and back through the eyes of his young female patron.

Life was not fair; yet it gave him a backhanded secondary education, for life's school was without walls that painted your life with colourful words that could ink you forever. The Prince of Peace was not in his heart in Paraclete; he bobbed and ebbed with the tides of life. Sally-Ann was doing well at school, with the help of a primary school educated hand. What irony of life! Surely, Sally-Ann would be tops when she sits her exams.

One afternoon she came home busy as a bumble bee; Doc was in the kitchen busy preparing something for supper. She came into the kitchen, which was not usual, for they generally met under the house or near to her hammock. "Boy look at this," she said animatedly pulling out a note from a little white envelope. It was the exam results and as predicted she was top of the class in all subjects and number one in her recitation. She stood there prating away with him in an unusually free and uneasy manner.

"Ah must thank you for your help, I must not forget that," she said. She took a deep breath and sighed.

"I couldn't stand you at first... but..." and she put her hand to her mouth as if she wanted to reprimand herself for confessing what she did. She felt she'd betrayed herself, her innermost thoughts.

"Ah know you din like me, you tried to push me around at first and I didn't ...."

"I wouldn't say that," she said, cutting in, defending herself.

"What is it then?" he challenged her.

"Ah didn't know you well – well... not good enough, you know. Ah sorr ...."

"You what?" he asked her. She laughed.

"Doh worry, come let me tell you something."

"What? Ah have to..." She began falteringly. "I have to... well... go and..."

She was standing near the kitchen window looking down at the road that would one day probably lead her away from home: to work, start her own life, raise her own family, build her future... Doc went and leaned against the window too, his heart beating a cadence on its own that had nothing to do with the dinner he had to prepare, its drumming racing down the streams of shadow in the valley. He didn't touch her at first but was close enough to put his arm around her shoulder, a curious Western smile jamming the corners of his mouth. Outside the birds played in the evening sun, as they do every day God made. He tried to kiss her. "Doc," she said in an emotional voice, her heart shaking at the young cage of her ribs to get out. Get out what? Get out of what? She shivered like a frightened bird caught in a trap; she was too scared and shocked even to shout. He pressed her against the window with the full weight of his body.

"Sally-Ann?" a voice called from outside.

"Dots coming!" she said nervously to Doc. As he released her, the crumpled school envelope fell to the ground like a flake of sin. The wind blew nature's evening music through the kitchen window and she flew upstairs to her bedroom, scarcely glancing at Dotlyn on the way, confused about what Doc did, what she should think, what she should feel, what she should do regarding Doc: their yard boy and her friend and tutor, not certified. Doc is a deck hand... he crossed the line... Why are boys like that? Before they could talk to you, get to know you good, they are ready to jump you, like some animal. I like him but I don't know that I love him. Why would he force me, if he respects me, really loves me?

Weeks went by after the incident. Sally-Ann never spoke about it to anyone. Her admiration and growing affection for him, and maybe even the feeling of tenderness she felt regarding him were vanished completely. From that day, she double checked her resolution and determination towards her education. What would have happened to her if Dothlyn didn't call? She was disappointed in Doc and so she went back to her natural stage of imperial haughtiness; it was her social safety net.

She returned to her old ways, head held high, and walked with rapid studious steps and square shoulders, nose pointing forward like a sailfish, piercing the air and anything that came too close. She, unlike Velma, carried her bag of books against her chest like a righteous breastplate of studiousness, her arms crossed protectively over them. These demonstrations were more pronounced when Doc was around. Now, not only the incident fixed a gulf between them; but the books, her parents' assets, her station, her Catholic education, her confusion...

Velma's parents put on a short leash on her since her dance with Doc. If they happened to meet, she would be with a friend, or her younger sister. It was as if circumstances of life had chaperoned him out of hers. As for Doc, the boring menial chores began to deaden his nerve, his soul and his spirit. For a short time both Sally-Ann and Velma were emotional balms of distractions that took his youthful sensuous mind away from his job. Then the waves of yard boy chores would gallop in again, deadening his mind and breaking his spirit. His indecision jockeyed him in the Briggs' long circular racetrack of chores.

When would be the right time to leave this job? Is there ever a right time to leave a job like this one? Some people remain yard boys all their lives, Mr. Joseph said, growing old and never growing up really, just decayin' like the breadfruit skin one would throw in the fig stools of time to manure them.

Why should I be fertilising other people's lives alone, while mine stay stuck in menial tasks? Look at Sally-Ann, part of her success at school is mine. My name should be on her report too, come to think of it. Now she is Princess Sally-Ann or Juliette, and me the Caesar not yet emperor of his domain. Yet she's always there hovering about, vague, like a spirit... Girls are strange creatures to hang around "frogs and snails and puppy dog tails..."

From time to time, Velma danced with him in the dance hall of his memory... the kiss... sparks of youthful desire... flames of youthful passion... love... The Briggs came in too and joined the dance. How will he tell them he had to leave their job? What would become of him? The terrifying face of poverty stood grinning at him, waltzing around him, through him, growling, snarling, ethereal and naked. Mama Misère never seemed so close, baring her merciless hungry fangs! Ah got to get out. I'm a young man. My future is ahead of me. I have to leave. It is best to leave now... soon... now.

The thought came to him: "If you dissatisfy wid a job, change it." There was no future for him with this job. He thanked Ms. Catherine for trying to help him out; it had plugged a little economic hole for him and his family. His eyes were more opened now; he had met some nice people but the job itself had outlived it usefulness. He had to move on. It had not yet dawned on him that he came to the Briggs as a young yard-boy; but was leaving an experienced yard-boy cook. He was not matured enough to make full sense of either his history or his experience.

One morning, when Mr. Briggs was out and the children gone to school, he knocked at the back door of the house, and Mrs. Briggs told him to enter. He went to where she was in the sitting room, on her favourite mahogany rocking chair, leaving some comfortable distance between them. Before he could speak, she said, "What you want? You should be..."

Cutting her short, Doc said to her, "Ah know Ma'am. Ah jus want you to know ah leaving de work by de end of de month, so you go have to find another yard boy."

"What you sayin?" she said, genuinely surprised.

"Thank you Mam for de work, but de work too hard, and ah does be tired and there is not much money in it and no future for me here and ah want to go and learn a trade or something."

"What you sayin' boy? You want to go out?" she said, trying to make sense of his decision or maybe to confuse him.

"No, Mam. Ah leaving de work," he continued. "De work too hard and de money small..." By now the effect of what Doc was saying began to sink in, like a stone thrown into the big river basin under the colonial bridge built over the Paradise River. She got up from her rocking chair where time was quietly, painfully settling into her. She came towards him in a state of discomfiture, her glasses hanging around her neck. Her steps were feeble and determined.

"Tell me, is it really de money? Ah thought you di like it here? All de help you givin' Sally-Ann with her Recitation..." She was trying to feel him out, to see if something had transpired between them, for she had noticed a distance between them for some time now. Something must have happened, something important, something hot or cold or in-between. She could not put her finger on it; her daughter was the same size and her monthlies were in order.

"Ah have to move on Mrs. Briggs. There is no future for me here, Ma'am."

"You want more money?" she asked excitedly – a state in which Doc had never seen her before. She had money and power over him. She thought that she had him to hold now. Money, money always draws people, controls people, make people do what they don't normally want to. She had always been so calm and in control. Now she seemed so ruffled and unsure of herself.

"We can see how we can improve your pay, with a little more responsibilities, of course," she continued.

"No tanks Mam," he replied matter of fact. "I ha' to move on."

She felt powerless in the face of his decision. There was no way of persuading him to change his mind; change was his mind, rolled into a firm circular ball and ready to roll, down the hill, like the gingerbread man.

"Excuse me Mam. Ah goin an do me chores now, if dat is OK wid you." She made a gesture with her hand for him to leave and he walked out the room, down the backstairs and into the small servants' kitchen behind the house to continue his domestic chores. He washed the breakfast dishes and scrubbed the pots and pans, then the kitchen floor. Later in the day he prepared the dogs' food and made preparations for the family supper, as usual. He attended to his work as thoughtfully and as methodically, even though he had slated himself to leave at the end of the month.

That night during supper, Mrs. Briggs shared the information of his intended departure with the house circle. There were whisperings of: "Why?" "What wrong?" "Who interfered with him?" Clarissa looked at Doc with sadness in her eyes, while Sally-Ann put on an air of: "I don't care"; then soon after, she excluded herself from the supper table. For the rest of the month, there was an air of artificial excitement and enforced politeness at the Briggs'. Whatever the social bond that might have developed between them, it was broken. Doc started feeling like a stranger once more, working under a cloud that was sometimes shaded with tolerable resentment.

But nothing bothered him beyond measure for he had smelted himself into the armour of his decision and the prospect of another life, a better life, somewhere else. His turtleback hardened under his yard-boy responsibilities.

At last, the day of his departure arrived. The sun came up as usual, unhindered – here and there some curtains of cumulous clouds. No breeze. Humidity high. He said goodbye to Mrs. Briggs, for she was the only member of the family present. He did not really listen to her response, because he did not want to be softened by negotiations nor deterred from his mission, so, picking up his bag, he walked down the hill from the yard onto the main road that would take him home to Telescope. He looked up at Velma's house. He wanted to see her to tell her about their time together on the dance floor the night of the concert and about his leaving and much more. But he knew she was at school, so holding his bag in one hand he pushed the other into his pocket, straightened his Beep-bop cap and headed down the long lonesome road with a mixed up heart.

Winding his way along the road, he passed hog plum trees with their ripened fruits pattering on the road; mango trees with their fruits in various stages of maturity: ripe, yellow and green, tantalizing and mouth-watering to behold. There were cocoa, bluggoe and plantain, with their green leaves covering parts of the road and providing a welcome shade from the scorching sun. Was the sky angry with him or him with the sky? Times had changed but life remained the same.

Every step along the Paraclete road took him closer to home and family. He finally reached Telescope, home, arriving there with a mixture of joy and sadness not only about Velma, but Sally-Ann too. Most important, at the time, his mind was fixed on the problems of existence and the uncertainty of his future. Poverty stood starkly and frighteningly ahead of him.

Toiling, rejoycing, sorrowing
onward through life he goes –
Each morning sees some task begin
Each evening sees it closed
Something attempted, something done
Have earned a nights repose.

LONGFELLOW

Book Two

THE TAILOR SHOP

- I -

On returning home, Doc came to realise that the road ahead is paved with bitter hardship; some large iron boulders had to be removed for him to go forward. Two major issues had to be confronted; first, the gripping hands of poverty were digging into his flesh and kept beckoning fiercely at him. Secondly, he was also beginning to be consumed by the fiery coals of love for Velma and Sally-Ann too, apart from her imperious haughtiness which hovered in some corner of his heart. Thus his romantic heart became agitated and restless.

Armed as he was in his crusading state of mind, Doc decided to meet all those difficulties, to overcome them and crush them. He had no regrets of leaving the job; he had outgrown that position. But his change had other consequences. Most of all, he was passionately in love with Velma and he knew that she was in love with him. When she left him that night of the concert, almost being marched out the hall by her mother, Velma was thinking about the way he put his arms around her, his touch made her lose a little self-control. The passionate kiss was proof of their love.

"Come on girl, you sleeping on the boy shoulder in the middle of the dance floor," said her mother nervously. "What you think people go say." Velma said nothing but lazily continued their way home. She made some apologies to her mother and went into her room. It was late in the night when she fell asleep; she had a restless night; Doc overcrowded her sleep throughout the night.

Doc, too, missed the meetings by the bridge; their meetings on the bridge were not planned. The bridge was the first meeting place and it came to symbolize something special, something unique and something very dear for both of them. The bridge was their unspoken romantic shrine, it bonded them together. Doc liked meeting with her there; he liked the way she held her bag with wooden handles packed with books. At home, he was thinking of them dancing together and of the moment when she abandoned herself in his arms dreamily on his shoulders and then the long unending kisses alone together on the dance floor.

Unknown to themselves, they were demonstrating an unrehearsed romantic performance where their bodies, hearts and minds were one in unison. They were oblivious of everyone around them; it was a time of blissful forgetfulness as they floated away with only the music of their hearts until they were rudely awakened by Velma mother's hand on her shoulders and her angry voice saying, "It's time to leave."

For some time though, Doc began to question his judgement. Perhaps, he thought if I didn't leave, things might have improved for me at the Briggs. Then Sally Ann's shadow fleeted past him and his mind returned to Velma. He wished he had a chance to talk about their love. To tell her how much he love to see the freckles on her face and a lot of other things. These doubts and uncertainties, these rising and fallings of the emotional barometer, these swings of optimism and pessimism would plague him on and off for a very long period in his early life.

A few days after his arrival, his mother said, "Ah running down de road to come back; I have to see my God brother." After she left Doc went to see Ghost; they had to talk. He passed in the back of the garden under the golden apple tree where he met Vicklyn, Ghost's younger sister, playing with a ragged doll and eating a mango.

"He dey home?"

Without a reply she shouted her brother's name saying in a weak voice, "Doc come."

On seeing him, Ghost said, "You looking good, man, Parcelete agree with you in a kind of way man, how was the work?" Doc explained that it was hard, but he managed.

"Well ah could see dat, you looking real good; ah hear you have a girl," and he slapped him on his back. They both laughed a chummy laugh which seemed to affirm Ghost's statement about the girl.

"Who is she? Is she the one with the tack-tack marks on her face?"

"Yes her name is Velma; ah sure you see her already; she goes to the convent, bright as a shilling." Doc explained about Velma, the freckled-faced girl. He told Ghost that they use to meet by the bridge every time he was on the way to the shop and when she was coming from school. He didn't want to elaborate a great deal about Velma.

Then he continued, "But there is another one; her name is Sally-Ann; you know her, she comes down by her aunt sometimes. Ah think she likes me, but, ah doh know; she kiss me on my forehead once or twice under the house."

"What boy! You striking good oil already; two chicks in a short time," Ghost said with some joviality. He was pleased to hear that side of Doc's Story.

"But ah doh know," said Doc. "Then you know ah de go to the concert and thing, man; ah even dance, yes boy, ah dance with Velma and we kissed and when the music stopped we were dancing until her mother came and told her it's time to go."

"You mean you mash she toe? Ha! Ha! Ha!" Ghost laughed, it seemed funny to him.

"Well she mash mine too; but it was nice, everybody was looking at us dancing without music."

"You turning man, you going to dance and dancing and kissing too, you ain't easy."

Then they strolled up the road until they came to the ball pitch, where they picked mandarins and tangerines from Ms. Ethel's tree and they sat under a coconut tree and feasted. Following this, they exchanged stories about their lives over the past few months. Ghost told him that he was trying to become a mason, but work was slow.

"Since you left all ah had was two weeks building a dead wall all the way in Conference." Cold Coucou Face saw them and came over to join them. Doc gave him an edited version of his life story over the past few months. He never mentioned Velma or Sally Ann. The Sun was quite hot by then but they thought of a game of cricket. The wickets were under the coconut branches where they always hid them after a game. There were two bats there too, but there was no ball.

"And is only three of us," said Coucou Face.

"Well that's good enough, one bowling one batting, one keeping wicket." Ghost was firm on that.

Somehow, Ghost never liked to be dictated to by Cold Coucou Face. He never liked to follow his lead or anyone's for that matter, except Doc's. "What you say, Doc?"

Doc said they should play. "Out ah man for your bat," then added, "ah wish we could ah play ah two for two."

"Well leh we wait then until somebody come across," said Ghost quietly. They ate their fruits in silence until they saw Mud Mask, who immediately joined them. He too, was glad to see Doc. When he questioned him, Doc gave him a more limited version of his stay in Paraclete.

"Ah glad to see you back; all this working business is not good. Now we can lime when we want."

"Now we go play two a side," said Ghost. "Me and Doc and you and Mud Mask," pointing at Cold Coucou Face. Ghost went over to Mr. John's land and picked some young breadfruit because they couldn't find their wooden knot ball. They played until they were quite exhausted from the midday sun. Then Mud Mask had to go and give the cows water. When he left Cold Coucou Face took his exit. Following this, Ghost wanted to know what Doc was going to do. Doc told him that his mom wanted him to go and learn a trade - Tailoring.

"What! Dat good boy, ah better come too, een ha' much mason work around."

"Well come, you think your grandmother go want you to do that," said Doc. "Ah doh think she go mind, and tailoring is clean and we go see a lot of girls passing and ting," said Ghost.

"And doh forget you learning to sew as well," he reminded Ghost.

"Oh yes," Ghost said as he thought about the fact of learning to sew and they were not really going to look for girls but to become Tailors!

"I have to start on Monday."

"Monday! You doh waste time?"

"Well you know mum she said she agreed for me to start on Monday."

"Okay then, Monday" said Ghost.

The rest of the week past by quickly. When Monday came, Doc was dressed up in his new pants and shirt and his new Jim boots. He was now on his next job, learning to sew. Ghost was standing in front of his gap waiting for him. His feet was well oiled and his face was shining like a six pence ah fus he had oil on them. He too, had on a new outfit. For the moment they didn't feel like Doc and Ghost, the Rocky Boys. In fact they were not even wearing their Rocky Boys cap; they left them at home.

There was no lazy drawling walk heaving one foot far ahead from the other taking their own time, with their hands deep in their pockets. They were not rocking, there was no loud talking. Ghost didn't even call out any of the girls by their nick names. They met Lorna, and normally Ghost would shout at her 'Cocoa wood foot', but they passed her unmolested on her way to school. She looked surprised. They were just cool, making their way to the tailor shop.

They arrived at Brother Noble's shop which was upstairs his house. They greeted him with a loud and unusual "Good

Morning!" Ghost stuttered a bit as if he had tight tongue, Brother Noble greeted him warmly but was surprised to see Ghost. He wasn't expecting him. However, he didn't mind as long as he was serious about the business of learning a trade.

The tailor shop was in a big square shaped room. There was one single machine, a long table with half made clothes on it, on the side of the table there was a big iron with smoke coming out from the back. There was a man with a long pants and a serious face know as 'shark eye' to the boys. He was sewing on the machine while Brother Noble was measuring with the tape measure hanging from his neck. He had a pair of large scissors in his hand.

He measured the fabric on the table; put a little cut or a little notch here and a little notch there. This was the first thing that caught their eyes. "Sit down and take a five" he said in an amiable voice. They sat down on high stools. "So you want to be a Tailor," said Brother Noble in a friendly voice while carrying on with his measuring and markings.

"Yes," said Doc. "We want to learn to sew just like you, sir".

"Ah glad to hear dat," lifting his eyes to look at Ghost a little dubiously. "Let's have juice", he said. Soon after, all four of them had juice from a tin can. Shark Eye looked up and down at Ghost critically, thinking in his mind, 'I doubt you are tailoring material I sure don't think you will make it.' Then Ghost met his eyes. Brother Noble was a medium built man with a serious, studious expression on his face. He had long thin fingers with a mark on his thumb that the constant use of the scissors left there.

He sat relaxed as he took his juice interval and introduced Doc and Ghost to his assistant whose name was Winston but known to Doc and Ghost as 'Shark Eye'. They both knew him and were glad to be introduced to him as Winston. Ghost was muffling a laugh because he liked to call up Shark Eye but he tried to keep a straight even face. Doc was thinking, “In truth, in truth a new phase of my life has begun and ah go go for it.”

After the juice interval, which lasted about fifteen minutes, Brother Noble called them to the table to explain a few things as a tailor which they must learn. He said, eyeing Ghost critically, “The first thing you have to learn is to make button holes, then hem, then to peddle the machine”, pointing to the single machine in the corner.

“You understand what ah saying”, they both answered yes together.

“You boys would have to make the juice; somebody will go down the road and get ice from Mrs. Billy. There is a little room in the back where I keep the sugar, lime, gospo and orange, that would do; everybody can bring something, you will have to buy your own cakes or bread and salt fish though.” They all laughed and Winston made an impression like a laugh.

Brother Noble took two pieces of Khaki fabric and showed them how to cut a button hole. “You cut it like so”, he held it up to show them, “not a big cut you see here,” he pointed at the part of the material where he made the cut. “After you cut you base it like so”, and taking up the needle he placed his finger under that fabric then based around the cut hole. “Doh worry,” he said. “You go get the hang of it in no time, in the meantime put on these thimbles and come and look at me and see what I am doing, look at how ah making button holes and learn to use the thimbles.” They put on the thimbles and then he showed them how to bend their fingers to get behind the needles. The thimbles, he said is to protect their fingers especially when they were sewing tough fabrics with their hands, especially khaki drill.

They spent the greater part of the morning making button holes, learning the use of the thimbles and learning to hem. Many of the button holes were 'pig eyes' but brother Noble assured them that it was not too bad, and it will take a while to get the hang of it. "Patience is a virtue, don't worry," he said.

In the afternoon they did almost the same thing, except that Ghost had to make juice and Doc had to light up the iron. This routine continued with little variation for a number of weeks. During that time they became quite skilled in mastering the use of the thimbles and making button holes. Their hemming too, was neat. Even the herring bone stitches were well presented and they were commended by Brother Noble for the way they caught on so fast. Even Shark Eye agreed that they were quick. "And dey work is neat too, especially Doc's buttonholes and his hemming" said Shark Eye grinning and darting an eye in Ghost's direction.

One evening on the way home after Ghost pelted down some mangoes over the road near Mrs, Charles shop and washed them under the pipe by Mrs. Alexander, Ghost became very reflective after a bite or two of a large juicy mango. Then he said, "We doh getting no pay you know, not even a little something to go to matinee." "But man it's good we learning a trade," said Doc." "Alright, anyhow too much sitting down and way we sit up dey we could hardly see anyone passing." "You mean any girls." "Yes," replied Ghost with his mouth full of mangoes. "Well anyway," said Doc, "I would like to see Velma." "In the meantime leh we just work at it." Doc added reflectively thinking about the night of the concert. "Velma or Sally-Ann? Which one of them or is it two of them together, Ha! Ha!" "Just Velma."

Ghost said Doc should choose carefully but he like Velma. Then he crossed over to the other side of the road, threw the mango seed in the drain, washed his hands at the stand pipe and wiped them with his handkerchief. Then they made a slow progress up the Canal road.

Weeks went by; and Doc settled down to his tailoring beginning truly to enjoy it and reminded himself of what his grandmother use to say: nothing ventured nothing gained. By now he'd mastered the art of the button hole and hemming. Then he learned to stitch; before that he learned to thread the machine. He found the peddling of the machine very hard. It kept going backwards and forwards and bursting up the thread and breaking the needles. However, with time, patience and constant practice he mastered the art of stitching which when he did he performed with great dexterity and was commended by Shark Eye for his newly learned skill.

"Boy you is fast like lightening but try and make the stitches straight," said Shark Eye by way of advice. "Okay, ah go remember; ah go try to make them straight," said Doc. Doc felt good and kept quiet. 'You coming to come', he thought and was determined to improve his work. "In three months' time I must learn to sew pants and shirts. Coming to come is not good enough. I want to come good, get my work done properly; ah want to reach the top, get to the winning pole, dats what ah want." Doc was determined to put himself under some heavy manners; as far as he was concerned tailoring was another one of the many rivers he had to cross in his life. The first happened to be yard boy, now it's tailoring, but deep down he knew that was not all. Time was moving on and he wanted to move with the time. After tailoring, what? He hadn't the faintest idea. It is tailoring now though, and come what may he was sure he would make the best of it.

Ghost did not take to the tailoring as Doc did. Every now and then he would have an excuse for being absent from the shop. Doc began to ignore his excuses; he never even told Brother Noble about them any longer.

One evening, he said to Doc, "This tailoring is making me lazy. Everything is ah sitting down ah sitting down, me blood go turn water and ah go get old before me time; ah think ah going back to mason work man." Doc told him he would continue the tailoring. Ghost's decision to leave tailoring did not come as a big surprise to Doc. He felt from the beginning that Ghost was only going along with him, that Ghost had no serious commitment to tailoring and in truth and in fact his heart was with the task of masonry, so he encouraged Ghost to move on. And Ghost moved on and Doc remained.

"Go on man, take it; to besides you will earn some money, as long as we doh waste time. You doing something that you would like and I'm doing something that I would like. We is still we." So Ghost moved on back to masonry and Doc remained with tailoring. But Doc also wanted to move to another tailor shop where his cousin was working. One morning he arrived at work much earlier than usual, thanked Brother Noble and Shark Eye for their help and said he wanted to join his cousin down by Murray's. They wondered if they said or did something he didn't like. "No", he said. "Ah just want to be near my cousin."

Not long after, Uncle Charles, "Charlo" the local builder, offered Ghost two weeks in construction where he was building a bridge that was washed away by floods after the heavy rains in October. This was in Upper Capitol. Doc went by Mr Gilbert's shop where he joined his cousin Raymond not far from Brother Noble.

When he told his mother about his decision to move she said to him, "Ah hope you don't go and get into any foolishness, you must put your hand to the grindstone and don't flinch." Doc said he won't get into any foolishness.

"Mr Gilbert's has a real tailor shop and he does not mind having me especially when he knows that Raymond is my cousin. In this shop everybody can see you and you can see many people, you don't feel lonely as if you hiding away; ah go see my friends and them and ah go want to learn even faster."

"Ah hope you know what you doing" said his mother. She was thinking about the school children especially the girls from secondary school and St. Joseph's Convent who usually attend piano lessons upstairs Murray's store. It is a popular place for young people to lime in the afternoon on their way home from school and it was right opposite Mr. Gilbert's tailor shop.

This new tailor shop was spacious, it was not linked to any house, and there were four people in the shop with him at any one time. There were three machines and two cutting tables. Mr. Gilbert and Mr. Sawney were partners and they owned the place. They had four young men working with them each one an accomplished Tailor and one was fast learning to cut and design jackets. Raymond, Doc's cousin from Dry River, was a very good, popular tailor, but he was not able to sew jackets as yet. Once they knew he was Raymond's cousin they showed him a great deal of appreciation. He had a lot of hand work to do; it was a serious place and he worked hard and fast. Work was constantly pouring into the shop. Every man, when Friday or Saturday came, gave him a little something, some pocket money.

"Doh mind," said his mother "if it's a quarter it's better than water, keep at it."

Within a short time Doc was able to stitch up a complete shirt; he was quite capable of sewing pants as well, except for the pockets. Not long after that he was able to complete both pants and shirt without help and to take measurements and cut and stitch all by himself. He even made a pair of jeans for himself without assistance. His first long pants! Everyone congratulated him. They made juice and bought him roti from the Indian lady Ma, who sells for them and they all had a little fete before he went home.

He worked for the boss and the others, continuing the hand work, pressing and keeping the iron well lit, especially when there was a big job: a suit or some uniforms. He did herring bone stitch, sewed buttons, soaked and dried khaki materials. When he completed sewing he cut off all the base threads then he pressed and folded them and made them ready for customers' collection; but he never got any job of his own for a long time. He continued though, to collect a little something, a few dollars here a few dollars there, but he had no regular income.

Uncertainty and extreme poverty continued to dog his trail. He felt himself spinning in a current of uncertainties about his future. "Ah wonder how ah go make a living?" Doc asked himself one day. He thought perhaps he was born to see trouble. "Is so de world is, ah din crucify Christ. All wey ah turn things bad. All these children coming from Secondary School with their boots and stockings going to piano lessons boys meeting up with girls and thing and they holding hand talking nice talk and thing and I am much older than these boys and they ain't drive a nail yet. But me, yard boy and apprentice Tailor." Doc reflected despairingly about his future. Then his mind raced back to the time he went to the doctor, Doctor Mc Sween in Grand Bras. Although he had a very severe griping pain, he still had time to read these words written on a plaque in the doctor's office in front of his desk:

Some men are born great, some achieve greatness

And some have greatness bestowed upon them.

He asked the doctor what it all meant, but the doctor had no time for him; he wanted him out of his office as soon as possible especially when he knew that this little ragga muffin little boy ten toes knocking could even read and now this dry foot country boy want me to analyse and explain this important quotation full of intellectual meaning and all that; he wants me to explain it to him. The doctor wondered what the hell this world coming to.

But Doc never forgot this quote. It stuck in his head longer than if a mason had put it there. And so he recalled it now: "Ah sure ah go achieve greatness, in for a penny, in for a pound, ah go achieve greatness," as grandmother used to say; "one thing for sure you have an English tongue in your mouth and whatever one man can do another can do," he reflected with a hopeful sigh.

Doc felt he was heading toward the achievement of Greatness. He didn't know how or what road he would take. He had no education to speak of but he could read the Royal Reader up to number six. At least, it's a start he can read. And didn't he use to read his friend's letters for him when he was just twelve or thirteen? His friend was in his twenties but could not read. So when his girlfriend wrote him from Trinidad, his friend Barry, who use to work on a public truck, marked 'PWD' Public Works Department, or as the Rocky Boys called it, 'Poor People Work and Dead.' For that, Barry use to allow him to ride his new racer bicycle and Doc would go sometimes to his house somewhere in La Bay when Barry was at work and have a good ride. It was a kind of payment. He could read even better now and couldn't see why anything should hold him back in his pursuit of greatness.

Doc decided to give tailoring nine months to a year and see what happened during that time. He would also be on the lookout for something to go with it, something that could bring in some money fast, so he would be able to buy a pair of shoes, a shirt or two and contribute something to his poverty stricken parents. It would be nice to be able to buy some fish at least once a week. With such thoughts, his spirits were lifted when he went back inside the shop.

Not long after, as if someone heard his yearning, he got his first tailoring job; a neighbour wanted him to sew a pair of pants for him. On his way to the shop next morning he stopped, took out his tape measure and his little black notebook with a piece of elastic around it and he measured up his neighbour. He wrote the measurement down in his little black notebook with the elastic band attached, then he put the book in his shirt pocket with the needle on it; he had a thimble on his little finger like a real Tailor. For the moment he was happy, he was in goat heaven. In the afternoon when everyone left, Doc and Raymond remained behind. Raymond promised to supervise his cutting. On his way out, Mr. Gilbert said to him, "If you not too sure about something Ray go help you." Doc told him that Raymond was staying with him. "Everything go be alright then, ah go see you in the morning." "Goodnight Sir," replied Doc as Mr. Gilbert, right hand in pocket, cigarette in the corner of his mouth, hat tilted on one side of his head, crossed over the road and headed for home.

Mr. Gilbert was a short man with a thick moustache and a broad box-like chest. He had a peculiar musty smell as if he had remained around some of the old clothes hanging on the rack too long and he had acquired its scent. He was a man of measured speech. He never said more than he had to and that was very little. He smoked many packs of Phoenix cigarettes a day; he had that faraway and often dull look about him. He acted like a mouse that would scuttle off at any sound or movement. He often rushed off to the club across the road and played cards; he gambled and drank. When he got a big job everyone was happy for him. At that time he became light-hearted; talked a little more and drank a little more.

Returning from the rum shop he would generally be whistling and singing. His favourite tune was: "Tilly gal, your nylon has a hole in the centre." Then he whistled light, light as a bird, he chirped along as a bird, he hopped lightly too; like a bird from branch to branch. But Mr. Gilbert was a serious man. When he was instructing his number one about the style he was designing for the job, his voice was firm and authoritative. Sometimes you would hear him say, "You see that boy; ah want you to do the sleeves just so," pointing to the crayon mark on the material. "And then ah want you to cut and mount up the back."

"Yes sir," his number one would answer with a smile. He was a very affable and jovial young man who always seemed to be happy and girls were always visiting him, then he would say, "Alright Chief, ah get it Chief." He and Mr. Gilbert worked very well together.

When Doc completed sewing the pants he pressed and folded it and tied it with a long piece of scrap material, then he folded it up and put it in a piece of brown paper and wrote the person's name on it with a red crayon, but Ray took it out from the bag and gave it a final overlooking to his satisfaction. That being done, everyone was happy. It was now late and time to leave. They closed the shop, locked it and left the keys in the usual place. They had a little chat in front of the shop after closure then Ray asked him what he was doing on Sunday. "Well, nothing special; we going down to the river and have our usual swim, after that we just liming until dinner time," said Doc." Or perhaps we might go to matinee, dey showing a good ranch at the De Luxe." "Why don't you come to the Christening on Sunday then? It's in Harford Village."

"Ah wonder boy". "Yes ah think ah go make that instead, but ah go have to walk, you know the bicycle tube is bad and ah doh have the money to buy one; it is about three weeks ah doh ride it." "Well leave early then, ah really want you to come, de house is down in Two Congo, near to the man who makes fibre brooms. It is up on the hill with all the red mud, you know it?" "Yes ah know the place, man," said Doc. Doc agreed that he would go to the christening.

He told Ghost about his invitation and about the bike. Ghost gave him $2.00 towards the inner tube. He made up the rest of the money and they got up early the next day. First cock crow. Ghost came and helped him fix up the bike before they went to the river for their usual early morning swim. As soon as they returned from swimming, instead of heading towards the pasture, he went home and had breakfast. His mother was surprised to see him home so early, so during breakfast he told her about the invitation from Cousin Raymond.

"You should go and enjoy yourself, Ray is alright; he is a nice young man; he won't lead you astray," said his mother in an honest voice.

"Okay Mum, I have to leave early, it's in the Village down by Two Congo."

"Put on your good shirt, the one that your aunt sent you from Trinidad, the New Yorker Junior, it look nice on you."

"You press it?"

"Yes ah press it long, and it hanging up on the back of the room door."

"Well ah going and brush me teeth and get dressed." He put on the pants he made, combed up his hair and thing, and bathing himself in alcolado he felt refreshed, real good and ready for the lime. The bicycle 'Desire Me' was standing by the grafted mango tree not far from the house. Ghost washed and shined it too. Doc jumped on his bike and rode up to the Village then down to Two Congo.

He had no problems finding the house. From far off, he could hear the music. It was a scorching hot afternoon. When he arrived there, he was perspiring like a pig. Someone asked him if he wanted some juice, he said he wanted some water. Dorothy went into the tent which was a little from the house and brought him juice in one hand water in the other. He drank the water but she kept holding the juice in front of him.

"Ah bring it just in case."

"You drink it for me", he said.

Everybody was in their Sunday best, all dressed up and looking good and thing. The Christening Ceremony was going on inside the house, speeches were being made, glasses were tinkling and there was a lot of hand clapping and singing; merriment was in the air. Ray was glad to see him and introduced him to his friend the baby's father. He was a man about Raymond's age, about twenty-two or twenty-three or somewhere in between, thought Doc.

Larry (for that was his name) was a short man with a huge smile, broad shoulders, wide eyes and cool, black skin. He was wearing a white shirt and gabardine pants neatly pressed which fell neatly over his two-toned shoes. He had a banjo hanging from his right shoulder. He was a friendly young man who oozed with happiness and was really enjoying life. He was in the pink of form, as they would say.

Larry extended his hand and squeezed Doc's own, then hugged and squeezed him saying, "Ah hear about you from your cousin, ah know you go be a little test. Have a drink, eat cake and food, and it have a lot of beautiful chicks around; make yourself comfortable. We'll catch up later. Ah have to circulate, like the breeze. You know what I mean little guy? Ah have to circulate." And he moved towards another knot of guests.

There was a great deal to eat and drink and the guests paid full justice to their host. There was a selection of drinks: mauby, ginger beer, sky-high cola, lime juice and much more. Cakes of all descriptions and lots of food: rice and peas, plain rice, yam, sweet potatoes, oil down and so on and so forth. Chicken roasted, chicken stewed, stewed pork and beef, curry goat plus the "hard stuff;" rum for so! Everyone was happy, eating, drinking, laughing, talking and kissing with steel band music topping up the merry making event with some calypsos.

The yard was ablaze with merriment. Doc was jostled, here, jostled there, but it was cool, he didn't mind. When he left the tent he went over by the leafy cutlet tree. Dorothy, one of the young girls he met before, left the group and went up to him and asked, "You okay?"

"Yes the Christening is real good, lively and thing." Dorothy knew his sister; they were all good friends, but she didn't know him or even remember meeting him before today.

"You was born in Trinidad or you live in Trinidad?" she asked good naturedly handing him a glass of juice; then they started a little old talk.

"I made this juice, ah sure you never drink a better juice than that", she said, without waiting for a reply to her former question.

Returning to her former question he said a long "noooooooo!" then he had a large gulp from her juice and agreed with her that it was the best juice that he ever drank, then he said, "I was born right here in Grenada and ah never been to Trinidad."

"But- well how ah never see you, your girlfriend keeping you under wraps? You too young to have woman keeping you under wraps already," said Dorothy jovially. Doc almost choked on his drink; he coughed and laughed at the same time which seemed to please Dorothy no end.

Then he replied: "Ah doh have a girlfriend."

"You doh serious. Ah thought ah hear they say there is a girl in convent who is mad about you."

"Ah tell you ah doh have a girl."

"What! Ah nice boy like you?" she replied, half jesting, half serious.

He was thinking, could she be serious about this girl in convent thing, when she said she didn't know him? He thought she was just trying something. By the time Doc got around figuring out whether Dorothy was jesting or otherwise, Larry returned with Raymond. Larry was now holding his banjo in his hand saying, "Let me play something for you fellas, man."

"What about the girls?" someone shouted.

"We can't live without them you know, said Larry. So ah go play for everybody. "That's what I mean in the first place." He was a little tipsy.

"We go have a little song and thing," he said, opening his eyes very wide and sporting and unsteady gaze. He struck up a cord on the banjo.

"What you go sing boy the same old song you does sing over and over?" asked Grey in a sparring mood."

"No that's a new one it's a love song."

"Ah din know you could sing love song, ah thought was only calypso."

"What happen to this little girl, she playing big woman, bantering with me," said Larry groggily. But at last everyone was quiet and Larry corded up, cleared this throat and started up:

"Once I had a secret love....." everyone began to laugh and Dorothy laughed out the loudest; she seemed to be enjoying Larry's confusion more than most. In her enthusiasm, she continued to slap Doc on his back and hugged him around his neck and waist in a familiar manner.

"Go on man, go on and doh bother with dem, especially this little madam," someone encouraged from the crowd.

.... *"That lived within the heart of me, and all too soon my secret love, became impatient to be free........."*

Serious laughter started again.

"So you sentimental then?" asked Myrna, Larry's girlfriend, the mother of his son James.

"Boy you never sing ah love song like that for me," she said accusingly. More laughter. For Larry had problems making the high notes.

From the crowd, "you bust man you better pack it up and try something else." Doc thought he would never hear the end of that song, he was right, Larry gave up. Soon, someone came around with a mouth-watering set of refreshments and what with all the interruptions, secret love was returned to its secret place. Not long after that, Ray said, "give us a calypso man you know you good at that,"

Dorothy agreed, "Something hot and spicy" she added.

"OK, Ok give me ah chance, give me ah chance, and hear this one:"

'Mammy, Mammy, where is my daddy?

In de dew and cold your daddy sleep on the cattle pole."

Larry tapped his feet, shuffled along and really opened up on the banjo strings with electrifying rhythm which set the place alight. Soon, everyone started to whine up and do their own thing. The rum was flowing like water, the music was hot like fire, then two other guys picked up an empty rum bottle and a spoon and joined in; another one came with a piece of iron and a big nail, then one pulled a comb with a piece of silver paper, and music was blasting in the air in a serious way. Ah whole orchestra was in motion; with this impromptu orchestral band everyone swinging to the rhythms.

They whined and jumped up, holding on to one another. They just leggo dey self and everybody began to feel nice, nice. The party moved up and down, in and out and everyone was just whining their waist. This attracted more and more people who came and joined in the fun. By now the crowd was thick and the christening was in good shape. But it was late and Doc wasn't sure if the lights on the bike were working, so he was thinking of leaving. Raymond saw him moving away from the crowd with Dorothy at his heels.

"Y.....You are leaving already?"

"Well not right now, but I'm thinking about it, you see my lights?"

"Forget that man; come, we must have a drink together. You eat?

"What you saying man, ah eat for so!"

"Well now it's time to have ah rum, insisted Cousin Ray."

"Ah never drink rum before and ah doh want to get drunk."

"Now Mister, you go have your first drink ah rum today."

"Ok, not a lot and ah want water with it."

"Anything you want, just taste the stuff."

"Ah hear dey call it the 'fire water', and ah fraid."

"Doh worry, you won't get drunk, ah go see to that," said Cousin Ray reassuringly. He fetched two glasses and a bottle of coconut water and ice. Ray poured his first into his glass.

Then he said to Doc, "listen, let me tell you, take a little, it's your first time eh?' Take an inch, ah have two inches in me glass." He showed him.

"Now take half of that and drink it in one go, just throw it back in your throat and drink some water immediately, you won't feel anything at all. Look", and Ray gave him the demonstration by swallowing down the contents of his glass then drinking some water soon after.

Doc then lifted his glass to his head, inhaling the rum in doing so which made him cough. He dispatched it down his throat, drank some water then coughed a few times again; his mouth was on fire so he had some more water. After a while, his head began to feel as if it was as big as a base drum and didn't really belong to him. Then he felt as if he was floating in the air. He blinked and smacked his lips; his head continued to spin for some more time but he came round okay. Dorothy came from somewhere, where he did not know, and she gave him a glass of juice with some ice.

"You playing ah big man you drinking rum," then she walked off in the same way she came. She didn't give him any time to reply. After a while, the party quiet down, the baby James with two lovely dimples clenched fist and wide bright eyes were shown around proudly by his father – like most fathers do. Many people placed silver coins in his hand, and when they fall out his dad picked them up and put them in his pocket calling them James coins. Then Myrna demanded them saying she could save them for him.

"His education begins with these," she said, holding up a fist full of coins for the crowd to see.

"You know," said an elderly member of the crowd, "crossing the baby's hand with silver is an African custom, it good you know.....it go bring him plenty luck."

"Is that so, Grandma, anything else?" said the young woman with red eyes.

"Yes," said Grandma. "Now, you see, if we never eat salt we woulda fly back to Africa and escape from slavery. That is the truth, the God's truth," emphasized grandma, anticipating doubts then continued, "We African people know how to do plenty things you know and one of them is to fly."

"That might be so, but we doh have wings to fly," said someone half drunk. Gradually, everything cooled down, then the music started up again but not with as much zest as before. Larry put down the banjo and his mate did the same with his guitar and the rest followed with their musical instruments and the party gradually fizzled out.

Doc was quite sober again. His head was back to normal. He was, however, in a shifty mood. He was thinking it was time to make a move. He had enjoyed the christening, the people and his cousin Raymond and the young attentive Dorothy added to his enjoyment; in fact, everyone did. The time for his departure finally came, and he left.

Taking farewell, of Raymond in particular they slapped each other on the back, then Doc said "okay bye" and Ray said "ah go see you tomorrow."

He said bye to Dorothy who held on to his hand for a long time saying, "You is a nice boy; ah go see you again," then she reluctantly let go of his hand and darted off to the kitchen.

When he left Two Congo, it was almost dark; the sun had long gone to rest. There was quite a sprinkling of stars in the heavens. Fire flies flitted about briskly and the soft noises from the nocturnal insects were musically calming. The sweet scented night flowers perfumed the air with great profusion; it was a calm lovely night and Doc just allowed the bike to cruise; he didn't have to peddle too much for most part of the journey was down hill.

On arrival, he leaned his bike on the outhouse as customary. The dogs greeted him in their usual frisky manner. He said good night to his parents, his mother replied softly but his father was sitting below the breadfruit tree in the front of the yard playing draughts with his friend Mr. Lewis. They were both great draughtsmen who could make one game last for hours, and when they were on the board they were in their own world. They could neither see nor hear anyone. So Doc's good night fell on deaf ears.

Mr. Lewis and his father were playing with torch to light them and the wind continued to fan the torch in front of them which, when this happened, it made Mr. Lewis quite vex because he tended to make mistakes with his moves. Then they would knock the board quite hard when they 'eat' each other's knobs. When either of them made a big "eat" you could hear a big laugh and the shout of "draught board, man, draught board!"

When he went indoors, his mother followed and hoped he had a good time. "How is me Cousin Raymond? Did he tell you how Cousin Ricker and Jim was?" Raymond had said nothing about his mother and father and as usual Doc took it for granted that all was well with them.

He showered, towelled himself and then sprinkled Limacol all over his body and when he said prayers, shouted good night to them, and went to bed. Just before he left for work the next morning, he recited, "Tell me not in mournful numbers, life is but an empty dream. Ah think today is a good day to work on the other pants and finish it off." As soon as he arrived he told Ray how great the christening was. Raymond was glad he enjoyed himself.

"The machines are not busy today," he said, "so we should finish it off, you get the cutting scissors and the crayon and put your best foot forward."

"Ok," said Doc. "Ah want to finish it today."

"Well that's nothing; you would finish it in a short time." So Doc worked and finished the pants before lunch. After lunch in the early afternoon, he sat in front the shop near the pavement where everyone passing could see him and did all the handwork. People saw him as they passed and they called out to him. Some of the children called out by his nickname, "Hi Doc," or just 'Doc'. Others waved to him from across the road.

Those going to Murray's piano lessons neither waved nor said anything to him. They were the rich, stylish ones, children whose parents were well off. Although they never said anything to him, he liked them. They looked good, well dressed and thing, especially the girls. They walked stylishly and talked like some people on the screen; they "haw hawed," and constructed their sentences in proper grammatical order; in Concord, with Subject Verb agreement, things like that.

At times, however, Doc thought they could be stale, artificial, soulless and spineless, too peppered with pretentiousness, especially when they knew that they had an audience. At that time everything that they learnt from books just jumped out from their mouths. There was, however, one girl that he really liked. She was tall and lean with two big flowing ribbons in her hair. Her name was Nora. She often walked by herself although she saw him, she never said anything to him, not even a wave, a hi or hello.

When Doc completed the handwork, Raymond told him to press it, and then he folded it again, tied it up and marked Mr. Baldwin on the paper and took it with him on his way home. Doc's heart gladdened as he approached Mr. Baldwin's house.

"Where is your father?" he asked Mr. Baldwin's son, a child about nine or ten who was sitting on the cocoa branch eating roast breadfruit.

Speaking with his mouth full young Baldwin said, "He gone in the garden for grass."

"When he comes back give him this pants," and he handed the parcel to young Baldwin.

The next morning he collected his $20.00 from Mr. Baldwin who was pleased with the job, for it fitted him very well.

"You go do well as a Tailor; ah could see dat; ah like the way you do this you know the ting in the back pocket," said Mr. Baldwin.

"The tag."

"Yes, How you call it?"

"It's a tag; a kind of hook over your pocket to prevent someone from stealing your wallet," he explained to Mr. Baldwin with kind of superior professional pride.

"It's a good thing, it's a good thing," said Mr Baldwin who played with the tag much as a child fondle a new toy. He buttoned and unbuttoned it then pressed it down with the flat of his hand. Then Doc said good bye after receiving his first payment as a tailor, and things can only get better and better.

"Well done Doc," he said to himself, but continued with his morning lament.

"Not enjoyment and not sorrow is our destined end our way,

but to act that each tomorrow find us further than today."

Then he repeated, *"find us further than today."*

- II -

"Ah must achieve greatness," he said optimistically. "Ah must," he repeated to himself as if he was trying to reassure himself of his own existence as a person, as if he wanted to anchor himself somewhere on this earth to give him stability and substance and some reason for being. However, despite his optimistic flashes of brightness and his hopes for achieving greatness and his self-uplifting work from the psalm of life, it was not long into the morning when the cloak of pessimism eventually enveloped him. His vision of Hope slowly and sadly turned into a vision of despondency.

After leaving Mr. Baldwin's, despite his promise to get him customers beginning with his son, that blanket of depression just had him wrapped up. Everything around him became dark and oppressive, the day gradually turned into an artificial night, he worked out the cost of the material and the cost of the pants, the time taken to sew it and then he thought, "nothing much here for me it's only $20.00 dollars."

This added to his depression. Then other things bothered him, mainly Velma, "I love Velma" and he debated about Sally Ann thinking she too stylish and frontish. "Ah doh know," anyhow he thought, it good to know that he is ah Tailor, "you have something in your head and nobody could take it away from you. I is not ah yard boy anymore, I is ah Tailor but still"......."

Doc felt dissatisfied and impatient with himself; he wanted more and he wanted it now. He felt he was not moving on fast enough. He liked the trade; he liked being a tailor to be seen outside the tailor shop doing his hand work; he felt cool about that no doubt about that at all and as for returning to his previous job that was unthinkable. What do you take me for? Although sometimes it crossed his mind that maybe he could go back, he thought briefly that he use to get his meals but should he return to the Egyptian flesh pot? No! He decided against it; he will take his chances in the wilderness; it is his life; nobody have to tell him what to do.

His mind returned to Velma and their first dance and a kiss in the floor when her mother came to claim her away from him and it galled him; it was a bitter pill, though. Then he wondered: maybe she would not like to be seen with him in the future knowing that he was a yard boy, had a menial job. She would love me for me, my own self. Well ah doh know, ah can't say," opening and closing his fist. "Ah think it is always better to have a trade."

And so he continued to wrestle with what had become a doubting and contrasting situation in this new light; he wondered if he had thrown away his first chance: being at the Briggs; "if ah did stay at the Briggs after sometime they would ah give me another job, something like Raydon. Ah would a go in the mountain, pick up nutmeg and thing, walk around the big house in the evening and thing, cut some fire wood and get some grass for the goats and them and then go home," he opined bleakly. Then he added, "Perhaps me and Sally-Ann coulda get married!

It was the first time he had thought seriously about Sally-Ann after he left Paraclete and his job with the Briggs and he thought about Sally-Ann as his wife! How he came to think about that, Sally-Ann, like a tall, dry giraffe standing over him and perhaps calling him to order! That was a piece of nightmarish reflection; he couldn't be serious; it must be a nightmare, and he dismissed it as such. What is happening to him? So Doc walked down another street away from the tailor shop. He was in no mood to go into the shop at this time. Instead, he wanted to find a quiet spot where he could sit down by himself and try to resolve his dilemma, his conflict of feelings that had been cluttering his head since leaving Mr. Baldwin and receiving his Twenty dollars.

But he could not get Mr. Briggs off his mind. He went back to them. He compared his previous job with being a Tailor Boy and wondered what advantages he would have had, had he remained working for the Briggs'. Sally-Ann, he reasoned, could have been his Trojan Horse for entering the Briggs family. They defiantly could have married; he tried to convince himself once more about the fact that she did show some fondness for him for she even kissed him twice on his forehead; that is a good start; and then the episode in the kitchen. She said nothing to her parents about it; she would have come around, she could have come around. One day she would have given him a real good real kiss on his lips; he would have continued to take her up on Recitation and even some other part of her school work, History and Geography.

"Ah coulda work me way up. Ah could a become the conductor on 'Our Favourite', ah never seen any regular conductor dey. And once they see that Sally-Ann likes me and ah help her and she became me real girlfriend after she leave school, ah sure they woulda help me make something of me life."

And so Doc continued with his catalogue of lamentation. The bright sun of optimism that blazed his mental horizon earlier in the morning and opened up a vista of Hope, with the passing of the morning, had all but vanished, turning grey, even dark and stormy as the day wore on. "A bad hand had been dealt to me or maybe to my ancestors before me." The sad song of lamentation had now become his chorus; he became pensive, moody and morose. He was wrapped up in the blanket of sadness and depression which covered the last vestige of his earlier optimism. Again pessimism reigned!

He walked down Albert Street, crossed over a little puddle of mud and came to the back of the cinema where he sat down near the ticket house. He remained there, oblivious of anyone. He pressed himself up against the wall, forcing himself against it as though he wanted to push the wall open and enter into it, and hide himself away from the world. All his visions of hope were burnt up by the midday sun. He stuck himself there as if he was erected by a mason.

The bell rang for lunch in the school on the hill, the Methodist school. From where he was sitting he could hear the noise of the children in the playground; joyous, feeble, weak, loving and happy voices, full of hope and youthful innocence for the future. Lunch time came and went. School resumed, but Doc was unmoved; he was wrapped up with the chain of sadness, and hopes blighted away.

"It seems like the dice has staked high against me. This life... this bitter life…it's not right ….some people born with gold spoon in their mouth…….. Some born to suck salt."

Doc recalled to mind the many times when his mother had to go to the mountain to pick up the one, one grain of nutmegs to sell to buy salt fish and other simple food. He and the other children were too young to make the journey with her. The mountain was far, far in the Clabony near the sulphur spring, but before she left she would cook them some provision. That's all there was, bluggoe, fig, breadfruit, yam and things like that which they would have with salt fish and coconut oil for their lunch.

"When the sun is right over head, when your foot mashing your shadow, it's 12:00 it's lunch time. Ah mean that's the time you should eat your lunch," his mother would say with an impassive face. Then she would take up her wide bamboo basket, put her cutlass inside of it and hold the basket to her waist, locking it with her elbow.

Then she would say, "Ah running in the mountain to come back. Doh go in the people's land you know. If you get hungry, suck a cocoa, ah coming back soon." Soon usually meant when it was dark; any time between six and eight. What could she do? All she had to depend on was number 11. Her feet. All foot, uphill, downhill; through the ditches all foot, she alone and God.

The morsel of food she left them would be devoured almost as soon as she went out the gap. They felt famished since the night before and the cup of the bush tea they had with a piece of roast breadfruit didn't pass through their teeth hole. They were hungry as soon as they finished their breakfast. It was customary for them to be hungry. Hunger was the stock in trade. They lived a hungry life; they knew nothing different. They went to school hungry to church hungry and they even may die hungry; even the little games they played they did so on half empty stomachs.

When mangoes were in season well that was different. They had a treat every day, but that is only for a short time once a year. In the normal course of events, however, being hungry was the order of the day; it was the way things were. Sometimes the neighbours come to the rescue; often however, it would be cocoa, half ripe golden apples, dried coconut or whatever else they could scrounge, they would make a meal of it. But they never complained. They assumed that, that's the way the world is; they accepted their lot stoically.

What was there to complain about? So what if they didn't have a childhood? So what if they never knew when it was their birthday? What if they didn't have a birthday party? A gift? A hug? What if they never experienced hearing the words 'I love you?' Life is like that.

Then Doc asked himself, "Why is it that some people are born to suffer? If so, why, why me?"

He remained grappling with the question of why life should treat him so harshly. Even life had no right to mash him up so, to rub his mouth in the ground, to batter his teeth and push them down his throat and make his knees buckled down to the ground! No! Life had no right to do that to him...... and with both hands he covered his face and cried, sobbing pitifully, like a child and with tears pouring down his face like Annandale Waterfall.

"What ah go do, what ah go do!" he shouted mournfully.

Now weak, depressed and emotionally drained he drifted off into a kind of trance, half- asleep and was transported to another world as it were. His eyes were almost sealed shut, and all he can "see," discern, make out, in that state were myriads of tiny orange-coloured lights, floating, jumping, lifting in a spacey motion in a void-emptiness. All was emptiness. Yet, through and between these indefinable sometimes dark yellowish pin-tips lights; Doc in this lamentable state saw the word "HOPE." HOPE! He recalled his grandmother reading from the bible: '*although he put his mouth in the dust, there is still hope*'.

Doc blinked his eyes, felt his hand to make sure that he was real. Gradually, slowly as it were, he came back to life if one must say so. A strong surge of energy seeped through him. His body and his mind were energised. The emotional barometer swung upwards once again, for now at least. And now......optimism was now on the cards.

After a good long while, he stretched and walked towards the stand pipe in the corner of the cinema and washed and wiped his face. Now, as if awakening from a long sleep, he rubbed all the muscles and smooth away the signs of depression as best he could. He gradually came back to life from a long sleep. He then strolled to the front of the cinema and wandered around looking at the forthcoming attractions. Two other boys were there arguing over a certain film but he did not hang around. It was time to go home for the sun was fast sinking and soon the lamplighter would be out with his ladder climbing up the lamp pole to pump up the lights and get them going. On his way, he avoided passing in front of the tailor shop; he wanted to avoid everyone.

So he passed in a shortcut and when he reached by Ghost's house he didn't call him. He didn't even give him a special whistle to say: "well ah passing". He went home and straight under the cocoa, where he remained until supper. After supper, he pushed his hands in his pocket and found the $20.00. He had forgotten all about it, the same $20.00 he was paid for the pants he had sewn for Mr. Baldwin.

Going up to his mother he said, "Mum this is for the pants ah sew for Mr. Baldwin," and he handed her the money.

"So yuh start to make for yuh sewing den." She said light-heartedly.

She was then moved to say, "You can't give me all the money you must hold something in your pocket."

"No mum, you must keep it; you know how to spend it."

"It's not right for me to do that, ah mustn't keep all. You're a good child, George, and you kind, ah go join a su-su for $5 a month and ah go put in the $2.50 for you, but you must still keep a little something in your pocket just in case."

"Alright mum." He heeded his mother's request. She thought he did well; he could sew; he sewed complete pants all by himself in less than a day and earned a whole $20.00

"It's only a few months ago you started to sew, started learning trade" she said speaking with a fish bone half chewed in her mouth. "Very well, and you could sew already you even earning money" she coughed, for the small pieces of bones were irritating her throat.

That morning, as he dressed in one of his old ragged shirt and tear up pants, he checked out Ghost and said, "Leh we go and knock about man."

Ghost was at home doing nothing for many weeks now. The little job he had with Charlo, learning to be a mason came to an end within two weeks. He was waiting, just waiting for something to turn up. Things though, never seemed to turn up, except once in a blue moon. So Ghost was at home with a lot of time on his hands and waiting for the moon to turn blue. When Doc told him that they should spend the day liming and gallivanting, Ghost wanted no better sport. It was a long time they had spent time knocking about. It would be a treat.

"So yuh dingo down to the shop today den," said Ghost, to fill in the silence. He didn't expect Doc to say anything. Doc just opened both his hands, as if to say, "Well as you can see."

"Way we going?" asked Ghost. "Ah mean, way we starting from?" he said again after a longish pause, speaking and yawning at the same time, opening his mouth wide like a donkey when it's braying.

"We could go and set trap in Grugu. We could shoot up some crabs and thing wid we catapult. Afterwards we could go down by the Grand Stand, where we go meet up with Cold Coucou Face, and Mud Mask. You know they come down dey in the evening grazing cow and thing."

"Yuh thinking of spending de whole day?"

"Well maybe, we go see. When we meet up with the rest of the boys, we go play a game of 'stick up' as well."

"I will be Rocky Lane?"

"I know yuh is always Rocky Lane and me Rod Cameron" Ghost didn't mind. Any port for a storm......why not? "We have time like bush," he thought.

"Well that good enough for me." He said, beaming.

"Ah better hold me cutlass. Wey is yours? We'll have to get grass for the cattle and we have to pick jelly and ting. You need your blade. Go back for it, man."

Doc sprinted back and took his blade, which was leaning up in the corner of the kitchen. He was in and out in a flash, before his mother could ask him about his whereabouts. They walked side by side down the well- known path leading to the Grugu. They cut off the heads and branches of trees as they strolled idly on. Ghost told him that when he saw him passing yesterday evening he knew that things were not all right with him.

"Ah see yuh pass me house straight, straight, straight yesterday evening not even a little whistle. Ah say to me self, "me partner doh looking well."

"In ah way yuh right. All day yesterday a din go to the shop."

"Why?"

"Something just came over me, man. Things though; pressure."

"Yuh fed up?"

"Ah like tailoring, but as I said something like bitterness boy, yuh know after I finish wid me first job and ting, and ah see what ah get and tings hard like hell......yuh dig what ah mean? Yuh working hard, hard and in the end yuh get next to nothing. Yuh can't see yuh way. Big iron stones blocking it; like those big stones in Telescope Point. Yuh know?" Ghost opened his eyes wide with surprise.

"Man yuh have to take it easy. Yuh have to creep before yuh could walk. Its early days. You is a man wid patience. Take it easy man; doh rush the brush; you go get dab."

"Ah know man, but after Paraclete.....and Mr. Baldwin's job......."

"Man listen, Paraclete was one kind of experience. Just cool it wid de tailoring and ting, you go get jobs. Ah know ah man like yuh could do anything," said Ghost in an unusual serious tone.

"Yuh think so? Ah doh know."

"Ah know yuh is a serious man, Doc is me yuh talking to yuh know. Ah man like you have stick ability. Look at all the boys around. Dey all look up to yuh...dey doh tell yuh dat, but it's true. All ah we does say so. Yuh always take the lead to do something.

That's why I like yuh; wid me, ah doh stick one thing for long. But yuh........." and Ghost chopped on the ground with his cutlass.

"Ah doh know what come over me, sometimes ah feel...... well everything seems so dark."

"Man listen, yuh is ah man wid ambition. When yuh say yuh go do something, yuh do it. Yuh do something man!" Ghost emphasized in that unusual serious tone, that was new to Doc.

"Doc yuh is not like us, yuh know de usual boys? Yuh is not like us. We is only blow hard. Yuh know, mouth open and words jump out. You're different. Yuh hardly open yuh mouth, but when yuh do so, tings happen. Yuh do tings; when yuh talk action flows."

Doc chopped on a piece of cutlet wood with his blade thoughtfully, taking in Ghost's speech. He knew that Ghost was making sense. He had to listen; it wasn't often that Ghost would speak with such seriousness.

"Doh give up man," said Ghost after a pause. "Yuh have it in yuh man." He paused.

".....Man that is just temporary, just for a while. Ah know yuh have it in yuh. Is me yuh talking to, yuh know. We know one another since we was little, little boys running around in shirt tails. No pants or just a tear up, tear up piece of blue pants and tings like dat. We go in river, we swim, we go in the sea, we swim, we never fraid nothing. Ah know you, Doc; you have stomata. I am just a little older than you but ah always look up to yuh from since we meet up. Ah always like to lime wid yuh more dan anyone else. Yuh and me is real bouf."

Doc was Ghost's role model, but Doc never knew.

"Me and yuh is real bouf man, just hold the wheel," he said perspiring and passing the back of his hand across his brow and wiping off the sweat. Doc began to think of Ghost's words with seriousness and began to see him in a new light. He thought of him as being deeper than he Doc imagined him to be. Ghost didn't let up; as if he knew his friend needed some inspiration. He needed some help. On the other hand, he loved him. They had been close friends from childhood and although Ghost usually cursed everyone, including Cold CouCou Face and others, he was never that way with Doc. When Ghost got really bad and unbuttoned his shirt, he would push his chest in front of somebody to beat it: his chest.

"Come see here, beat me chest. If yuh bad beat me chest!" he would taunt. He taunted Cold Coucou Face and the others, but not Doc. He respects him. He liked him; he and Doc were special pals: "Bouf." This was an opportunity to do something uplifting for his friend Doc and Ghost didn't waste time and words.

"Look at the cricket team," he said, "all of us talk about it. We all know it's you put the team together and hold it together as well. When everybody fumbling and couldn't make up their mind, yuh just organize us. Yuh say who is Bowler, who is Wicket keeper and who go open bat. We beat the strongest team in the area, Dumferline. All because yuh talk wid us and make us practice real hard, you organize us, that's what made us successful."

"Well yuh make de bats and soak the ball and collect the subs for the ball and refreshments........"

"Dat was nuttin. Dat was nuttin. Ah make the bats and ting, but it was yuh who organize us, tell us to save towards the ball and ting. Yuh tell us we must buy a good leather ball and learn to use it, all about the shine and ting. Yuh tell us we must never practice wid a new leather ball, so we use the wood knots and the cork balls. Yuh make us the toughest youth team in the area.

When people hear about the 'Ahsanti Boys', dey fraid like hell! Not only the cricket team, yuh did the same wid the football team too. Yuh make us proud; de baddest team in the area. Nuff respect we get," said Ghost with an unusual eloquence.

"But that was not all, yuh remember when all of us went down to Mango Row and we had to say who we want for captain? Everybody, all five of us, except for Cold Coucou Face, say that yuh have to be the captain of the cricket team too."

Ghost told him to hold a slack end tight. Before long, tings go change; he go make it.

"Doh fraid, you go be ah real good Tailor, watch and yuh go see! Doh rush tings! Yuh think ah doh know tings hard on the home front. All the close neighbours know dat too. But doh rush the brush. It's only a few months since you learn to sew and yuh could sew pants and shirt already. Yuh good Doc....yuh good man!" Ghost ended by throwing up his arms around Doc's shoulders.

Then they both embraced. Doc was tight lipped and thinking hard. Ghost was elevated in Doc's estimation and he felt proud to have him as a friend.

Aaron John Milton, known to our readers as Ghost, was two years older than Doc. He was a medium built boy with a broad chest, slanting eyes and a medium structured face. Ghost was a boy of few words, except when it came to 'calling up' someone, teasing and provoking him. He earned his nickname because of his agility and nimbleness. He was fast on his feet, as brave as a panther and as swift as lightening. Ghost was often called 'Mouth Almighty' as well, because he was full of chat and bravado. No one took chances with him. He was bad.

He would unbutton his shirt and dare anyone to "beat me chest, beat me chest, if they call yuh man. Anybody who is badder than me come look here," he would spout with gritted teeth.

"Come look here, beat me chest, beat it up, beat it up! If they call you man beat it up!" As could be imagined no one dared. One day Mud Mask tried to 'beat up his chest'.

Within a few minutes, Mud Mask was lying on the ground and Ghost was strutting around saying, "anyone else like to try?" No one dared; they only looked on in cowering amazement. Ghost would tease anyone: men, women, girls and boys. The young girls in particular were his favourite targets.

"Yvette yuh ent see how yuh foot look like ah piece of cocoa wood," he would say with bitter venom.

To Theresa, "Yuh foot have more spot than a leopard."

And with equal relish, "Thomas de dam ass."

As for the man from Trinidad living in the cocoa, who walked with a kind of 'jerk you waist', Ghost nicknamed him, 'the steel band man.'

It was Ghost who gave Winston the name 'Cold Coucou Face.' On their way for water one morning, Winston just grabbed a large chunk of last night's coucou from his bucket and started to devour it making his face as serious as a judge. Of course Ghost gave him some sticks with his tongue and nicknamed him there and then. That's how he got the nickname.

Ghost was the best bowler on the cricket team, the best fielder, the best all-rounder. Doc, who was the captain of the team, often put him to play at Long On, but Ghost was all over the place. As soon as you hit the ball, he would be at mid-field, gathering the ball and often striking the wicket too. He was very straight with the ball. He was good at stoning down mangoes, and even better with knocking down the middle stump with the ball. Ghost was as brave as a lion. If you had an army, Ghost would be in the front line. He would be in the vanguard, at the head, leading the attack. He was fearless. He would charge bravely and furiously. He was hard, tough and stubborn. He would be behind enemy lines too, sabotaging and destroying communications. Just show him the target and he would be going for it - a man of little or no delicacy, but Doc's honest, loyal and trustworthy friend.

There was an understanding between them since the very infancy of their friendship. So when Doc began to wilter and started to be fainthearted and dithering about his trade, Ghost knew it was necessary to stretch a supporting hand to his friend. His pal. It was an unusual role for him to play but necessary at the moment; and he performed it in a heroic manner. Doc was grateful; he needed this support. He appreciated it and from then on Ghost rose higher in Doc's estimation; the bond of friendship became even stronger - inseparable.

"We is we and anybody coming between us is weevils," he said, picking up his cutlass from the ground. They continued their journey to Grugu in silence. Ghost picked guavas here and there from the short low lying guava trees. Doc was preoccupied with cashew nuts; they both shared their spoils with each other. When they arrived in Grugu, they went separate ways to check their crab traps; they had six traps each and found that they had caught four crabs each.

Leaving Grugu, they went down by the Johnson's place to see if they would find traps to raid, but they met up with Hard Wedge, one of the local boys from around Johnson's place. They both feared Hard Wedge and changed their minds about raiding the traps. Instead they shoot some jazz about football and thing. Hard wedge was the captain of his local football team. After a while, it began to rain and they took off their clothes, covered them with coconut branches and went into the water and swam.

While the rain was falling on their heads, the rest of their bodies were under the water. They loved it!

After a while the sun came out, but it was still drizzling lightly, so Ghost began singing:

"Rain and sun jumbie marrying behind the door!"

Then Doc asked him if he has ever seen a jumbie. Ghost shook his head.

"But ah know of ah lot of people who've seen one doh."

When they left the beach, it was late. The morning was far spent and the day was creeping into the afternoon, so they abandoned their plans to go down to the grandstand. Ghost climbed a coconut tree and cut down a bunch of jelly coconuts.

"God even put water in the tree for us," said Ghost, sliding down the coconut tree. They drank coconut water and ate the soft fresh jelly, until they were full, then they went back home.

"We go catch up later," said Ghost, as he turned to go to his house. Doc gave him a short wave as they separated.

When Doc got home, he felt cold since his clothes were damp. He untied his crabs and put them in an oil drum with other crabs; they all began scuttling fiercely, trying in vain to escape. But instead, all they did was climb on each another's back and bite each other in their futile attempt to get out of the drum. When he looked up he saw his mother sitting on the steps looking at him. She must have been sitting there for some time but he hadn't seen her before. She was looking sad and distraught.

"Mum you okay?" he asked. "Ah din see yuh dey when ah came."

"Ah was here; ah was just looking at you. Ah sit down here thinking and wondering where you been."

"Me and Ghost just went down by we trap and ting and ah had something to tell Ghost."

"Nutting wrong?" He ignored the question, pretending he hadn't heard.

"Ah going and take out dese wet clothes." He had a shower and changed.

"Something happen? Yuh fedup wid the trade?" asked mother.

"Nutting mum, noting happen......well...."

"Doh give up on the trade, you know. Yuh must not give up."

"Mum ah won't give up on tailoring. Is okay. Ah cool..... Ghost and me was talking and after dat....well, me and Ghost didn't have a talk for a long time. So after the trap we sit down and talk and ting. Yuh know, and we had a swim."

"Yesterday ah notice yuh look sad, ah taught, well ah say something wrong and yuh doh want to tell me. Ah say well it must be dat yuh fed up wid de trade."

"Nugh mum, yesterday ah was thinking...... well ah de feeling ah little low in spirit eh......."

"Ah taught so. A know something wasn't right. It showed on yuh face when yuh come in yesterday evening, but as you din say nutting, ah keep quiet; ah doh want to shove me nose in girlfriend and boyfriend business."

"It wasn't nutting like dat mum! After ah get the money for the pants and tings......" He began to falter here because he didn't want to let out on what actually caused him to be in that mood yesterday.

"Ah see how tings hard wid yuh. Life hard; we doh have much coming in. Well it cross me mind that ah could get two weeks in the road, in travo, ah could work in the road, yuh know, to help out.

Ah din go in the shop at all yesterday. Ah din feel too well in me mind, so ah went and siddown in the back of the theatre all day thinking and wondering, trying to find answers, some kind of answers to our pitiful plight; ah know we doh live on estate land and nobody could move us, but the little piece of land we have can't support us."

There was a sad pitiful look on her face while listening to his story, but Doc felt a little better, now that he had shared his problem, not only with Ghost but more importantly his mother.

"Son, ah sorry," she said sadly. "Ah sorry to see that you have to go through this, yuh have to walk such a difficult road, but ah know tings will be better. One ting is sure; Tailoring is much better than the last job. Doh think ah doh know life is hard for yuh. But it always darkest before dawn. So yuh see son….."

Now, going up to him she embraced him.

"Ah have to take night and make day and me mudder before had to start from scratch, in truth, to be honest…." She paused.

"In truth she had to find something to start, to scratch, for her parents before her and so……… well……. were stolen from Africa and they had nothing except their strength." She took a deep breath.

"Yuh see son, it seems life has dealt us a bitter card. A painful hand. It's the way life is for some people. I didn't expect yuh…. Well it's not right for yuh to suck the same bitter fruits we had. Yuh shouldn't have to share in it, but it go change…. God give me yuh all and ah know ah have to bear the burden. 'Cattle horn is never too heavy for its head'. Ah go stand up wid yuh and all the rest. Ah go carry my own burden by the hook or the crook, because wid God me burden is light. He go help me, yuh all growing up good.... God never gives us more than we can carry. He knows things will be better. You getting big, God bless yuh to have a trade because yuh have a good mind....."

Then she broke into further convulsive sobs, while holding on to his shoulder with a firm grip; afterwards she left and went inside and Doc went and sat under the short mango tree in the yard.

- III -

Once again the see-saw life of Doc continued to move upwards. Again the stars of optimism began to shine his way. The next morning, before cock crow, as you would say, bright and early he was up like the proverbial bird searching for the best worms. He whistled for Ghost and they went and checked on their traps; afterwards they had a swim and then headed home.

Back at work he entered the shop timidly wondering about the reaction of his boss and the boys. The boys were glad to see him and gave him a friendly welcome, wondering whether he was sick or seriously indisposed in any way. Ray was very keen to find out about his health. Doc assured him that everything was okay.

"I okay man. Ah din feel too well these past few days, that's why I wasn't here…."

"But now….."

"Hold on, ah see the boss coming ah must apologise to him."

Mr. Gilbert came forward with an extra spring in his step; his lips were puckered, pressed together, he was whistling, for he was in a happy mood - he had gotten a big job. He entered the shop with his hat leaning to the far left of his head, his shirt tucked neatly in his pants and his moustache neatly trimmed. He was looking as a new, minted shilling. The first thing he did after greeting the boys was to talk to his partner about the series 'Second Spring' the last episode of which they both followed with great interest.

After they had exhausted 'Second Spring', Doc seized his opportunity to make his apology for his absence for the previous two days. He said he wasn't too well; there was no way to get the message to him; that his mother was also indisposed and that it happened suddenly. He was somewhat sad because he didn't want to tell an untruth to his boss.

"Alright, alright, glad to see you back and hope it's nothing too serious. Is it a girl?"

"No sah, not a girl. Ha!"

The rest of the boys raised their heads and whispered loud enough for Doc to hear.

"These young razor blades and dem not easy," coming from Congo.

"And now that you're back," said Mr. Gilbert, light heartedly, "Ah have some handwork waiting for you." Then he reached for a grey flannel pants on the line and handed it to him.

"Ah want you to cut all those loose thread, and then hem the waist lining, the turn-ups and the foot. Ah want you to herring bone dem. Then put on the fly buttons, and also the buttons on the flaps of the two seat pockets. When you finish de handwork, press it and hang it up on the line. Ah go fold it myself. When Ricky finishes the work on the jackets, do the handwork on them as well."

The instructions were firm but friendly in Mr. Gilbert's light hearted non-dogmatic manner. Doc just kept saying, "Yes Mr. Gilbert," "Yes Sah," to each piece of instruction. Then he set to work immediately without hesitation. He pulled out his needle from across his shirt pocket, found the thread, double threaded the needle with waxed thread, took his favourite tall stool with the bars around where he rested his feet, went outside and sat in front of the shop and burrowed through his work. For the rest of the morning he sat there working alone with a determined single-mindedness, with furrowed brows and a singular concentration.

Whilst thus engaged, everyone including his friends passing to and from town called out to him but he never lifted his head, except occasionally. Now and then he would raise his head in acknowledgement but by and large he kept his head down to the grindstone of tailoring life. After he had completed the pants in the morning Mr. Gilbert gave him both sleeves for the jacket to do the hand work as instructed before.

"Then put it on the special stand and press it when you finish the hand work. Ah know you could do it."

"Yes Sah, ah go try me best," said Doc. He was in a fine frame of mind and now he was not learning for himself alone. He had seen his mum cry yesterday.

It was about 3:30 when a slow sweet lingering voice said:

"H-E-L-L-O D-O-C!"

"Hello," he replied in the same manner as before without looking up. Again the same voice said "H-e-l-l-o D-o-c, yuh doh want to see me?" At last he looked up from his work and saw Velma staring down at him with her wholesome looking face.

"Velma!" he blurted out when he saw her. For a moment Doc lost his sense of proportion. He fidgeted awkwardly. This was not part of his plan, part of his schedule of things for the day. Today he pledged to himself, committed himself to get on with his work with all seriousness, without distractions and his mind concentrated on achieving greatness. He'd planned to 'work like a beast' to make up for his two days in the Wilderness and now Velma! She was an emotional balm, but right now he was a little embarrassed and it showed on him.

"Velma, how is yuh? We din see since the night of the concert."

"Yes, ah know...."

The simple truth was this: Doc did not know where to begin to reconnect with the girl of his dreams after those many months of not seeing her. Although the experience on that memorable night never left him, it was a strain to reconnect the relationship and move it on. He would go back to the Paraclete bridge setting and their hellos and kisses and the shopping bags and basket in his hand. He found it difficult to reconnect with her, away from the Paraclete bridge environment and a yard boy's thinking. He couldn't yet relate to her in his new setting and as a young and upcoming Tailor Boy.

That was his dilemma, because both his circumstance and his status had changed during those many months; this was what he had to understand. Things had changed and so was he; although he didn't as yet fully understand that; what Doc finally realised was that Velma never thought of him in any other way than the boy she loves. He was just Doc to her and she loved him just for being Doc, himself. She watched him as he got off the stool holding on nervously to the jacket sleeves. She had the undisguised cheerfulness about her, as she eyed him in his new situation.

"How are yuh Doc?" she asked again for the umpteenth time without taking her eyes off him as if he were a piece of newly found jewellery.

"Yuh like……well, hem…… I miss not seeing yuh these many months. I'd long to see yuh so very much Doc," She said calmly. Doc returned warm greetings as best he could in his present situation. In the shop all eyes were on him, as it were he was dithering; his response was jerky.

"I miss yuh too, although…..although…….well I am happy to see yuh again," he said. Finally, beginning to warm towards her while in his mind and manner working out a new level to relocate himself with her, finding a new approach if you like, it was necessary, he thought.

He would have liked to stop all he was doing, forget about everything else and take the hand of his loved one and walk over to the Anglican school with her, sit on the back of the school steps facing the sea in the cool afternoon and pick up the pieces from where they left off on the dance floor that memorable night in Paraclete but he was a responsible young man, he had a job to complete.

He'd been away for two days and his boss had been lenient with him. He owed something to his mother, respect for his employer and a commitment to himself to move towards greatness of which he believed he was destined. So the task at hand came first, he's almost finished, just to press the sleeves of the jacket of which he had to be extra careful. Would she wait? He believed she would.

He was trying to find something to say, although it wasn't necessary, she already decided she wouldn't leave without him. She came closer to him. He fidgeted some more. She touched his shirt playfully as if she was examining her newly found piece of precious jewellery. The boys were looking out at him. She was talking to him but he didn't hear. Velma's voice was soft and sweet. She had spoken to him for a short time before, a few minutes while in his embrace on the dance floor where for some time they were making and dancing to their own music. She'd longed to see him and was overjoyed and delightfully pleased and happy to meet with him again. Doc felt her close, delightfully close. He felt as though he had stepped out into a new daylight; day had just dawned for him, although he was still in a state of confusion.

He glanced at her. Her poise was easy and cool, her manner calm and refreshing with that honest look on her face; not imperious and confrontational as Sally Ann's. Velma had that noble modesty and sweet simplicity that had always endeared her to him even when he couldn't describe it and did not fully understand it. She looked particularly lovely standing there with expectant eyes following his every move, still holding her bag with wooden handles with a hole to push her hand through to make carrying easy. She touched him playfully on his shoulders again. She had an irresistible urge to play with him, to hold and fondle him.

"Yuh nearly finished?" she asked in a soft voice.

"Ah just have the pressing to do now; you go wait?"

"Yes, yes ah waiting. Ah doh have to go far. We living in La Fillette now, you know".

"True?"

"Yes that's why I doh have to hurry. Dey expect me home late, because ah had to stay for lessons, but the teacher is not well today, so ah have time. And then ah so glad to see you, we meet up again. I am very glad."

"Okay den ah almost finish."

"It's awright don't hurry too much." Sniggerings came from inside the shop. Now and again a head would appear at the door.

Doc took a long look at her as he was about to re-renter the shop and said: "You go wait here or......"

"Ah waiting right here," she said positioning herself close to the steps that led to the upstairs of the building. Doc offered her the stool he was sitting on before, but she refused. She leaned up against the step still holding up her bag. "I okay", she reassured him. All eyes were on him as he went into the shop. They all seemed to encourage him on; so they made space for him to complete his work.

"She waiting for you eh?" Asked 'Big and Tough'. A tall thickset man with large muscles.

"Your girl-friend?" ask the thickset man.

"She is my friend", answered Doc quietly. Doc was standing by the table waiting for the iron to press the jacket sleeves as was instructed earlier by the boss. It was not long before he got the space and he did the sleeves. This finally completed all the jobs that were given to him earlier by Mr. Gilbert. When he handed it to the boss, he looked it over carefully and seemed well pleased with it. He examined the pants then the jacket sleeves and was satisfied.

"Well done boy, good job, you can leave now, you can go home now. Ah go see you in the morning, please God," said the boss, almost gratefully.

"Thank yuh, Mr. Gilbert," he said, moving along more confidently now. The boys looked at him with quiet admiration and pride, as he wished them all good evening.

"Alright, alright, ah know yuh have business to attend to," said the muscular man, ironically. Finally, before he left the shop, he pinned his needle on his shirt pocket and pushed his thimble on his left small finger as the experienced Tailors do. Velma saw when he came out and she joined him.

"That was not long," she said. "I thought ah had to be here for hours." Two of her school friends passed her and waved knowingly. Those pupils from the secondary school going for piano lessons opposite the tailor shop kept gazing curiously at her walking up the road with Doc. They looked very surprised, nudging one another and talking, gesticulating about and opening their eyes wide.

"It's a long time ah din see you" she said passing Mr. Mc Laren's Bakery. She was walking on the inside and Doc was walking on the outside of the road.

"Yuh missed me?" he asked after a while.

"Ah missed yuh a lot! Ah use to look out for yuh on my way home. Ah get accustom to seeing yuh. Every time I approach the iron bridge, just below de bridge dey, where we used to pass each other, my heart use to run on yuh and miss a beat," said Velma. She continued, "And yuh said nutting until the night of the concert. I loved the time we had dancing, hugging and those kisses, Doc" she said.

"That's true" he replied. "But we said a lot that night though, by our actions."

"Yuh know maybe we din have to say anything before," she said briskly.

"Why?"

"Ah bet we said it here," touching the spot where his heart is, "and I'm at school all day and yuh have your work and ting."

"What is in we heart must come out sometime and de work, well, ah was just holding on."

"Some time," she replied, looking straight ahead "and I'm not mentioning anything about work."

Further up the road they stood looking at each other, but saying nothing. Then he asked, "Wey yuh living now?"

"My grandmother died and we left Paraclete. My father has land in La Fillette, so he built a house dey and that's where we live now. We give the house in Paraclete to a cousin."

"Oh ho, is that so? Yuh like La Fillette?"

"Ah like it more than Paraclete. For one, its nearer school, ah could walk, ah doh bound to get a ride. Another thing too, ah have my own room and we have a pipe in the house and it's not a board house. We have concrete post and some other parts of the downstairs are concrete too. It's better than the one in Paraclete."

"Yuh seem happy wid it and glad to leave Paraclete. How far up is it?"

"About half way up the long stretch, near to teacher Reason. Yuh know where teacher Reason living? Well it between him and the big bakery," said Velma cheerfully. She was indeed happy, elated, and it reflected on her face. There was a spring in her step too. She had reason to be in that mood. She was happy to move, no one knew that better than she did.

It was her hopes too, that when she met up with Doc again (as she knew she would) she would find time to be around him without too much worry about getting home. She made a full declaration of her love for Doc. No doubt about it, for she felt a warm flame burning inside her. When they reached by the bridge on the Great River, Doc took her bag. She was glad. The bag was heavier than he thought. He looked inside. He had never seen so many books in all his life and wondered how she could read all of them and what they had in them. When they passed the bridge they stopped and he took out some of the books; many were ink stained and smelt musty.

"What's it yuh looking for? Let me help you."

"Nothing special," he said. "Ah just looking. So many books; ah never see so many books before. Yuh is a bright girl."

"Ah try to study hard. It's important, Doc."

What?"

"Education."

"Yes; ah could see that from all these," he said, pointing to her mobile library.

"How far you reaching with me? And when we going to see again?"

"So much questions.... Ah won't run away you know."

"Ah know yuh won't run away, but yuh left Paraclete without a word to me. Why didn't yuh tell me yuh was leaving? Ah couldn't sleep well for a long time after I heard yuh were gone. Why didn't yuh tell me?" she repeated with sadness in her voice.

"Ah left in a hurry. Ah thought that if ah told anyone or if ah delayed, ah wouldn't want to leave. Besides, ah didn't see yuh and ah couldn't come to yuh house. But den ah din know yuh wanted me to tell yuh. Ah thought...... well ah thought.... I was thinking.... Ah doh know what ah was thinking..... We never said much that night." She looked at him and they both sighed deeply.

He rambled on somewhat incoherently, still not saying what he wanted to say. In fact he didn't know exactly what he wanted to say.

"Ah went home, stayed in my room and cried all afternoon when ah hear yuh left. I not seeing yuh, yuh know. I love you Doc. Well.... I like you very much....well," she burst out. "Ah love you, yes, ah love you a lot a lot," said Velma with feeling. "And the way you held me that night and out....and oh..."

She covered her face with both her hands and turned towards the northern end of the river. After a short while, they continued on their slow journey once more.

Then she spoke again, facing him, she said, "Ah ask Sally Ann for yuh one day, because I couldn't stand it anymore; she just watched me cut eye, as if I do her something. Then when I ask her if yuh sick she tell me to mind my own business, ah too fas'."

"She could ah tell yuh that ah leave the work."

"Sally Ann like yuh? Ah have a mind she likes yuh. One day she told me that yuh used to help her wid her Recitation and that you read good, doh mind yuh is a yard boy."

"So yuh all did talk about me?"

"Nah, she jus tell me that one day when I ask her for yuh. Ah think it was a way of telling me something."

"Like what?"

"Like she loves yuh." Doc paused for a while, and then he told her he was never sure about Sally Ann, but one thing he was certain about, that she was very haughty and too proud for his liking.

"But she also like books and ah like that about her."

"Yuh like her? Yuh used to help her with her Recitation in truth?"

"Yes, ah like her, but not in the same way as I like you. Ah tell yuh; ah think she is very proud. But ah used to like to listen to her when she reciting. Well, she asked me to tell her if she was going right and ting, yuh know, so ah use to listen and then test her. It helped to pass the time. It made a good change for me. Ah used to feel bored; de work was boring, so it was a way of passing de time, especially in the rainy season." Velma looked somewhat surprised at his declaration, and that was not all.

"Sally Ann wanted to come first in Test, so she wanted me to help her do so. We use to say recitation together under the house. At first her parents objected. Dey din want her close to me like dat, especially to be alone under the house. Ah use to like to hear her recite Shakespeare, especially Romeo and Juliet. She is very bright, but not like you. She likes to show off," said Doc, becoming hot.

"What else you all use to recite together?" asked Velma with strong emphasis on the 'together'."

"At times, she would recite Julius Caesar. You know what ah mean? She use to recite poems by Wordsworth and Longfellow and others. Ah can't remember all of dem."

"So all you spend a lot of time together doing those things?"

"No, not a lot of time. This use to happen once in a while, and sometimes on Sundays."

"Which one of the poems did you like to hear most?"

"Her favourite one was Romeo and Juliet. One evening when she finished reciting she asked me if I ever kissed a girl. I told her 'no', and then she said to me the first kiss was very important. It must be special and it must have a lot of sweetness and passion in it."

"Why didn't you tell her that you kissed me? Well, we kissed."

"That time we din kiss yet."

"Why would she tell you all of that if she din love you?"

"Ah tink she was showing off; trying to tell me that she reads a lot of books. Ah tink some of that come out from what she reads."

"Ah tink," said Velma, who by now was somewhat overwhelmed by the discussion.

"Ah tink Sally Ann wanted to tell you she loves you, to be talking like that."

"Ah wouldn't say that," said Doc apologetically.

"You see when ah was working for dem, she was the only one who never try to give me orders and tell me to do dis and dat. She did try but not for long. She use to make me feel dat I could be more than a yard boy, although she never said so. You know what ah mean?"

"I'm trying to see what you driving at."

"Okay, when she recited a stanza from Julius Caesar to me...... the way she say it use to inspire me; especially this passage," and Doc recited:

Men at sometimes are masters of their fates.

The fault, dear Brutus, is not in our stars;

but in ourselves that we are underlings.

"When she recited this passage, it used to make me feel ah could improve myself and dat ah doh have to be a yard boy all my life. Ah din tell her dat," said Doc.

He was not only hot, but becoming emotional as well.

"But some of the poems she recited, especially dis passage, helped me to make up my mind sooner about leaving her parent's work. Ah feel ah had to take my life in my hand there and then, come what may. Ah thought ah could better myself."

Velma was amazed by this revelation. She thought that 'this Doc is not easy. He is no fly-bite. He is not a sock, there is substance in him', she realized.

"So she inspired you to leave; that's why you leave without telling me?"

Doc said, "you know ah couldn't come to your house. And we din meet up. Anyway, ah just wanted to leave, and leave as quickly as I could, and that's what I did. I love you Velma," said Doc in a contrite voice he repeated, "I love you."

"So you don't love Sally Ann then?"

"Ah can't say dat; ah just like her. When we use to talk and ting, ah never use to feel dat. I was working in dat job, you know? She use to make me feel good in myself and the job did not feel so.... boring and menial. When ah say ah was leaving she did look a little sad, because we were friends in a kind a way."

"The same thing I was saying all the time. She cares for you a lot; if not she wouldn't act in this way. You see her since you left their work?"

"No," replied Doc, with a distant look and wondering whether she did not pick up at least an indication from him that he had some strong admiration for Sally Ann.

This admiration was very close to the margin of affection. In actual fact, this was exactly what Velma was thinking about. He also recalled the episode with Sally Ann in the kitchen. Was that a love act or the prelude to one? He felt guilty about it, but he studiously avoided it. Doc said a lot that made her think, reciting love poems, talk about first kiss, their being together alone under the house. In Velma's mind all the social ingredients pointed to love. Doc sensed that, so he tried to get on their (he and Velma's) personal track.

"Velma!" he said in a powerful voice, we talk about Sally Ann long enough. Why we doh talk about us, when we go see again? We are coming near to your house. Ah want to reach you by the junction; ah doh want to go up to La Fillette Road."

"Ah want to show you our new house; don't you want to see it? Ah want you to see it, Doc," she appealed quietly.

"Listen Velma," said Doc in a fatigued voice, "ah really doh want to go too close to your house. Well, ah din plan to....well, your parents...... Ah mean maybe another time." Velma shook her head in a sign of disbelief. A bus passed them; it was 'Our Favourite', Sally Ann father's bus. Sally Ann was sitting in front.

By the time Sally Ann recognized him, the bus was far up the road. She, however, threw her head back and waved frantically to Doc. Velma just looked on unbelievably when Doc returned eager greetings to Sally Ann. However, she remained cool in that stately, even graceful demeanour of hers.

"Are you going back now?" she said, in the same serene composure.

"Ah tink ah should……. You are almost home, and as I said, ah doh want to go too close to your home."

"Well reach me by the tall mango tree. You know the one just by the parlour, in the junction with Santopee Street?"

Doc agreed, and they silently continued their journey. They were not far from their destination and in actual fact, if they had pursued their journey in a normal way, they could have completed it in less than an hour. But they were in love, and young love in particular must find ways in making a journey and the issues surrounding it interesting, making dull events colourful, monotonous journeys must be spiced up, and the two of them had more than enough affectionate ingredients to season up a dull hour's walk, making it into two. This they did.

They were reluctant to part from each other, and despite Doc's protestation that he did not want to go near her home, he could not resist wanting and hoping to see her house. He wanted to imagine her there in her room. He was curious, plus, there was that affectionate cement that invisibly bonded them together; they were both aware even before the concert that they were inseparably linked.

"Come, talk to me, you vex?"

"I am not vex. It just come back to my mind all that we were talking about before…about you and Sally Ann. And ah tink, if you don't love her, she must be in love with you."

"Why can't we forget about Sally Ann? Stop talkin about her and think about us. Leh we talk about us. Ah asking yuh once more, when we go meet up again?"

"Yes Doc, ah know. I want to concentrate on us, but I can't get Sally Ann out of my mind, and her interest in you. Ah stop just now, but soon after she passed on the bus, waving to you like mad, your attitude changed. Your attention was divided between Sally Ann and me. Your face get tight, tight and very serious. You should ah see yourself."

Doc dithered for a while uneasily and uncomfortably, but he did not want to continue down the Sally Ann trail. However, it left a strong impression on Velma and it was not easy for her to get off that road, so the discussion with its uneasiness, was once more brought back on the table. It was contentious, like the Dragon's teeth. It seemed to have taken root, and it took up much of their valuable time, time that should be spent exploring where they go from here. They hadn't seen each other for months; they hadn't spoken about the dance, about themselves on that memorable night.

Doc silently conceded that Velma was jealous. He reasoned that she had right to be. A lot had been said about he and Sally Ann, and now she just passed, and his response! It somehow dirtied the water between himself and Velma. Velma was right to be jealous, he conceded to himself; and worst of all, if Velma should learn about he and Sally Ann in the kitchen, that would be terrifying and may even destroy their love in its infancy.

He was honest enough to concede that he had found something unique in Sally Ann. There was an attraction about Sally Ann that fascinated him. Although she was what she was, there was something curiously magical which dragged him back into her orbit; like sitting upon a piece of rock; dangerous, but one is drawn to it. The sea, the water, ebbing and flowing, the rocks and the rough waves threatening. But dangerous though they are, somehow it does tempt and dare you, perhaps to try a plunge.

Maybe nothing would happen, and the experience, if it does not turn out to be tragic, could serve you for a lifetime. Unthinkable, but possible; daringly so. Doc was attracted to her, because she had inspired him more than she had repulsed him. Doc loved her in his own way because of these qualities, and if, up against the window in the kitchen with Sally Ann, if that episode had run its full course, who knows what would have happened? But that, Velma wouldn't understand..... well not now. And if he had told her the full story, he would lose her, and he didn't want to lose Velma, so he put that into the back of his mind for the time being, hoping to tell her the full story one day.

"Before you go," he said....... "Before you go, leh me tell you about this dream I had about three weeks ago." She held a straight face.

"Come on girl, relax," he tugged at her skirt. "Leh me help you," and he took her bag of books away from her again. He pushed his hands through the wooden handles, and coming up to her face, eye to eye, he said, "I like those little stars on your face...... Black stars," he said, laughing. She smiled too, she was happy he was thinking about her in that way. No one had ever seen her freckles as stars.

"Your face looks very nice. When we use to just pass one another on the bridge, ah use to go home and in the nights I use to think of you. I use to call you my 'Black Star Venus'."

She laughed out loudly, deep and very sweet. They were now standing by the junction near Santopee Street. That's where they agreed to part. Three men passed by, walking behind a donkey with a crook on its back, carrying grass on one side of the crook, and a bag of nutmeg, some bananas and bluggoes, on the other side of the crook.

The young man called out to her by name and blew her a kiss, holding up a cutlass in his hand. He was a short man with a pushy kind of walk, as though he was heaving his chest in front of him as he walked. The other two men, who were older, walked slower with exhausted steps, looking tired coming from the mountain and holding up the cutlass in the crook of their elbows like a Pharaoh's sceptre.

"Ah dream," continued Doc, who, after a long pause decided to pursue his course about sharing his dream with her.

"Yuh had a car and yuh drive; well ah think fly, to Trinidad."

"Yuh was in the car?"

"Of course I was there!"

"When we got to Trinidad, we din know anybody and we say leh we go to England, where we go see castles and ting, yuh know the tings we read about England. When we get dey ah wake up," said Doc, smiling away as though he was still having that experience.

"That's a good dream but really, car can't drive to England but den it's a dream!"

"Yes" he said, "it's only ah dream." She looked at him keenly and then she brushed off an imaginary particle of dirt from his shirt.

"Yuh going back now? When we go see?"

"Yuh ever dream about me?"

"Ah have homework to do; we must go now."

"What did yuh dream?" insisted Doc.

"Ah tell yuh......leh we go."

Once again she pleaded with him to leave her alone. Her mind was again drawn back to Sally Ann. She was very unsettled from the time she saw that wave Sally Ann gave to Doc and his response. She wanted to go home; she was confused, uneasy and felt threatened, but still she could not drag herself away from him, like a magic spell just held her there. In his presence, it was hard to let go of him, that invisible bond was at work.

"Tell me den, tell me….."

"Ah day dream about yuh, well if yuh insist yuh want to know, ah always day dream about us, from the time I use to meet you by the bridge. Yuh don't realize Doc, I love yuh almost the instant ah saw yuh. What ah day dream about I can't tell yuh now….well it's a secret for now. Ah go tell you….years from now, den I won't feel shame."

"Ah go look forward to that day, even if is fifty years from now." She was glad when he said that…….. " 'Fifty years from now'."

"Yuh know where ah learning trade now. Ah go look out for yuh after school, whenever possible."

They stood under the tall mango tree. It was in blossom and the birds flitted up and down the branches and bees were busy too as bees are. Under the mango tree, they stood facing each other. What to say and what to do now, parting was not easy. They were filled with mixed emotions that developed soon after 'Our Favourite' passed. They were glad to be reunited and things like that after months of separation. They were both experiencing feelings of deeper love….but they were still innocent. They were both novices and Sally Ann created many doubts in Velma's mind. Despite all that, when she weighed it all up she knew that Doc was in love with her and not with Sally Ann. With such feelings her doubts subsided. She threw fear to the wind.

"We only kissed once the night of the concert." She said. "Nobody coming, hug me up and kiss me again before you go and leave me tonight. Hug me up." She repeated in a quiet firm voice. They hugged and kissed long and deliciously.

"Ah thought yuh had to go and do yuh homework? Look at the time, it's late already."

"Doh waste it den," she said to Doc and he hugged her and they shared some passionate kisses.

"Anyhow, I don't care how late it is Doc, as long as I'm near yuh, in yuh arms, all the clocks in the world could stop," she said with a kind of drunken passion.

They embraced each other again. As they held onto each other her heart was thumping away, but she nestled in his embrace and he too never wanted to let her go. Then she said good night in a faltering voice as they kissed again; then they extricated themselves and she caught her breath.

"Good night again," she said, taking hold of her bag and holding it to her stomach with both hands. She hurried home. Doc watched her until she disappeared into her gap and into her house. Then he turned back and redirected his steps towards home sweet home.

Velma slept badly that night. Her mind was confused. There was a torment going on in her, although she felt his arms around her and his damp lips still resting on hers; she had troubled dreams. She dreamt that she was being chased by a herd of cattle and one of them with exceptionally long horns and very big eyes, chased her and attempted to butt her. But she escaped it by dodging and hiding herself behind a large cashew nut tree. When it made the attempt on her life, it struck the tree instead and then it groaned and dropped dead. She woke up with a cold sweat.

- IV -

Doc went back into his tailoring routine, but as time rolled on his mind remained divided about it. Since after his two day disappearance, in fact from the time he completed his first job for Mr. Baldwin and received his twenty dollars, his commitment to tailoring had changed. He began to view it in relative terms and not a job for life; it was too pedestrian, too sedate, now he'd got it, he wanted more, another challenge, a bigger and more taxing experience.

One morning his mother saw that 'faraway look' on his face just before he left for work. She approached him.

"Doh look well dis morning, something wrong wid yuh? Something bothering yuh?" she asked with concern.

"Ah wish ah had another job, mum. Look at us. Tings will get better, you'd say, but same old story.... hard work and nothing to show for it..."

"George stop dat! You worry too much. Have patience. Patience brings results. You go get your reward. You doh even take your eighteen birthday yet, and you want to put the problems of the world on your shoulders. You is not Atlas you know! Take it easy. Tink of Velma, son, she is a nice girl."

"Ah tink of her mum! She reads a lot of books. She is very bright, and one day...... Who told you about her mum?"

"Ah young man like you mustn't only think about one thing. You alone can't right the wrongs of the world you know."

"So you know...."

"The place is small. Everybody know about the night of the concert in Paraclete."

"Oh yes, yes, her school friends and ting."

"Listen son, take it from me. I is your mudder. I see a lotta ting and plenty trouble, and listen to people make plenty plenty promises. Dis world, son, promises plenty, but when push comes to shove, we get very little. If dey de leave us in Africa, instead of dragging us here as slaves, and make us work from sun up to sun down, tings woulda be better for us. Dey say some people start from scratch. But we didn't even have anything to scratch. We had to find something and then start to scratch.

Donkey say the world is crooked, but is man dat crooked, man, man! Some ah dem looking nice, nice in de church and ting even dem. Man make dis world God give, man make it like a hell, especially for de poor people. For them hell is right on this earth, because man made it so." She spoke with feelings of sadness.

His mother tried again to encourage him to stick to his trade.

"A go try, mum. Ah go continue to work hard and one day ah go change tings, ah know dat."

"Just keep on at your job and hold your head up high. You go be awright, ah tell you dat awready. You go make man.... you must make man. Tings doh stay the same way all the time. Empires rise and fall. How could we be poor forever?" she said rhetorically. He touched her hands as she sat there looking downcast and exhausted. The sunlight shone through the cocoa trees and it glittered through the coconut branches and things seemed brighter with the sunshine. He went down to work in a happier state, mindful this time about what his mother said. She surprised him. She seemed to understand everything, although she could hardly read.

"Some people start from scratch. But we didn't even have anything to scratch," his mother had said. He was more determined now to fight against the odds. What are the odds anyway? His mother had always been fighting against the odds and she was always winning.

He would find another way, another job. Yes. He can't complain he shouldn't. Since Mr. Baldwin, quite a few jobs had been coming in. He even used his mother's sewing machine sometimes on Sundays after mass; he made adjustments, general alterations, and children's clothes (boys).

He even sewed a few Peddle Pushers that just came into fashion. The first one was for a girl named Jane. She liked him. That's why she gave him the job. After that, her friends came. He even did one for a big woman in Seamoon. Slowly..... well not too slowly, he was moving on. The boys in the shop were pleased for him. Ray helped him to design new styles of Peddle Pushers and the young girls loved the new styles. At the end of most weeks, he went home with twenty dollars and more. The men in the shop continued to give him his 'little ting' at the end of the week. His boss congratulated him for learning the trade as quickly as he did.

He said he showed remarkable promise and he was proud of him. There was a great future for him in tailoring.

"Ah come across some boys who use to come and siddown, days after days, weeks after weeks and months after months. After all dat time dey couldn't make a decent button hole, or hem ah pants..... well they could do it, but how?" he said, looking at Doc with a pleased eye. His partner joined in and gave a host of examples of such people.....

"An after a few months, dey leave. Dey come with an empty head and dey go with an empty head."

One of the senior boys added, "Well dey din come wid empty head, dey come wid dey head full of saw dust. That's why they couldn't take in anything, Ha! Ha! Ha!" said Congo, with a huge grin from the muscular man.

For the short time, things did pick up. A ray of hope shone through. He was riding on the wave, and yet for him, now almost nine months older than when he left Paraclete and his yard boying job, things should move faster. He felt good within himself, shoving and pushing himself along like a rocket will be his limit. Tailoring was definitely too pedestrian for him, too slow.

Now that he was almost an accomplished Tailor, tailoring began to look and feel lazy. He agreed that it was a nice, good, clean skill but you're not busy, that is, when there are no customers, all you have to do is just sit down and shoot jazz, old talk and ting, walk around. Just lime. Yes, you just lime. But at the end of the day, at the end of the week you broke. The lime doh have juice.

Doc thought that he wouldn't abandon tailoring, he could do it at home and at weekends, or in his spare time. Therefore, he resolved to find another job. He was too energetic and he was becoming quite restless all around, to be chained down in the shop, attractive though it was. He must get a job soon, to go with his sewing. He could sew already. He could cut, and work out measurements, what more does he want? He will continue to develop and advance himself by practice. 'Practice makes perfect'; so he decided to burn his candle on both ends. He will have two jobs.

Happy to be a Tailor boy he was, without a doubt. In fact he was very proud of being a Tailor. He might be poor, but his mind was not poor. Didn't his teacher tell him that he can do anything he wants, but he must always read. Yes, he is not poor-minded. He felt good that he had a skill. He could hold his own. He didn't feel too intimidated by the pupils going for piano lessons anymore. Afterwards, they might soon be coming to him to sew for them. Even if he didn't have their education and didn't speak like them, he was sure that from now on they couldn't cut style on him. Instead, he will cut style for them.

To Doc, that was just a start. He would not rest on his tailoring laurels. No....not Doc. He wouldn't, he wouldn't put all his economic eggs in one basket. No way. That doesn't make sense. He go get work, any work, that would further launch him into orbit. He vowed to achieve Greatness and the only way he knew and understood how to be Great was to work towards it with absolute determination and singular concentration. That is the way to Greatness.

On his way down to the shop one morning, he passed in Plant Protection Depot. He'd always seen people going in and coming out from the office, but he was never too sure what the whole thing was all about. The sign on the office read 'Plant Protection Depot: Enquires'.

That morning, he decided to go in and find out if they had any jobs. The man he met at Enquires told him that this was a job were men, especially men of his age, and in their early twenties, go around spraying bananas. The government, he told him, give them spraying machines, and a Land Rover to take them from one place to another. The spraying is for protecting the leaf spots and to protect the fruits from diseases, which often killed the whole banana tree if it is not protected by this spraying. It's a good permanent job, but he will have to see the secretary and find out if there were any vacancies.

He went into the office, and met the secretary. She was not busy, so Miss Gladys (that's her name) could speak with him at once. She told him that there were no vacancies at the moment. "However," she said, getting up from her seat and yawning, "I'm sorry" she said, and continued, "We are expanding. We hope to get two machines anytime now for our area, so we will have four vacancies to be filled (two men to a machine). If you like, I could put your name down, and you could pass in from time to time and check," she said encouragingly with a dull, sleepy look on her face. Doc agreed for her to put his name down. "Why not?" He asked himself.

"Ah man like me who doh born wid any gold spoon in me mouth awready, ah doh have nothing to lose. Ah mus move on by the hook or by the crook. Ah mus build me mudder a good house. Ah could spray bananas, and ah could sew as well. Ah could handle dat," he said to himself, feeling quite elated as though he had the new job already.

Meanwhile, things in the shop continued in the same unvarying manner. He did his handwork, did his own jobs, and helped anyone who needed his help. That was his tailoring life. He was an apprentice. He was still learning, and he was willing to do his share. As a rule, he was never very busy, but active enough.

Now that Velma had found him, (and he her), she paid him occasional visits. They chatted and continued from where they left off in La Fillette, except that she didn't have time - not much - to spend with him. She often brought him a fruit, a banana mostly, sometimes a special Julie Mango from their garden.

"I picked this mango with a lot of love because I know it is for you." He would smile and squeeze her hand. She smiled at him in her usual peculiar manner of sweetness. She teased him, gave him chat, (more light hearted now) about Sally Ann, but they just laughed it off. She was more at ease now. She was assured within herself that Sally Ann was no threat. She was now very busy though because examination was just around the corner.

"Ah have to hurry home, in fact, ah getting a ride up. But everything is for a time, as you know. We go have a lot of time to roam about after the exam. You go take me for a ride on your bicycle." She looked at it parked against the shop. It had a stand like a motorbike and was quite imposing. Its name, "Desire Me", was quite eye-catching too, written in Old English, in white on a black background and edged in an impressive red. It was very stylish.

Velma giggled: "What a funny name? 'Desire Me' Ha! Ha! Ha! You happy! Ah go see you, yes boy!" She was off reflectively, holding her bag of books (with the wooden handles) in front of her. Doc looked at her as she walked off and smiled a sentimentally charged smile.

- V -

Weeks after Doc left, Sally Ann remained obscure. For a long time nothing bothered her. She didn't even worry too much about school, and snapped at everyone who tried to talk to her and make her happy. After passing him in La Fillette that afternoon, her spirits were raised. She was excited and very happy. When she got home, her father told the rest of the family that the sighting of Doc was the remedy. But no one mentioned Doc to her personally. In fact, discussion about him was not very welcomed at home.

"He's jus pick up and leave us," was Mrs. Briggs' dry comment.

Sally Ann, however, had a longing to see more of him. This boy, whom at first she started to order around the house, and later found that she didn't want to be living without him. Funny!

'But ah think he might have given himself airs and graces.'

When she was in her room, she often compared him with the Sobers' boy, who never left her alone. He always wanted to touch her, especially around her chest. He was forward, she thought. But Doc is not here, and that Sobers' boy always turned up like a bad penny. He always 'appear' out of nowhere like a spirit. He always wanted to help her do something.

"Sweet darling angel, let me help you with your books," he would tease her.

One afternoon she got so vex with him, she could have split open in two, and if you opened her you wouldn't find a drop of blood in her, ah fuss she was vexed.

"Come sweet sugar apple Sally Ann, come let me tie your shoe lace for you, all ah want from you is a kiss from those rosy lips."

She pushed him away, ran and vowed never to talk to him again. But David was okay. He was bright. He was one of the boys from the country, who just passed the Islands Scholarship. He was just breezing out before he went to Presentation College in Town. She didn't dislike him, although he had all the credentials, in a way....only not in a way that she desired. Apart from his brain, his family were well off, well, more than well off....she would say rich; they employed both yard boy and a servant girl who had her own little house near their big wall house. He was a good match, thought Sally Ann. But, dis Mr. Doc kept nagging at her brain!!

Whatever could be said about Sally Ann, no one could deny her appreciation for her studies, and her determination to reach the highest rung of the ladder. Her ambition was to become a lawyer, and without doubt, she was poised for it. These were some of the qualities, no doubt, that Doc admired in her. But they were only some of the qualities. Doc liked her mouth, the movement of her lips when she was reciting. Doc found them to be very tantalizing. He often thought about them, especially having felt them on his forehead once or twice, they felt soft, cool and balmy. But, he thought, she can't be compared with Velma, she was studious too and her lips were the most delicious in the world.

It was a wet, rainy afternoon when he left the shop. There was a big football match being played in Victoria Park, between Green Street and Spartans. The two teams were playing a knockout match; the one that won this match would take home the Trophy. No one in the shop wanted to miss this match. The shop was closed early that afternoon; the boys headed towards Victoria Park. The streets were alive with great expectation for the local team. Mr. Gilbert did put a little something on Spartan to win in his local club.

Everyone was hoping that Spartan would give them licks. However, everyone knew that the boys from Town were giants. They were good; they even beat teams from away. They were more skilful than the boys in the country. Green Street was a team from Town, St. George's, with an impeccable reputation for quality football. Spartans were the best in the country teams. Many of the players were Spartans in both name and nature. They were tough, hardy men of the soil. They walked bare feet, often trained bare feet, and often covered many miles without shoes, carrying heavy loads on their crowns. These guys ate hard food, like yam, bluggoe, breadfruit and things like dat, with a lot of good fresh fish and lambie water. They were strong and they trained hard; they were no push over.

On the other hand, most of the Town boys were soft....well kinda soft, (although most of them originated from the country). Many of them were not as tough as the country boys. They ate too many pies, Irish potatoes and rice. That's what the country boys use to say.

Never-the-less, the boys from Town had advantages for training that the country boys could only dream about, and they made the most of it. Green Street was a team to be reckoned with; they were no small potatoes. Altogether though, both teams were well matched. The Town boys were skilful, well organized, well trained and disciplined. They were a Team and they worked like one. What the country boys lacked was skill, organization and training. They made up for it in sheer hardiness and dogged determination.

"When you going, go," that was part of their philosophy. "Doh hold back. Tackle de man and shoot," was part of their motto.

In the end, the contest was a goalless draw. Nil-Nil. Although overall, Green Street had more points than Spartan, so they won on average. After the match, steel band for so! Everyone was happy that Spartan didn't lose, although they didn't take the crown, but dey good, they did well. No holes in the wall.

'We tell them awready,

Spartans forever,

We go play de game till we dead:

(Chorus) Spartans forever'.

A crowd began gathering around the steel band and they joined in the chorus. The drinks began to flow, hard drinks, soft drinks, in between drinks were lavishly swallowed down. Some men, in the heat of it all, unbuttoned their shirts, threw back their heads, stretched out their hands and turned on some serious whine, often, right down to the ground. Women joined too, and before long, a spontaneous party was born. Doc and his cousin Raymond stood and watched as the impromptu party swung until at last, rain threatening, he had no mudguard on his bike, he decided to leave.

"Listen man, we go see in the morning, ah go hit de road."

"How you hurrying so? Ent yuh riding?"

"Yes, but....."

"Well why don't you hang around for a little while still? Look at these nice chicks around," said Ray, Pointing to a bevy of beautiful girls preening themselves.

"Ah could see. Ah know what you mean man, but Ghost waiting, we have to go and torch crabs tonight."

"Awright den, we go ketch , ah let you off dis time."

"Awright, awright," said Doc, "tomorrow den." On leaving his cousin and special friend, Raymond, Doc headed off and picked up is bike, which was under the stand. He was going home, passing Rivulet's Lane, when he heard:

"Doc! Doc! Wait for me."

It was Sally Ann who came running towards him.

"Hello Mr. Doc," she said in her firm, pert manner.

"One minute ah see you talking, the next minute, when ah turn around, you disappear. I run all the way from the stand to catch up with you. Is a lucky thing you were not riding," she said breathlessly.

Doc looked at her with surprise, and smiled a good welcoming smile, which said, 'I'm glad to see you.'

Sally Ann went on about being actually glad to see him too. She said she just wanted to talk with him for a little while, and she hoped that he would listen to her. She was not too mindful of whether he said anything or not. She started off, and went on speaking nervously for a long time before she was interrupted, and before Doc was able to get in a word:

"Why did you leave Doc? Ah wonder if you know how this affected me. And now is the first time we meet up face to face since you take yourself up and just walk out...ah see you and Velma...."

"Well hold a minute nugh, you doh want to hear what ah have to say? You act...."

"You go have your say," said she, paying very little attention to him.

"Why didn't you tell me you were planning to leave? Eh? Tell me that! You din think about how I feel? You just pick up and go, leaving me there....eh, jus leaving me there wondering....thinking, thinking. For days ah didn't eat, couldn't eat. You din dey to help me. Ah wanted you...and tell me you never thought of that day in the kitchen, suppose...." Then she paused and said sadly,

"Ah bet you told Velma you were leaving though."

"No I didn't tell her I was leaving. Ah didn't tell anyone. As you said, ah jus pick up and leave. It was necessary for me to go and learn a trade. In the kitchen, well... nothing happened as you know."

"If you did stay with us, you coulda get anything you want."

"How do you know?'

"Ah coulda - well we coulda..." she said vaguely, wondering.

"Well....well you coulda just tell me you going. Ah woulda keep it a secret. Our secret. Our special secret.... But no...."

"Take it cool. Remember after that episode in the kitchen you didn't talk to me, well not much, you became all stuck up again."

"Ah sure you have someone to talk to already."

"Who is dat?"

"You know who. Ah even see you in La Fillette walking her home. Ah bet she's glad that she lives down there now."

"Who you talking about?" insisted Doc, pretending ignorance.

"Okay, okay, if you want me to spit it out, it's Miss Velma! Yes, Miss Velma! And doh pretend to be stupid with me, because ah know very well that you are not stupid. Ah know that long, days after you started working for us. So don't pretend with me!" There was a mixture of interest and concern in her voice.

"Ah suspect Velma loved you a long time, she hides it. She is good at that. She is sly and underneath. Ah try to get her to speak about you many times after you left, but ah never get anything....."

"Well you know," interrupted Doc, "Love not to talk, love not to boast."

"Yes ah know dat, but....she was planning...."

"Planning what?"

"You know, planning to take you....well"

And she began sobbing like a child.

"What you crying for?" asked Doc, in a contrite and caring voice.

"Doh cry; you is a nice girl, and you getting more and more beautiful every day. Ah glad to see you, ah really glad to see you."

"An you leave, and you din tell me, and is Velma you always chatting up, and walking home with, an what if anything had happen in the kitchen, eh?"

"Well you know, we din get far wit dat" and he took her hand.

He parked his bicycle on its stand near the drain, out of the way, for people were hurrying away from the Park and rain was drizzling heavier now. From where they were, they could see the large cinema building and its forthcoming attraction on the billboards. She ran her hand over the seat of 'Desire Me' during the longish silence.

Then he asked, "How you getting home? It getting late!" he said with some concern, knowing that she had a good long way to go to Paraclete and there was no bus at this time.

"I'm not in Paraclete tonight, I'm staying down by my Aunt. I'm spending time with my cousins. They are in the stand now. They know I came to see you, so they know I'm all right. They bigger than me; they will take care of me."

"Well that's alright den. We could talk a little more."

"Ah doh say a lot of recitation at home anymore."

"Why?"

"Because you not dey to take me up, an listen to me, an since ah hear that you and Velma like ring on finger…well…ah think I won't like to say."

"Ah wish you would say…but…well if you don't want to say…. who tell you Velma and me like ring on finger?"

"Ah know, ah have me pick up around de place and they tell me everything," said she in a very positive voice

"How is your school work?" said Doc, trying to steer away from her concentration on he and Velma.

"You doh want to talk about you and Velma?"

"Ah thought you wanted to talk about us."

"Ah hear she is your girlfriend," pursued Sally Ann.

"How is your recitation?" again asked Doc.

"Ah told you, since you left with no one to take me up, ah fall back. Well ah doh do much again. You use to make me feel ah want to do it. Ah use to feel real good when you were listening. You help me a lot. I miss you...ah mean," she tried hard to make an unconvincing amendment of her true feelings.

"Ah miss you recitation too, well the passages." He went on, "Sometimes.....well at first, you use to hurt my feelings by some of the things you use to say to me."

"Ah sorry, ah din know you too well.... and...and you was working..."

"Yes ah know I was working for your parents."

"It's not that I want to say. Ah don't know how to say it," she said awkwardly.

"Let me tell you, Sally Ann; you use to say a lot of things that gave me encouragement and inspiration too, you know."

"Ah din realize dat."

"Yes you did. Listen to this passage from Julius Caesar: *"Every bondman in his own hand bears the power to cancel his captivity." And again "The fault dear Brutus, is not in our stars, But in ourselves, that we are underlings."*

"Ah like the way you recited that. It was very inspirational. It use to make me feel that I could do better than just being a Yard Boy," said Doc with sincere feelings.

Hands covering her face...."And it took you away from me," she returned.

"No, we are here again, now. We are here now," said he firmly.

"I know we are together now. But you could have been home. Dad would have let you drive the bus," she said.

"Don't come wit dat; you know your parents, especially your mother, would not have gone down dat road."

"What road?"

"You know, us together!"

"How you know? They woulda do what was best for me."

"Ah doh tink dey woulda agreed to dis one though. Us... ah doubt it," said Doc. A long spell of silence followed again. They now stood facing each other, people were hurrying along and the rain began pelting down.

"It's late. Time for us to go."

"We go see again? Or you don't have time for me now?" said Sally Ann, with one hand on his shoulder. The rain suddenly ceased, but threatening clouds and overcast skies persisted.

"Ah go have time for you, starting from now."

"Come here," he said, "it's my turn to kiss you now." They embraced. He kissed her, not on the forehead as she did to him months past. He kissed her firmly and lingeringly on her lips.

Then she gasped and pushed him off.

"You know, he said, "that will be our first and last kiss."

"Ah wonder what Velma would say if she see you now?" she said softly.

Doc said nothing, but wondered penitently about his loved one as well, and about the consequences.

"The lamplighter is here awready. Time to go."

"We go see again?" she shouted, as she strolled off back down the Lane into the stand where her cousins were waiting for her. She found them engaged in conversation with two young men, one wearing a tie with a pen in his shirt pocket. She'd seen both of them before. They all, all five of them strolled lazily across the park into the main road.

After Sally Ann left Doc, he remained standing there holding his bicycle by the handle bar, and wondered about her and his relationship with her. He felt disloyal to Velma. He found himself thinking hard about kissing Sally Ann. However, he hadn't the time to resolve this new issue. He felt it had to happen. Sally Ann had given him something, an intangible something which he cherished.

Doc loved Sally Ann in a fascinating, tragic manner. There was that tragically tantalizing dangerousness about her, which, by her very being, could lead one into his death straight onto loadstone rock. You know, the chances are you will die if you follow your inclination to have that which she places before you. And yet, in spite of the danger, you want too…well, be tempted to challenge Fate. You want to take the plunge down the jagged precipitous rock.

Sally Ann uncompromisingly put Doc to the test, by compelling him with her very presence, which said: 'love me, I'm yours, have me.' And Doc, looking at her, thought: "and die. No, I love Velma." He resisted the temptation and escaped the tragedy of plunging down the rock of no return; and his love for Velma was the only reason for not loving Sally Ann fully.

He had to meet with Ghost and it was past their appointed time. He jumped on his bike and rode down Gladstone Road, passing the Lamplighter pumping up the gaslight next to Rapier's Shop.

"Good night, Mr. Thomas," he said to the Lamplighter, who had his straw hat buried down on his head and was busily pumping away at the gaslight.

Raising his head to see who it was, he responded, "Boy, wey you come out boy? Aaron was here waiting for you so long; he left about ten minutes now, vex, vex, vex. You better have a good excuse."

He met Ghost waiting for him by the café where they usually bought their milk and rock cakes, near the entrance to the market.

"Doh tell me nothing," said Ghost, and put his hand over his ear. "Ah doh want to hear," anticipating Doc's excuse.

"Ah know who hold you up, who you spend your time with. Ah see her, and ah tell meself, 'Doc go be late today, today.' You playing test. One day two ah dem go meet up wid you at the same time, and ah want to see how you go get out of it. What you go do?"

"Ah didn't expect to see Sally Ann. Ah was on me way on time...."

"Okay, okay, forget it. Ah buy de kerosene awready. You have twenty-five cents for me."

"What time you tink we should leave?" asked Ghost after a gulp of milk.

"We leave as soon as it make dark man, about seven."

"Well dat good. You have a good bag home? Tonight is really crab night. Crab like bush. So come wid a good bag, and you cutlass."

"Okay den, seven."

They left to go and torch crab at the agreed time. It was pouring down with rain. It was a good night for torching, because crab can't stay in their holes....too much water. When they reached Grugu, the place being flat, was like a lake; water was everywhere. They dragged and splashed along in their water proofs, one holding the bag, and the other the torch.

Sometimes they each took their own route, each with his bag and torch. There were other crab catchers there that night too. At the end of that stay, by the time they were ready to go, they had enough crabs to feed the whole of Grenada. As usual, when they got home, they shared their spoils.

Before Doc left, Ghost brought out bread and saltfish cake. They ate hungrily, but Doc had to leave. They were wet, and he had to get changed.

The following night, they called up the rest of boys. Cold Coucou Face, Mud Mask, Scall-up, Boostie and a whole group of them. About six or eight altogether, and they made a cook, crab and dumplings. The boys brought flour and other things. The dumplings were stiff and hard. Ghost made them. Some plain, some mixed with corn flour that when you bite them, they go 'kicks', and sometimes your teeth got stuck in them.

Cold Coucou Face went home for his piece of pan. He played and sang in the pale moonlight. Then everyone joined in. The Boys had a good time. In the dark, with full bellies, they started to tell jokes, shoot jazz, old talk, and ting. Ghost called up a few people going home. Short Man and Mr. Thomas came under his attack. "School boy", he shouted a number of times as they came along. "Why don't you go back to school."

As for Mr. Thomas, the boys had it that his wife was 'ruling' him. He was a slightly built, quiet man. She was plump and had a sharp tongue. The boys nicknamed him 'Tom De Ass', and so Ghost called him up, 'Tom De Ass, wey you come from dis hour?.....She go beat you."

Then one of the boys said, "Nugh man, she just put him in a corner and siddown on him," and they laughed. Then they all left and went and sat on the ticket gate and continued their fun. A heavy shower of rain drove them under the coconut trees. When the shower passed, they went back to the ticket gate. Not long after, the moonlight came out, bright as day. Down by the Danda Kayo tree, over the road, something started to sway up and down as the wind blew, glittering like a bright light, up and down and flashing occasionally. Everyone got scared.

There was old talk about things under the plum tree, which was near to the Danda Kayo tree, so someone shouted out, "Ah spirit, ah spirit." They all scampered off to their homes in an instant, but it was only a wet bluggoe leaf glittering and moving from left to right in the moonlight as the wind blew.

Back in the Tailor shop next morning, the discussion about the football match between Spartan and Green Street continued. Doc didn't have much work of his own that week. Things were slow. He helped Mr. Gilbert, who had some and had come to rely on Doc's good quality handwork. Doc assisted Raymond too. He was getting to know the men and the job as well. He was also gaining experience, helping those who helped him. It was good. That's the way it was.

- VI -

On her way home from school one afternoon, Velma brought him a groundnut sugar cake. By now the boys were used to seeing her regularly. They liked her and they gave Doc 'sticks', telling him, "She is a nice girl" and things like that, "Don't fool around with her you know" She was in and out in a flash. She was too busy.........

"Ah can't stop. My father is at Hutchinson buying groceries. He coming up jus now, and ah have to revise tonight. Chemistry in the morning," said she, hastily handing him the paper bag she had in her hand.

"Ah have a wedding to go to; my aunt is getting married."

"You going?"

"Ah have to. I'm Chief Bridesmaid. Ah go tell you more about it, because ah want you to come to the reception," she slapped his palm.

"We go ketch up. Love you, bye."

She hurried on home, clutching her bag of books to her stomach as she walked hurriedly along.

Three weeks after her exam came the wedding. It was sometime in June, when she completed the last paper. On her way home that afternoon, she told him how relieved she was.

"Studying is hard work you know, but I like it....it is very important. Mother Superior always keep telling us that it is the best thing we could ever do in our lives," she said enthusiastically, looking up at him.

"Anyhow, ah doh have to worry about school for a long time again. We go have time to spend together, now."

"For what?"

"You know for what, for me to see you. Let us walk fast, it's raining."

As it began to rain they passed two shops, where he wanted them to shelter, but she refused to go in, all because big people were there, and some of her school friends too. They ran under a cluster of trees that were over hanging the road, and remained there, until the heavy shower was over. It was the kind of rain that fell very heavily, furiously even...then stopped suddenly. A tall, leafy Cutlet tree overshadowed the cluster of smaller trees with over hanging branches.

The late afternoon sun came out soon after, and the trees glistened with a wet brilliance. The water from the leaves of the tree dripped merrily from the branches unto the undergrowth. They stood there close, and childishly comfortable, and kept looking at the drip, drip, d-r-i-p of water coming down from the leaves above unto the leaves below. After a long while they hugged each other as they stood quietly looking at the last of the raindrops.

"We must go," he said, "the rain stop."

She was even more relaxed now, dreamily so. She purred at Doc, and was as playful as a kitten, rubbing her damp face against his. At close up, the freckles on her face did not look so prominent. 'They are definitely little stars' thought Doc. They emerged from their tree house and headed home. As they walked along, she reminded him about the forthcoming family event, the wedding. The wedding, she told him, will be held in the Anglican Church, in Grenville, on Sunday, the 15th July at 3 o'clock, and the reception will be at the La Fillette School.

"I will be Chief Bridesmaid, could you imagine me?! Chief Bridesmaid. Ha! Ha! Ha!" she laughed ecstatically, with that peculiar laugh of hers.....sometimes dry and cynical, sometimes warm, loving and melodious. Doc wanted to know where to fit it (the laugh), at this moment in time. But he saw she was happy and he was glad for her. Now she can have a rest, the exam is out of the way.

"You don't have to come in the church, but you must be at the church for when we going in and coming out. Ah want you to see me in my bridesmaid dress and the veil over my face, and the hat and ting! Ha!"

"I will be there by the church with the rest of the people that come to see weddings. I'm coming only to see you."

"You have to be at the reception, you know. After ah change we go have a lotta time to talk and ting." His mind ran ahead of him anticipation of them being alone together.

"Ah told mum and my Aunt about you awready. And you know mum remembers you from the night when we were dancing in Paraclete.....you remember? Months now."

"Yes, I do remember her. She came and took you away from me." They exchanged knowing looks as they walked along. She told him that a band would be coming from Town, because her Aunt doesn't want steel band alone. Steel band will come in, at the late half, 'The Grenville Syncopaters', they will play until the early hours. But the 'St. George's All Star Band' will provide most of the music to begin with. They will open up the dancing at the reception after the speeches, and after people toast the bride and groom and things like that.

"It go be a big, big ting you know, and will go until morning." Then she open her eyes wide, wide and said, "Perhaps, just perhaps, we may get away. Some way. You could take me for ride on 'Desire Me', Ha! Ha! Ha! Ah go sit sideways on the cross bar."

'There must be something funny about my bicycle's name?' he thought, so he asked, "What's the joke?"

"Nugh, only.....well, ha! Well only your bike. Ha! Ha! Ha! The name. Ha! Ha! Ha!" She tried stifling a laugh. She said nothing further. She was used to him now and it brought out the funny side of her. "Let's hope it doesn't rain," he said, ignoring the funny side about his means of transport; but still thinking, and trying to see the funny side. 'The name' he concluded.

"Fred Sam ah de wedding sweet, the marriage sweet, but the after blows behind," announced the wedding from the bride's car horn. Everyone knew of this unique piece of music from Fred Sam, the local business man who rented out vehicles for weddings. As soon as people heard this piece of music, they at once knew a wedding was on. The men would say, "Somebody going and hang he self today. Ah wonder who?" The music continued to play from the time they left home until they reached the church, and after the ceremony, to see them on their way home. *"Fred Sam say...."*

This announced that Aunt Muriel's wedding was on its way to the church. Sam's car, with the singing horn, announced the unmistaken event. Its distinctiveness was always instantly recognizable. Doc was one of the large crowd of people outside the church, waiting to get a glimpse of the happy couple. Never mind the after blows. Well, he only wanted to see 'his' bridesmaid. They waited at the church which was lined on either side with palm trees from the entrance to the end of the building.

The bride was in a long white lacy dress, white hat, and elbow length white gloves, a white veil and she also carried a bouquet of flowers. She was a medium built woman, who carried herself with elegance and grace, and smiled easily as most brides do on such an auspicious and memorable occasion.

The bridegroom was a medium built man too, with short forehead and strands of grey hair on his temples. He looked over-dressed and seemed to breathe with some difficulty. He looked ruffled up, dressed in a buttoned-up shirt and wearing an unaccustomed bow tie. He appeared uncomfortable in the hot afternoon sun; more like a stuffed, greased chicken ready for the oven. Never-the-less, despite his appearance and the seeming inconvenience, he maintained a good-natured, pleasing smile.

The bridesmaids were beautifully presented, looking like cherubs. They smiled a great deal in an innocent looking, childish manner. Velma was the most elegant of all. She walked quite stately in her high heeled white shoes, long dress, and gloves. Her eyes roved around, meeting up with Doc's. She gave him the most alluring smile that she could ever muster under the circumstances. It almost knocked Doc off balance. 'She could knock anyone off with this kind of smile,' he thought. As soon as the ceremony was over, he headed for home, showered and changed. He heard Fred Sam speeding the happy couple on their way home, with its now uncommon, peculiar siren:

"Fred Sam say the wedding sweet, the marriage sweet, but the after-blows behind......"

After dinner, he put on his new pants, one specially made for the occasion. It was a 'Whole Top and Hallow Bottom', a new style made from piece of fabric called 'Pick and Pick. It had no waist band and no turn-ups. Raymond helped him design the style. He was real hot. The pants was sharp, cutting nail! He had on one of his new shirts too. Only worn twice to matinee. He told his mother all about his invitation, and left home riding in style, with his legs open and out, and feet, mainly toes, touching the pedal.

When he arrived at the reception, his shirt was wet with perspiration. He parked 'Desire Me' under a Golden Apple tree by the side of the school, took out his handkerchief and fanned himself. Velma was in front of the school door, with a look of concerned expectation. A group of young beaus with bright eyes, hopeful looks and bulging thighs, glass in one hand, cake or sandwich or whatever in the other, surrounded her. They had that expectant, hopeful look. One was defiantly trying his luck with her. He held his glass of ice-cream in his hand and approaching, pleaded with her, Romeo-like, to have a taste.

"Have a little spoonful, ah tell you it is the best ice-cream you ever could taste," he said, laughing heartily, feeling as though he was in goat heaven. When he saw her go to embrace Doc, his face fell like ah over ripe paw paw.

He congratulated her on her dress, "You looked like an angel in the church, girl."

"Hi!" Doc said, and disarmed the hopeful beau by embracing her.

"You looking nice, eh," she said. "How you come so late? You din want to come again?" said she with a nervous smile.

By now the hopeful beaus had seen their hopes fading, or hopeless, so one by one they faded away.

"Ah had to go home and have a shower and change," replied Doc, still looking curiously around and focusing hard on the young man with the glass of ice-cream, who was the last to leave.

The reception was well attended, as most wedding receptions are. People were everywhere, on the steps, inside the house, under the trees, knotted about in the yard and in the garden. This large crowd of people intimidated Doc somewhat, especially knowing that he was not connected with her.

"Come on let me introduce you," she said calmly.

"Your parents met me before."

"Yes, but they don't really know you; well you have been spoken for by me, and I know you saw them in Paraclete but you all have not been formally introduced," said Velma persuasively, squeezing his hand.

"Now, I want to let all of them know that we are friends. I want to let them know that by our presence," she strained, to impress a somewhat reluctant Doc.

"What kind of friends you want to tell them we are?" said he, as they walked through knots of people sipping drinks and eating.

"Serious friends, don't worry, come on, in any case, my Aunt don't know you, I want you to meet her. My parents know a lot about you, since Paraclete, but my Aunt, she must meet you," she said.

After some hesitation, and some pushing and buffeting in the crowd, they met up with Velma's parents. He was formally introduced to them. They shook hands with him. Her mother looked him over again closely. He was no stranger to her. She knew a lot about him from Velma and then from the dance-floor kissing. Not long after, he met Aunt Muriel, who had now changed from her bridal gown, and was wearing something less formal and more relaxing. She had a glass of punch in one hand, as she stretched out the other with eagerness when she met him.

"Hi Doc, she said in a relaxed, casual voice, "Velma tell me a lot about you. You enjoying yourself?"

Doc said he was glad to meet her, and that he was enjoying himself quite a lot. He commented on the wedding and congratulated her all at the same time, hoping that she would be very happy. He then moved closer to Velma.

"Ah go see you again Miss Muriel," he said, as he and Velma wandered around looking for Uncle Johnson, Aunt Muriel's newly wedded husband. But there was no sign of him. She asked a young man, a comical character, whether he'd seen the bridegroom, Uncle Johnson.

"Oh yes, your uncle now, ah hear he run away wid one of the bridesmaid." And grinning like a Cheshire cat, he went on his way. Velma was then buttonholed by some of her school friends, while Doc took the opportunity to get away from the crowd and into the school yard.

Velma became very engaged attending to her school friends and guests in a general way; she had more than her hands full. Hours passed and all Doc could have seen was a fleeting glance of her with a waiter in her hands, up and down the place until finally, they ran into each other.

Doc was sitting outside, under a small cluster of Sugar Apple trees, just liming with some friends. He was obviously enjoying himself with them. It was a mixture of boys and girls in the group.

They were giving one another old talk and ting. Happily and merrily shooting jazz, which ranged from Nansi stories to love. All sweetly spiced up in a flavour befitting the occasion, and much to their own taste. She went up to him unnoticed, touching him on the shoulder she said, "So here you are at last." She spoke with a measured, familiar, even and possessive air.

"Here, I bring a piece of wedding cake." She handed him a small wrapped parcel.

"I saved it specially for you. In fact, I had to hide it from some of these greedy people, who want to eat up everything. Like they never see food before. I'm fed up with them, and I'm tired too. I've been on my feet all day," she said.

"Thanks for the cake. Ah go put it in the cycle bag. Well take a five nugh. You look tired in truth," said Doc. The boys whispered among themselves and sniggered. The girls smiled knowingly to one another.

'She cares about him, and he cares about her' were written on all their faces.

"I can't right now, but about 7:30 I will, if not before," then she held his hand and said, "Come." They excused themselves and walked a little away, "You know what I'm thinking?" she said, in a quiet conspiratorial voice.

"No," said Doc in response, "I'm not a mind reader yet," he continued amusingly, as if he wanted her to understand that he was concerned about her, after seeing how worn-out she looked.

His manner was saying, "I do care about you. I believe you are working too hard. Why don't you take a rest? Ah doh like to see you like that, and besides, you just finish working so hard at you exams!"

"Listen," she said.

"I'm listening, both ears are yours,"

"Boy you know so much speech tonight, you swallow a dictionary? Since early, I wanted to tell you how much I like you 'bad' shirt and you Hallow Bottom pants. You in style!" She squeezed his hand and laughed heartily. "Anyhow," she continued once more, in that same conspiratorial voice. "The moon should rise between 6:30 and 7:00. It is two days before full moon."

"What you driving at?"

"You could take me for a spin. We could go for a ride on 'Desire Me', Ha! Ha!....." She covered her mouth to stifle the laugh. "We could go up Mt. Horne."

"Okay, but dey go miss you," said Doc.

"Ah doh think so. Dey getting ready for all night dancing an ting. The big people ting," she said, as they moved further away from the group. Doc didn't need much convincing about them being out on their own in some quiet place.

"Mt. Horne is uphill," he said, on reflection. "Ah doh think we should go up hills. We can't ride well up the hill forget the going up the hill. Anyhow, we go get away. We will go some way. Go back inside and finish what you was doing, and let your parents see you and ting. Ah go stay right here, or I'll be just around the corner waiting for you. Come back in half hour, and we go see what happen."

"Okay den," she said, and went back into the hall. When she went away, he re-joined what was left of the group. They gave him a little mouth and ting. He laughed it off in a good humouredly way. No fuss. No digging nothing, just nice and cool like.

"Your girlfriend is nice, ah bet she bad for you," said Alice, one of the girls who had been keeping a close eye on him all afternoon.

"Ah better doh stay around too long," followed Monah, staring at him with her beautiful big eyes. There were only two boys left, and one went off in search of his girlfriend. Gradually, they all drifted apart.

When Velma went back into the Hall, the reception was in full progress. Eating, drinking and dancing were the order of the night you may say. Everyone was holding something in their hands. A faint glow from the East, with the penetrating ray of light told its own story. The moon was making its slow progress towards lighting up the heavens. True to her word, Velma came out from the Hall, and into the yard with a paper bag full of refreshments in her hand.

"Let's put this in your saddlebag," she said "You doh want us to go Mt. Horne? We would enjoy watching the beautiful moon you know." She pointed to the much larger orb of light coming from the direction of Pearls.

"You see," he said, walking towards the bike with the parcel in his hand, while dodging a small group of people approaching....

"You see, although Mt. Horne is a good place, with a good view, it's up hill. We go either have to walk most of the way, or I will ride and you will have to walk."

"Where else can we go at this hour?"

"Let's ride down La Fillette stretch, turn left at the end of it and go through Dunfermline and we could rest up at the back of Pearls Airport; it has a good view dey too."

"Well okay," she agreed.

"Go on then, I'll meet you a little in front."

She met him in the junction not far off. He held the bike while she got on, and she sat sideways on the cross bar of 'Desire Me.'

"Hold the handle bar with both hands, and make yourself very comfortable," said Doc, encouragingly.

"It's good you looking after me Doc. But I'm comfortable already," said she, settling herself and ignoring the gaze from passers-by.

"Let's be off then. It is nice to get away from all these eyes," said he eagerly.

The bike was just coasting down La Fillette long stretch. All Doc had to do was just steer and regulate the speed. He hummed a tune, as cool breeze lovingly caressed their faces. Velma's head was close to his chin and her soft hair brushed lovingly against it. She was there, on 'Desire Me', cool and relaxed, surrounded and protected by his arms. He could see inside her sleeveless cotton bodice. She was not wearing any brassier; her two beautiful, firm breasts were very tempting. Her scent (which he lavished) wafted around him increasing the beat of his heart.

They continued down to the end of the road until they came to the junction. Then, as agreed, they turned left into the direction of Pearls, passing along the Dunfermline road. Once there, it was a stone's throw from lower Pearls. Passing the trace leading to the Rum distillery, they got over the bridge, and arrived at Lower Pearls junction, in less than twenty minutes. As they entered the junction, they met three boys who unashamedly gazed at her with sweeping eyes from top to toe, and began to giggle, nudging one another and pointing at Doc and Velma. Then they started to sing:

"Dorothy went and bade,

A Mermaid take she maid,

Dorothy, woe, yoh, yoh,

Dorothy gul you bad.

The boys laughed gleefully. They slapped their things and jumped up and down like Grand Etang monkeys. Doc and Velma walked on keeping a straight face, pretending they didn't notice them or hear anything. But the song 'Merry Maid take she maid' and their gleeful jesting lodged themselves in some part of Velma's brain and remained with her as they entered Pearls gap. They strolled along the stony dirt road which was thickly wooded with black-sage and cutlet trees on both sides of the road. There were thick vines and some sticky cherry trees. The whole area was creeping with water grass and walk fast; these luscious weeds/ bushes were spreading along the area in great abundance.

It was very quiet and the peacefulness was only interrupted by the nocturnal sounds of the night insects which in itself was not disturbing. Instead, it added to the general romantic atmosphere of the two lovers, who were still in their Juvenile years and in their hearts were secretly searching for a way to move on or develop from Paraclete. The evenings in Paraclete had never been discussed at any length before; they both probably found it wasn't necessary as they did when meeting and passing each other like ships in the night on Paraclete Bridge, apart from the concert.

Their stroll took them within sight of the runway where by now everything and everyone connected with the Airport had either long gone to sleep or sitting in some room awaiting the arrival of the first BOAC flight from Barbados. Doc leaned up his bike on its stand and wiped his brow. Velma dusted and straightened her dress and wiped her face while the silvery moon shone on them.

They continued to stroll along lazily and aimlessly as lovers do, but for them, they were searching for something to break the ice, but nothing in particular presented itself. So they kept walking slowly. A fallen star flickered across the sky. By now they were very close and alone together. Secretly, Velma recalled the night on the dance floor - dancing without music. She could still feel the touch of his arms around her waist and the feel of his breath upon her cheek, and their lips united together.

Then Doc said vaguely, "You all right V? I....I want to know. I feel..."

"I want to know how you feel?"

"Ah hungry."

"For what? Tell me what you hungry for."

"Something to eat and drink, smarty," she said, eyeing him curiously. For Doc felt unable to resist fondling her, which continued all through their aimless stroll. Whereas with Velma when they were not alone she often found it easier to touch and play with him and to fondle his dress, as it were. Alone together here, although reminiscing on Paraclete which was close to her heart, she had reservations. There was so much to try and understand.

The love had to grow; so far the seeds had been planted in her and, he thought, or believed that both their hearts and souls were united in one and waiting to be sealed with a kiss. Velma was hungry for some food which she requested. Then, defiant of her wishes, he said no to her request for some food.

"No, not yet; let's walk down a little further where we can get a better view of the moon; we'll find a nice place and sit down, then we'll eat." Velma went along with it in her even temper with his suggestion.

Not long afterwards though, she said imploringly, "Ah want something to drink now though; I've been up and down all day and ah thirsty."

"Oh gosh! Yes," he said, and fetched a bottle of ginger beer from the saddle bag of 'Desire Me' and handed it to her. She had a long drink, took one breath and then another drink, until her thirst was quenched, then handing him the remains. He eagerly gulped it down, then returned the bottle to the saddle bag, coming back to her. They both sat in an uneasy stillness, while a mild breath of air blew tenderly through them as they now lay down on a grassy area which was as soft as a bed. Still the uneasy silence reigned, as they peacefully lay there inhaling the fragrance of the night flowers.

Velma, who was on her feet almost all day enjoyed, even longed for these quiet moments under the light of the moon with Doc lying beside her but still indecisive of which road their love should follow. Then, having languished in a state of absolute peacefulness, their feelings deepened and their passion rose as they got to their feet facing each other. They held on to each other in a close, tight embrace. They sniffed, patted and petted each other playfully like children, then followed with a blissful thrilling kiss.

After this, he sat down again on the grass pulling her closely and wrapping her in his bosom. She shivered somewhat, then he released her and she sat a little away from him. He laid his head on her lap and she lovingly patted his head in the light of the silvery moon, humming quietly all the time:

"Love me tender, love me true, never let me go----"

Then almost abruptly, as if recalling something in the recess of her soul she said: "It's time for us to go, they might miss me."

"Awready?" said Doc with some surprise. He was lulled, as it were, into a state of seventh heaven even more so by the song which caught him and tied him there in her lap. He was thinking and believing that the evening had just started. Day just light, for when she suggested that they should go riding his imagination galloped at a rapid pace, believing that there was more to this 'ride', something like deep passionate love-making. He was disappointed when she lifted his head off her lap.

Then he raised himself slowly and lazily, stood up and brushed the pieces of dry grass off his pants. Velma also brushed and re-arranged her dress pulling here and there to get out the creases. At close up, Doc saw it was a peachy looking dress and the piping and trimming about the neckline were neat and fitted her tastefully. She looked very beautiful and tantalizing like a piece of chocolate cake - irresistible. He did not want to leave; he did not want to be separated from her at this moment, this golden opportunity, he thought, may never present itself again.

But Doc was young, and as with most young people, life must be hurried, everything must be done at once, right now. He felt that they must make love now - now or never kinda thing. Thinking that Velma was too shy to indicate her full or real desire and she, by making no reply to his earlier advances and now standing and facing each other again, he held her around her waist and drew her closer to him. He played with her hair and began fondling and kissing her.

For a moment she said nothing and seemed to be enjoying it as much as he did, and yet she was trying hard to fight off her passion; but it was difficult to keep such youthful flaming passion under cover and Doc, believing what he thought was a mutual desire for love said, "Come on."

"Where to?"

"Under the cherry tree."

"What for?"

"We can prove that we love each other like the big people," he whispered in her ears.

"What!" She exclaimed. "You want to have sex, that's what you want, that's the way you want us to prove we love each other? I don't think so!" Saying this with her arms folded across her chest, she paced the ground with rapid, vehement strides, mumbling something that he couldn't hear. "I thought," she said slowing down her strides, while Doc looked on in an unbelievable silence. "Ah thought we woulda wait until we older, wid a nice house and thing, get married you know, like in love stories and we could have children and….."

"And what? And when? Books is books; not everything you read in books................"

"But ah believe this," she said in anticipation. "Whatever, I don't think it is the right thing to do right now," said Velma firmly. And yet indecision tortured her, she felt a kind of disloyalty.

"When you say we'll go riding I thought, I thought................ because we are in love we would make love all the way, you know. You love me?"

"Ah love you plenty, a lot a lot, a sure of that." Then tears flowed down her cheeks like Concord Waterfall.

"I most certainly love you Doc," she said nervously.

"But"........... covering her face with both hands, she cried hysterically, shaking all the time. Doc did not go towards her in any comforting manner. He left her standing there for a while, only for a short while, then suddenly making an abrupt turn, he rushed and held her close.

"I would like for us to get married one day. Let's go; it's time; they go miss you."

A note of disappointment and sadness rang out in his voice. Velma made no response. Instead, she went and stood near the bicycle with her arms folded and in deep thought. A little while afterwards she called out to him in a strong pleading voice:

"Doc, why are you doing this to me? I love you dearly; don't let us kill our love in its infancy........Let us wait........give it a chance.............."

"Lock it up you mean."

"No, let it grow; give it some time"

"You mean put it in prison."

"No, no, no," she pleaded in exasperation. Then, unfolding her arms, she walked up to him with a penitent look in her eyes, and they both reached out to each other again, very demonstratively, they embraced and kissed passionately.

"I'm sorry if I hurt you," she mumbled quietly in his ears." "I am sorry."

"Let's pretend we married for tonight - well, you know, we'll make believe, eh?"

"And................?"

"We can make real love and when we are older we'll get married."

"Well eh eh; ah doh know...... school. Papa going to England and, and ah doh know, she said in a drunken, passionate state. As they by now were inching their way towards 'Desire Me'. For a moment she was drunk form the wine of love. In that state she agreed in a way to do anything Doc said.

"Yes, yes we go.........." and he led the way as she locked onto his arms and they both headed towards a mound where grass was spacious and the water grass was luxuriant and the leaves and twigs scattered plentifully around. There they sat, embracing and caressing, and he held her head in his arms and passionate kisses flew like sheets of rain. Then she lay quietly and drowsily on the ground, on a heap of water-grass and responded mechanically to his kisses. While she was in that state, he undid her underwear, and then she felt his muscles stiffen.

As he was about to enter her, somehow, as if by magic, she gathered all her super human strength and pushed him away. Extricating herself, she held onto her underpants and ran, just ran until she became tired and exhausted, then she sat down and dressed herself. Afterwards, she lay down on the ground feeling dull, weak and very frustrated. Doc lay on the ground, unsettled from the experience that happened in a flash, like the proverbial cup that slipped from his lips. All seemed to be going so well, and then....He lay there under the tree as the shadowy moonlight sprinkled through the branches, silhouetting him amongst the trees; there he was, full of mixed feelings and emotions about his loved one Velma. A great deal of time passed before she again took the lead to reopen dialogue. She went back to the spot where he lay and once again apologised.

"I'm sorry Doc." Although, in fact, she had nothing to be sorry about.

"I'm sorry," she said again in a contrite, almost inaudible voice.

"I....I love," she said fervently. "I love you!"

"It's alright," he said dully, still lying on the same spot where she left him in the peak of passion. He was just lying there with his pants half-down, trying now to understand this remarkable girl.

"I will always love you," she said softly, patting his head.

"Ah know....well....ah know. I will always love you too,"

"We're inseparable even though you think I locked the door of our love, but you know you alone have the key to unlock it."

"Yes. I am happy to know that I have that special privilege. Thanks."

"Yes, one cannot lock up love forever, but it takes time."

This was a salve to his wounded pride; but, in fact, Velma meant every word of it. To her, it was just not the right time. She held his hand, but he did not get up from his position on the ground; he lay there silently, remote and pensive.

"You vex. Don't vex with me, Doc. Have patience with me; wait a little while, trust me, am yours," she said, as if trying to atone for not yielding to him earlier. She ran her fingers along his arms reassuringly.

"We'll make real love one day. Sex is only a part of love. We'll do that, but it's not easy for me now."

"Why don't you unlock the door, let love fly out now ah mean......"

"Ah know what you mean, but what account would I give to God for my virginity?" said Velma in a burst of emotion, and that he had no answer to. He was kinda stumped, lost for words, if you like. Yes, he was burning up for her, and in her way she too was also being consumed for him, but she had to manage her desires, her feelings. As for Doc, he wanted her right now. He would at once, given the opportunity, strip her of her virginity.

He would not force himself on her against her will and make her yield under pressure, but making love now is what he wanted. This is what 'going for a ride' meant for him; he never thought of marriage at this stage; he felt they were much too young to think of conventional marriage before sex.

She, Velma, however, even in her state of weakness, believed in marriage before sex, not the other way around. It was her upbringing, the way her parents brought her up to think. Added to that, the nuns religiously – (Religiously) drummed it into the girls' heads, constantly warning them about one drop of that thing and she knew of at least two girls who failed to heed the warning and 'a drop of that thing' left them at the tender age of 14 or so, pregnant, although they disguised it very well and continued attending school for many months afterwards.

Velma loved Doc with a mixture of childish romanticism and as a young, maturing adolescent. Velma was in that changing state of development where she felt that the loss of her virginity was a form of personal sacrifice which she was not prepared to make at this time; and although caught in a moment of weakness and indecision, she found the inner powers to summon up her resolve just at the point when Doc was about to deflower her.

She was not prepared to yield her cherished jewel.....well not yet, although she knew that Doc was the man she would deliver such treasured possession to. She will surrender herself to him, although she had mixed feelings about it presently; so she came down on the side of caution and decided in the meantime that her virginity must be saved for that special day when they were married, and so it was, and time flew on.

By now the flaming coals of passion had burnt itself out and they both began to view their relationship with a more dispassionate eye. Amidst a mixture of sadness and joy, Doc felt his love deepen for her. He embraced her warmly for the umpteenth time and she drenched his shoulders with a combination of joyful and sorrowful tears. It was past time for them to go, and they quietly made their way towards 'Desire Me' and walked all the way from Pearls to Dunfermline gap, past the Rum Distillery, then they rode back to the school where the reception was being held. Doc said good night and she wished him well on his journey home. But by now the moon was covered with a thick blanket of cloud.

Feeling wan, tired and agitated, Velma made her way back to the reception.

"Where was you?" inquired her Aunt, "Your mother was looking for you. What's wrong? How you look like Frighten Friday so? Who bother you?"

"Where is mum? She gone home?"

"She is around; ah go tell her you okay when I see her."

And so saying, she got lost in the crowd. The party was still in full swing and showing no signs of abating; it seemed as if it would go on and on like Johnny Walker. But Velma was tired both physically and emotionally. She was drained and the past few hours with Doc stretched her to the limit all around.

She must sleep if or when she can, for she felt the time with Doc...... that very taxing emotional experience would deprive her of sleep and for Velma, it (sleep) turned out to be a commodity in short supply that night.

It was an uneasy ride returning home for Doc. He was unable to detach his mind from her and the new, widening experience. He lay down to sleep but like Velma, Pearls kept him awake until the early hours of the morning.

Back at work, things were quiet again. The suit was finished, collected and paid for, but the week was very young. He found himself in a restless and agitated mood like a dog scenting a manicou. He wanted movement, action, variety and change. His tailoring period he felt, was over. He had done well. The only thing he couldn't make was a jacket and that usually took years. He didn't have time for that, didn't want to be sitting around waiting. Jackets were not important; he was very good with shirts and pants so once again the time for movement and change had been beckoning to him.

It was not long afterwards that he met Ms. Gladys who told him that the machines long awaited had arrived and that they were in Town, in Tanteen and on Saturday Mr. DaCosta would be collecting two along with some other necessary spraying equipment. Following their arrival it would take a week or two to straighten up details, then at least four people would be employed. She said she had spoken to Plant Disease Inspector about him and all he had to do was wait, so he did, he waited.

In the meantime, he informed his mother about his impeding move. He told her he could do his sewing in the evenings and on weekends, Sundays after mass.

"You sure?" she pressed him with keen interest.

"I was thinking of paying down on a machine and renting a little place by Mr. Modest for you by the time you take twenty."

"Mum that's a long time, I won't be in tailoring so long."

"No. You in a hurry; Rome wasn't built in a day, you know, so take it easy."

"Yes, mum, ah know. It take a long time to build Rome, but tailoring is slow right now; ah could sew good already, all I need is practice and that would come when ah get me job and ting, ah doh have to be sitting around the tailor shop for dat."

His mother appeared dubiously satisfied. She was pleased about his new found enthusiasm and the fact that he began to make his own decision. She knew about this spraying; they had land in St. Cloud that was very regularly sprayed but she wondered how long that would last. She opined, with the tailor shop he would be his own boss and be employed in his profession for life; all he had to do was continue to improve himself; take a course and tings like that. But spraying with some machine on your back all the time so. To her, that was somewhat risky. But he was man and he had to chart a course for himself; all she could do was stand by him.

"Awright, awright," she said quietly on reflection. "Whatever you do, put God in front."

"Okay mum. Okay, ah go always remember that; ah know things go look up." And he jumped up on 'Desire Me' and made his way to the shop. Many weeks had passed away, and during the time he continued to make calls, continued to visit at the Plant Protection Depot on his way to the shop.

One morning, Ms. Gladys was waiting for him in front of the building, the downstairs of a house rented from Mr. Johnson. "Doc!" she said. "You doh mind if ah call you 'Doc'?"

"Oh no, Ms. Gladys, is me second name in a way."

"The PDI wants to see you soon. He tell me to tell you to come here on Monday at half past one; he want to interview you about the job."

That was Thursday morning. He entered the shop like a ray of morning sunlight - beaming. Friday morning, bright and early before cock crow, as you would say, he and Ghost went for an early morning swim down in the basin which was brief, and refreshing. Then they returned home after devouring some mangoes. Back at home, he had some man better man tea and then went down to the shop. He kept quiet about the interview.

Saturday came. It was usually half day at the shop. The other half day was just for liming, killing time, shooting jazz, old talk and ting, checking out girls and ting, eating rock cakes and drinking milk. They just dig the scene and take it cool. All the young beaus meet up as usual on Saturday afternoons at the regular spot by the entrance to the market where the owner Barz, took keen interest in their stories. The whole group of Rocky boys was there - Doc and Ghost, Right Pocket, Cold Coucou Face, Crab eye, Mud Mask plus two others, the whole gang was in Town, restlessly looking for something, like the lawless breed.

On leaving the café, they went into Everybody's Store to check out pants material. From there, to Bata to check out shoes, from there, over by Ms. Desousa to check the latest bad shirt from Trinidad. Feeling hungry, they bought bread and fishcake from Ms. Winnie, washed it down with some sky high drink. They only realised it was getting late when it was getting dark, for Mr. Earnest the lamplighter was busy pumping up the lamp by Rapier; they knew it was time to go home.

Sunday came and it was church first thing in the morning. After breakfast, which was Cocoa tea, bakes and salt fish, a few of them went to the river for the usual swim. Doc left and returned home early, earlier than usual, for he was thinking of tomorrow.

Monday came. He dressed smartly, took time off from lunch and went to the interview which was successful. He was told he'd be one of two men assigned to a spraying machine at any one time. One will be spraying and the other would be carrying oil, and this will alternate throughout the day. He was given an interview about the nature of the job. He would be given two weeks training and the pay would be fortnightly.

"Once you're employed, you would be on probation for two months. If you pass the probation, you would be given a permanent job," said Mr. Roland, the Plant Disease Inspector. He was a medium built, medium height, smooth black man, big, flattish face, bow legged and chicken hawked gazed as if he wanted to swoop down on him.

"You should give two weeks notice at the shop."

"Yes sir," returned Doc. "I will do so on Monday."

Doc told his mum about his success with the interview with measured humility. He thanked her for all her help and support. In reply, she quietly said she hoped he was doing the right thing. The next day, he told Mr. Gilbert about his decision to move on to try something new. Mr Gilbert listened to him attentively, said he was just getting used to him and so on and so on, but life is one of movement and change and he wished him all the success in the world. Then Doc told Ray, followed by the rest of the boys.

"Ah tell you," said Congo, "as soon as he could sew off he go; life here is too slow for him, ha!" said the muscular man.

His last day at the shop was a memorable one. The boys put some money together and had a little 'thing' for him. Speeches were made congratulating him and more praises for the way he took to the trade.

"But the only thing," said Congo. "There is always a little girl coming around with a paper bag standing up near 'Desire Me' Ha! Ha! Ha!" He grinned. They all laughed.

Ray stood in front of the shop as he was going out. They shook hands. They never seemed to want to let go. "One day," said Ray cryptically, "ah think we go do something real big. Perhaps go away; ah have ah uncle in England, you know, who knows, eh?" and Raymond smiled in the same mysterious manner.

"Who knows eh?" Then he confessed, "Ah go miss you boy." Then he slapped him on the back in a friendly way like.

"Come in and have a stitch anytime," said the boss. "We will be glad to see you", with a strong smell of rum reeking from off his breath.

Doc thanked them for all the help, advice and assistance he got from them. Then he did not know what else to say. He felt like running out of the shop because he was filled with emotion.

On a sad note, he said, with his back to them, "Good bye, we go catch up."

Then he jumped on 'Desire Me' and slowly and thoughtfully peddled his way home. With his needle still on his shirt pocket and his thimble made of brass which was smelly, on his right little finger.

And so came the end of the tailoring experience of George Awosu Williams, popularly known to his friends, and to our readers, as Doc. He'd completed another phase of his still very youthful life, and now was poised to begin a new one as a Spray Boy or Plant Protection Worker.

Out of the night that covers me
Black as the pit from pole to pole
I thank whatever god maybe
For my unconquerable soul.

W.E. HENLEY

Book Three

Plant Protection

- I -

It rained heavily the night before the day Doc had to begin work with Plant Protection. Then drizzling, followed by heavy short down pour, then back to the unending drizzle, drizzle, drizzle. Then it slackened and the yard was saturated. A new dawn was here marking the start of a new day and a new beginning with promise of new hopes and great expectations.

He got out of bed and yawned lazily, then he opened his window and looked out. The fowls and their young brood were chick-chick-ing. The chickens made their squeaking noises as they gathered around the yard for their morning feed.

The cocks strutted around, crowed and the hens fluffed their feathers flapped their wings and yielded to the cocks. The birds sang in their own special tuneful manner. The bees buzzed, hummed and whizzed from flower to flower, doing what they can do best: pollinating, assisting the provision of different foods necessary for humans; and possibly, most of all, the purest and one of the most nourishing of foods, honey. The early morning breeze was soft and cool. Then came the sun. That large orange fireball darted its early morning ray across a yellow sky patiently, imperceptibly, but inevitably lighting up the new day with that soft, early morning Caribbean sunrise.

"Lives of Great men all remind us...." Repeated Doc as he busied himself with his preparation for leaving. "Ah man must take a chance in dis world. Wherever you're planted you must grow", said he, after these uplifting thoughts of Great Men.

"Ah going, Mum."

"You pray?"

"Yes, Mum; ah say me prays"

She held him. Then said, "Go now and God bless you."

He left the house clutching a paper – bag with some fried bakes which he put into his jola. And on he went....it was short walk down to the Depot. He got there early; even Miss Gladys wasn't present as yet.

He waited outside while a number of passers-by greeted: "Hi Doc,", "Hello Doc" they all in their usual friendly manner shouted out his popular name, and he responded accordingly, being a little anxious. It broke the anxiety. He did not have long to wait, before the short, medium built slow – walking, heels clacking, staid gait of Miss Gladys made her appearance.

"Good morning, Doc, ah see you nice and early," said she as she breezed into her office. Doc acknowledged her greetings and hoped she was well this morning.

"Ah well, very well, Doc." She said again in an amiable, friendly manner. Just cool like.

Then: "You looking anxious. Doh worry the Rover coming soon; you go be alright."

Miss Gladys then sat down, rested her personal bag at the far end of her desk then she pulled out a chair and sat down. Not long after the Rover arrived. It was a dark green Land Rover with an open back.

The driver, a Mr DaCosta, was a short stocky man with a thick moustache and a stomach that went ahead of him. It was like a little wine cask. He hailed Miss Gladys in a familiar manner, flicked off a cigarette and coughed, hacked and spat: 'splat' on the wall. He touched his stomach and went towards Miss Gladys; who introduced them.

"Doc, this is Mr. DaCosta; he is the driver and the Mechanic."

Following this, she did the same with the driver:

"Mr. DaCosta, this is Doc the new worker who will be starting today and will be going up with you this morning."

DaCosta surveyed Doc neutrally, but did not offer his hand, then said:

"The boys call me Cos. Ah drive, and if anything happen to your machine, I look after them." Afterwards he went into the office and patted Miss Gladys on her shoulders.

She said, "behave, behave, day doh light yet, you start to molest me already."

Mr. DaCosta made no reply, went into the storeroom and took out a light blue painted machine, some spark plugs, some screws, nuts and some small rubbers, like shock absorbers.

Then he said to Doc: "Come help me put these in the rover." Doc assisted him in silence. When he'd finished he (the driver) shouted out something to Miss Gladys, closed the door of P421 and drove off.

On the way he gabbled something critical about the Plant Disease Inspector and his Team Leader, (TL), and turning his face to Doc, said that they were going to Mt Pleasant Estate, under Grand Etang Mountains. Doc nodded his head by way of acknowledgement. On their arrival, Doc was introduced to the Team Leader, Mr. Frederick, a medium height, slim, smooth, dark young man dressed in well ironed khaki shirt and pants, with a note book and pen in his shirt pocket. He spoke with a slight stutter as he extended his hand.

"I'm Frederick. The boys call me Wope, Wope, Sir."

"They call me Doc."

Then he told him that he will be working with Joseph, or Joe, who was standing nearby. He was a short affable young man, not much older than Doc; they both smiled at each other. After the formalities with Mr. Frederick, Joe said,

"Come, the machine is over there," pointing at a clump of trees not too far from where they were standing.

"You bring clothes to change?"

Doc said, "No."

"And what about lunch?"

"Well, ah have something in this paper bag here."

"Okay put it over there," pointing to the spot where all the lunches were. Doc followed his directions, putting down his lunch, and returned.

"Tomorrow you must bring your working clothes. Right now," said Joe, "we will be working with this machine and ah have to teach you how to spray, how to use the machine."

"Okay," said Doc looking a little uncomfortable, for the other machines were whirring noisily, and guzzling out spray oil over the rich banana plantation.

"Now then, Doc," said Joe, "before you start, even before you put on a machine on your back, ah want you to know something about it."

Joe was stooping down over the machine, a deep green and "Kickensdekker spraying machine" was written on the side; it came to be called 'the Dekker' for short. It was about eighteen inches high and about twenty inches wide, built in a slight curve with a pair of shoulder straps. It had a rubber nozzle about three feet, long with a metal point from where the fine spray comes out, which falls in a fine soft mist on the banana leaves.

Almost at the end of the nozzle there was a small 'on' and 'off' control button, so that the oil could be regulated, 'on' or 'off', while the machine itself is in motion. It had a small fan belt attached to the engine, which was at the back, a plug and a small petrol tank, also at the back. At the front, there were two small hooks where a circular oil container was attached; this was called 'the moon' by the boys. It was a very impressive and efficient looking piece of mechanical design which was made to be carried on one's back.

Joe patiently and exhaustively explained to Doc its method of operation. He even gave him tips on how to stop it (making it inoperable) when he wanted a 'five', and when 'the pusher', the Team Leader was not around. So he could 'stop' it and take a 'five' even if the Team Leader was around.

"Just take out the plug cap," he said, demonstrating by practical example.

"Take off the plug cap, and loosen the plug, then put it back. Give the ting a little knock and baps. It looking good again, no one could get the machine to start except the mechanic, and most of the time he is not around, so you can get a good rest. When you ready, just tighten up the plug again, and start you work. All of us do it. You must know all dese little ting and dem, if we have to work together," ended Joe on a proud, conspiratorial note.

Doc listened attentively to these asides of the job, and occasionally answered, "I see," "I understand" or just nodded his head.

"You must never take up a machine by yourself. Somebody must always be there to help you put it on your back."

Then he went on to demonstrate how it was done. Doc helped him to lift it onto his back by holding onto the back of the machine. Then handing him the leather straps. Having strapped it on, Doc gave him the oil container, or the moon, which was hooked in front with two clips and which rested on his chest, making him look like a space man.

With the machine on his back, the moon on his chest, and the nozzle held in one hand pointing forward or upward, with plastic shield to cover his face to protect it from oil, one indeed resembled a spaceman, landing, or about to land on the moon; and what made the sight more complete, the boys usually wore dungaree overalls.

Working in the banana fields with such an outfit, frightened many people during the early days of spraying. And with the intense whirring noise made by the motor, many young children often ran away crying hysterically, frightened by the men from outer space. Joe took his time detailing information about the motor for Doc's benefit. He was in no hurry to start spraying, although he saw that Doc was a little anxious to begin.

"Doh worry man; you will start just now," Joe said, seeing the anxious look on Doc's face.

"You have a lot of time man to get to work with 'Mr. Wright's' piece of tool," as they referred to the machine with some sarcasm. Then Joe told him to touch it, start it, and stop it, to get the 'feel' of it. Then he lifted it onto his back, Doc then set it down with his help. This continued for some time, while they were getting to know each other on a personal level. When all the preliminaries were fully exhausted to Joe's satisfaction, he said he would give Doc a demonstration; he would spray for Doc to see how it is done.

He did so saying: "You must always spray with the wind, not against it," as Doc helped him to set the machine down.

"Now let me see you spray," he told Doc to give him a demonstration to see how he got on. Doc started out, following the guidelines. He hadn't gone very far when Joe told him to stop.

"You spraying against the wind, man. Look," he said, "hold the nozzle up this way." He did it for Doc's benefit.

"Then gauge the direction from where the wind in coming, spray with the wind; when the wind change, close down the nozzle, switch off the oil," said Joe patiently, " or change to suit the wind."

The main objective was that, by spraying and following the direction of the wind, the wind takes the spray and scatters it as far as possible on the banana leaves the spray acts as a protection from the leaf-spot disease, thus enhancing the quality yield of the banana fruit. For the leaf spot is a disease that severely affected the quality of the fruits. Spraying helps to improve both the quality and quantity of the produce.

Doc was very attentive to all directions and to the information shared by Joe for he was anxious to learn. He wanted to do well in his new job, be a good spray boy, earn and save some money and build his mother a house, marry Velma and things like that.

"You is a good listener," said Joe, "and you go learn quick," looking up at Doc and wiping off the sweat from his forehead with the back of his hand.

"You explain real good, you know."

"By the time you have three months here, you go be the best spray boy – you go see." Doc felt real good and was pleased to have a pal like Joe as his workmate.

"Let's have another go before lunch. Ah want the Pusher to hear the machine before we sit down to eat; but ah sure he go come round before, though."

Saying this, he started the motor and helped Doc to get it on his back. The vibration shook him surprisingly again. When he did open the nozzle a few yards away, having gauged the wind, hundreds of fine, needle-like jets of spray flew out of the nozzle, some falling on the side of his face while a large, fine misty looking spray fell gently on the banana leaves. Doc began walking very fast, too fast; until Joe cried out, "Stop! Stop! You walking a little too fast; remember to change direction when the wind change, if not you go blind yourself. Too much oil coming back to you face. You go blind yourself and you doh get help from the Government if anything happen to you. You must take care of yourself. Walk slower." He told Doc to switch off the machine, and he helped him to rest it on the ground.

"Work won't dead, you know: you ever see they put work in coffin? Is man dey put in coffin, not work," said Joe, with a philosophical air.

"Take ah five' man, take ah five. They sat down on the grass to take a 'five.' As they both did so, sticks and straw in hand, Joe said, "You coming to come; you go get the hang of it soon, ah give you one or two months, then ah could see you giving it 'fire' for so."

While they were thus reposing, along came the 'Pusher'. The Team Leader affectionately called, 'Wope Sir!' With time, Doc discovered that 'Wope Sir!' was a generic name, a common name by which one member of the gang addressed or called to one another. 'Wope Sir!' came up to them. He walked up slowly to where they were sitting, and with a measured smile he said:

"You keeping 'little Wope Sir' all to yourself man. It will soon be lunch time. Let me have a chance to talk with Doc for a little while."

"Well, little Wope Sir, I'm glad to have a little time to spend with you before lunch" said Mr Frederick, smiling, in a friendly manner showing his white, well shaped teeth.

"Ah see you this morning, but we din have a chance to meet. I am Frederick. Everyone calls me Wope Sir, ah glad you come into our gang," said he, pulling out a handkerchief from his back pocket and wiping the perspiration off his face. Doc was well pleased to meet him formally

"Ah see you this morning," he said.

"Yes, ah know; we only had time for a quick 'hello'; ah had to tell the mechanic, Mr DaCosta, the one you came up with; ah had to tell him about one of our machines; he also had some parts for me. Ah usually hold some parts like plugs, fan belts and so on for the machines, so when the driver is not around, ah could put them on, or give them to the boys. So ah wanted to collect them as soon as he comes, because sometimes we forget, and he goes back with them in the Rover." It seemed as though Mr Frederick never wanted to stop talking to this man he'd just met.

"The machines must always be in good working condition at all times, like yours," he said lifting up the one in question.

"If they are not working good, they could affect the health of the workers. So the rubbers, the shock absorbers must be changed regularly. If not it could shake them up affecting their backs and you can't tell what could happen to them later on. It could make them sick with their lungs, or their kidneys. Ah know for sure it could affect their backs, so ah have to make sure they are in good shape," said he with a concerned look.

"The machine could be slack sometimes."

"I see," said Doc, still trying to follow all the details that were vague to him on his first day. However, Doc thought that he was a sensible and serious man, and that he (Doc), will have to be very circumspect, but was inclined to believe that Mr Frederick was taking the interest of the boy's health quite seriously.

Afterwards, in a more relaxed and less formal tone, Mr Frederick said he will soon get to understand the work; he has nothing to worry about. Then he sat down on the stump of a broken nutmeg tree, not far from where Doc was sitting. By now Joe had taken up the machine and left it some distance away, not far from where they had to start spraying after lunch.

"Is there anything you want to ask me?" said Wope Sir.

"Yes," said Doc enquiringly, "ah wanted to know how dis kind of work is done - well how regular we have to spray one place - well ..." Doc did not know exactly how to phrase the sentence to make his point, so Mr Frederick came to his assistance.

"Ah guess ah know what you want to find out."

Then Wope Sir said to him that it was coming up to lunch time and that they will have time to talk about the job in details some other time. Reassured that there was nothing to worry about, just yet, that Joe is one of the best spray boys, if not the best, and that he is in good hands, he will learn good, and much more besides, 'Wope Sir' asked him to join the rest of the team for lunch.

"You know little Wope Sir? All of us in the team siddown together and eat lunch. We is like one big family. So come with me. We having lunch in the back of the boucan, in the shade under the grapefruit trees. Come."

Doc, followed by Joe, met with other members of the team who had already assembled by the boucan. It was a spacious area with a thick undergrowth of water grass which made it very comfortable to sit down. They all sat down on the ground in a circular formation. Lunch was a grand affair, a small afternoon picnic. Each member of the gang ate from each other's food, as they unpacked their food carriers and opened them up to all. Everybody shared everybody's.

It was a grand feast, democratically executed, a grand melee, a demonstration of communal sharing and sensitivity, because it meant even if you were unable, or incapable of bringing lunch on a particular day, you were not excluded from partaking of whatever was on offer. Like, Wope Sir, at this time, and their motto was: **Plant Protection Boys Must Prevail.** The saying at lunch was, "*Make merry, make merry, make joy.*" There was no conflict, no antagonism and no fussing and fighting. It was 'make joy' and 'make merry'; share and share alike, kinda ting.

It was the opportune moment for the Team Leader once again to inform the gang about him. His paper bag with its dry roasted bakes was put amongst the other selection of food and it was sampled as well, although Doc was very self-conscious about his contribution. Joe got him a container and loaded it up with split peas and dumplings, and whatever else was going.

"When you finish you can take some more from anyone of the carriers, doh worry!" said Joe quietly.

Doc nodded. Wope Sir talked about him again to the team in between mouthfuls and they all acknowledged him in various stages of their luncheon. There was the on-going repetition of: *"Make joy, make joy, little Wope, make merry, all of us is one"* **and,** *"what is food? You put it in today, you pass it out tomorrow. It's nothing."*

And so Doc was integrated into the team and to bind it all, everyone offered him something, a piece of meat here, a dumpling there, a piece of breadfruit, or yam, or whatever, until he had to refuse their generosity because he had his fill. Everyone was kind and friendly and welcoming to him at this initial stage.

"That is how we is, man that's how we is, all of us is one," said Ken with bulging eyes.

After lunch, they washed and reassembled their containers. Then some had a little nap, while others had a game of cards, which they christened the 'gamblement', while others just aimlessly sat or drifted around. Doc walked around for some time, then sat under a grapefruit tree, where the Team Leader joined him for a small chat, wanting to know if he was alright, which Doc said he was... he thought the boys were very nice and friendly.

Not long afterwards, Wope Sir called out:

"Time up, let's make a start."

There was some grumbling from the sleepers, saying they just close their eyes and thing and making feeble protestations. They yawned and stretched, then slowly but surely everyone went back to his post and the machines could be heard singing again, deep into the large, rich banana plant. They ended the day by the small river at the bottom of the lower part of the road. The lower part had a great deal of breadfruit and orange trees in the midst of bananas.

The cleaning of the machines and safely storing them usually ended the day. Afterwards, the team washed and tidied themselves, then changed their clothes. Then it was time to leave. So they left. They did not have long to wait before the Rover came. The remainder of week, indeed, of the first month following on was not much different from the first day. Doc got the hang of it. He brought along his overalls, got a carrier or container for his meal, and learned the motto *"Plant Protection Boys Must Prevail" PPB, MP*. This motto was constantly repeated wherever and whenever two sprayers met, whether in the fields or on the road you can hear "PPB" and repetition of "MP" loud and clear.

In time, the Team Leader explained to him all about spraying and the keeping of the itinerary was like a quota to be completed, covering a certain area at least once a month, and it is the responsibility of the PDI (Plant Disease Inspector) and 'Wope', the Team Leader, to see that the team reached its target. And so, Doc inched, and at times pushed his way along with the Plant Protection Department, becoming a competent banana spray boy, leaf spots controller or whatever name one wants to call it. The first three months went by quite quickly.

During the course of that time, Doc became a very competent sprayer. He was able to 'read' the wind, and he showed a high level of understanding and willingness to learn and improve the standard of his work.

However, unbeknown to him, from the day he entered the post, he was looked upon speculatively by the PDI. It was the responsibility of the Plant Disease Inspector to observe and make reports about each new worker's performance in a general way; each attendance, his attitude towards authority and his industriousness. These reports were then sent to Town at the head office, detailing and explaining how he kept to the above guidelines, for his probation depended on it. Nothing could be found to fault him. And so, for the first three months or so, Doc had been riding upon a wave of success. Like Midas, everything he touched turned into gold. His hope was bright, too.

He thought that nothing could go wrong with him, but there was an undercurrent of fear and jealousy that had begun to run against him, faint and vague, but there it was, and just waiting. He had no knowledge of it, nor did most of the members of the team. However, it was whispered by one or two members who were very close to the ear of the PDI, that he, the Plant Disease Inspector viewed Doc with a very suspicious eye.

He thought Doc had an 'attitude toward authority'. He also thought he was argumentative and had 'ambition beyond his station' and that he asked too many questions. He was too inquisitive. Obviously, some members of the gang made a joke of it, that is, when he began talking and questioning them about the job, especially about safety etc. so they agreed with the PDI about that. They even jokingly referred to him as "the lawyer!"

It became clear that a number of them thought he was quiet,

did not make a lot of jokes but if he had something to say, he said it, and he was not submissive or stupid. Everyone admitted that he was hard working, patient and reliable. After he mastered the art of spraying, he performed his task with a high level of skill and dexterity; that sometimes the PDI hid behind bushes to watch or spy on him while he was spraying. He had nothing but praise for Doc.

"That Doc could spray damn good man, I wish all the boys could spray like him," he said to the Team Leader later.

The team leader nodded, and said, "For the short time he is here, he is one of the best."

These qualities set the standard that marked out our hero with the Plant Protection Department: hard working, patience, efficiency and reliability. These came from the pride he took in his job, coupled with self-discipline. This high standard started from day one, and developed during the many months of dedication, was refined and heightened, and it led to a successful probationary period. When he was told by the PDI that he had passed his probation, all he said was:

"I'm glad to hear sir."

"That's all you have to say?" ask the PDI.

"Yes Sir, ah glad."

He reserved a smile. The PDI just looked on and smiled. The high quality, the high standard that he laid down followed him throughout the eighteen months or so working with Plant Protection.

- II -

Doc remained the same after he passed his probation. He was not slack or irresponsible. If any changes followed, they had to do with his enquiring mind and a sense of justice. Doc always believed that the boys were paid inadequately for the work they did, and for the risks they took. The terrain was dangerous with machines on their backs and what he considered low wages. On the whole, he believed that occupational hazards were too many. The terrain was often undulated with hidden holes, stones and stumps.

On the other hand, there were hidden dangers of a long-term nature to one's health; the things spoken about by the Team Leader on the first day of Doc's arrival other people thought about them too, but remained quiet. Doc heard it whispered the first day but no one spoke openly to the PDI about such risks. They were scared to raise them with him, mainly for fear of losing their work.

Then came one day when he put his foot into the viper's nest. This happened one afternoon on the Bagatelle Estate. Fate has a way of playing all manner of unsuspecting tricks on us. One minute you could be riding on a cloud of peace and happiness. The next minute the sky will be covered with a thick, dark, dull blanket of cloud, thunder pealing out, cracking the skies; and lighting flashing and the wind howling at 100 miles an hour; soon this calm situation could change into a stormy one.

It was into a situation like that our hero found himself that afternoon on the Bagatelle Estate. That afternoon, the Team was completing their work, it was a difficult area to spray. The terrain was littered with large amount of unseen boulders, hidden drains, compounded with the noise from the machine. When the boys returned to the Rover after spraying, the driver and PDI were there leaning up against the vehicle.

When they were all together Doc said, "This is a rough place to spray yes boy."

Then John replied, "Ah hurt me foot on one big stone, ah nearly fall and buss up me mouth."

And it followed that most of the boys who were spraying that afternoon had something critical to say about that dangerous terrain. Then Doc asked the PDI what would happen if someone fell down with the heavy machine on his back and was seriously injured.

Everyone was surprised at his question to the boss. All eyes were on the PDI, who looked at Doc with a comical surprising look, shook his head and said nothing but the feelings of the gang were not secret anymore. On their way home that same afternoon, everyone was unusually quiet. Mr DaCosta tried to whistle, then hummed a tune: *"Melody d'amour, take this song my love one…."* But it was hollow and stale. The gloom remained. Some months later, in the same area somewhere in Walker, again it was after work on their way home when Doc asked the PDI if they don't get paid when a machine breaks down on the job.

The PDI returned a blank "NO!"

"Well why not? It's not their fault, Mr Roland, they should be paid."

Mr Roland said something about, that is how it is and he just come, nobody ever complained about it before.

"If you don't like the work you know what to do, there are many out there begging for it."

Doc said something about fair is fair, and the Team Leader coughed a kind of warning cough while looking in Doc's direction.

"I think," said Doc stoking the fire, "that the money we working for is not enough at all and not to be paid when your machine breaks down just makes it worse."

Some members of the Team began to whistle; some whispered to one another. He definitely heard someone say 'Shut up', but he paid then no mind.

"Mr Roland, every year I think we should get an increase," he pursued further.

"What you think you playing boy?" replied Mr. Roland.

Fuming, Terry said that was not a bad idea at all, and one or two members seemed to shake their heads in approval, but nothing more was said about the matter, and the poisonous reptile recoiled back to its nest; for the moment.

Many months passed and nothing was said, nothing was mentioned about what appeared to be that contentious issue, pay, conditions of work and so on. However, as the months went by, Doc was looked upon as disloyal and suspicious by the PDI and even by some members of the gang.

Many seemed to resent his popular notoriety; be it as it may, for his enquires, though necessary and well meaning, or well intentioned, the majority of the men were fearful of losing their jobs; they did not like it. They began to feel uneasy in his presence and some distanced themselves away from him.

One day an incident occurred at Nianganfiox Estate, another area with an unfriendly terrain, but a fertile plantation. The fruits were large and the land was covered with a sea of luscious green grass and vines. That day, a Tuesday, Doc's friend and a new work mate, Mano was in full control of the operation. The wind was blowing very favourably and spraying was easy to handle.

All was going well, until suddenly there was a crash followed by a loud scream by Mano, who had knocked his shin on a large boulder or stump, which was covered by the under-growth. Mano had a mighty fall and tumbled over, then rolled a little way down the gradient with the machine strapped to his back; with the oil came rushing out of the nozzle, spraying willy-nilly all over the place. As he fell, he knocked himself on an old nutmeg tree around his pelvis, and had another blow to his head by the machine. He was unable to move and all he did was moan and scream for help.

Doc was not far off and rushed to his assistance and he unhooked the machine releasing it from Mano's shoulders. However, Mano was still unable to move; he was badly hurt. Doc shouted for help.

"Help! Help! Mano fall and he can't get up. Help!" He screamed, trying to rub Mano's foot while continuing to free him from the machine.

In the height of his struggle to help Mano, whom did he see approaching? Mr. Shearer, the owner of the estate, who approached him like a lion on the loose, ready to pounce upon its prey. Doc was greeted by the following:

"What de hell is going on here?" Bayed Mr Shearer furiously.

And before Doc could recover from this bout of verbal attack, Mr Shearer fired another furious verbal volley at him.

"You boys are so damn stupid!" he bellowed. "So donkeyish, so dotish, can't you see that this damn hot oil from the machine is burning up the banana leaves? Now take yourself and this damn noisy machine and get outta me Estate."

By this time, with Mano on the ground bawling and Mr. Shearer shouting abuses, Doc was reeling, especially from Mr Shearer's verbal onslaught. His senses were jarred. Unable to collect his wits together, he offered a weak response to Shearer.

"He fall down and hurt himself and was unable to switch off the machine, Sir," said he nervously.

"What you mean he fall down? You idiot! He got eyes and he should look at where he is going," bawled Shearer.

"He was spraying, Sir," replied Doc, with some firmness, "and he has followed the direction of the wind. He had an accident. You mustn't shout – well, speak to me like that...."

"I can speak to you how ah very well like!" shouted Shearer. "Accident, accident me foot, you boys are so damn lazy you will do anything to get away from doing this work they pay you to do."

"You are a wicked man, Sir, to say such a thing," shouted Doc who by now had begun to find his tongue.

At this point, with Shearer's shouting, Mano's screaming, Doc's last response brought the Team Leader and some of the boys on the scene of the accident. Their first act was to assist Mano. They then enquired about the accident, which the Team Leader jotted down in his notebook. When Mr Shearer saw them, he toned down, and said to Doc in a more reasonable tone, that the first thing he should have done was to help Mano.

"That's what I was doing when you came along and began shouting and cussing me, sah."

Mr Shearer, a tall, lanky, elongated man, with greyish eyes and fixed gaze like a lizard and skin like a forced ripe golden apple, was wearing a white shirt and khaki pants with banana stain spots on the front of it. Looking at him more closely now, Doc thought that he'd seen him somewhere before. Maybe speaking at a meeting in the market; but he was not sure.

The Team Leader came up to him, followed by Terry (Mr. Know-all). Terry was the one who always seemed to know everything, always talking about Uncle Gairy. Always, Uncle Gairy this and Uncle Gairy that while pouring scorn on Uncle Gairy's opponents, such as one Anslem Smyth and Ian Johnson and many others whom Doc never heard about.

In the meantime, Mano was made fairly comfortable, and taken to a more convenient spot to await the arrival of the Rover. During the interim period, the Team Leader got some rotten bluggoe stalk (the old people say it is a good general remedy, especially for the relief of pains) and made a poultice by mixing it with some other leaves, then it was tired on Mano's sheen. Terry also rubbed some lime on Mano's foot.

Mr Shearer, (who was still around) felt very uncomfortable when he saw the support and assistance given to Mano, and the unity shown by the Team who kept repeating their motto: *'Plant Protection Boys Must Prevail!'* With this, Shearer made a swift retreat. As he left, Terry spat contemptuously on the ground, and speaking to no one in particular, shouted:

"Vermin! Wood ants! Bedbugs! Leech! Parasite!' Then he addressed the boys present saying:

"Dese people and dem doh have respect for the little people like us here in Grenada, and it's time people like him know that master day done, and Uncle Gairy say today we must be respected, today is not like before."

Joe said, "He should help Mano instead of shouting out abuses at Doc, insulting him and trying to make him feel small."

"At least," said the Team Leader, "he coulda get him something to put on his foot, and tie it up, and ask his servants to bring him some water."

By this time, everyone stopped working and stood around giving encouraging words to Mano, and sympathising with Doc.

"It coulda be anyone of us." That was Terry.

Then Godwin (Blue shirt) said, "Dese people and dem with all their big estate and ting, with servants and yard boy and ting, don't care one damn about poor people. You remember what happen in '51'? If they don't take care it go happen again, maybe worse too," said he, with some venom.

One member replied that he didn't know about '51', but "Ah hear about it from my father."

It was in the early afternoon when the PDI arrived with the driver. They were told about the incident and Mr DaCosta, who was holding a ripe banana in one hand and a sandwich in the other, while chewing on the other half, rested the remainder of the sandwich and the banana on the bonnet of the jeep, and went over to Mr Shearer's house and got some First Aid Bandages and ointment for Mano. The PDI was then given a fuller account of the accident by the Team Leader, with Doc's active support, including the behaviour of Mr Shearer.

Soon after that, Blue Shirt and Terry shouted "Plantation Boys Must Prevail!", and Doc repeated, "Must Prevail!"

Then the boys clapped and said Doc did a good job. He had helped Mano and stood up to Shearer. Then they shouted out again (louder this time), *"PPB! MP!"* which resounded like a defiant echo through the mountain. It was an aggressive show of solidarity and it acted as a gauntlet thrown down to Mr Shearer and in Doc's mind, to the PDI as well. Then he shouted loudly:

"Master day done!"

The PDI looked a little flabbergasted, even shocked. The Team Leader, who had been very angry at Mr Shearer's behaviour from the start, stepped in with a long caustic speech about a meeting which he attended with his grandmother when he was about 16.

"About eight years ago," He began in a firm voice, "when I was just 16, I went to a meeting in the market in Grenville with my Grandmother who is a member of the Union....."

"Which Union?" interrupted Terry.

"There is only one Union in this country for the labouring people, as far as I can see; and it is the Grenada Manual and Mental Workers Union," said Wope proudly. "The only one," he repeated.

"At that meeting," he continued, "ah remember Uncle Gairy talking about the process of cocoa and how it affected the labourers some years ago. He told us that one time, not so long ago, that cocoa prices fell on the world market, you know the overseas manufacturing countries and ting, for Grenada doh have any machines for manufacturing cocoa; all we do is grow it and send it away.

Anyhow, when the prices fell that time," said Wope, beginning to sweat while the PDI, the driver and the rest of the team waited impatiently for him to come to the point.

"Well, when the price went down, when dat happen," said he wiping off the perspiration with the back of his hand, "the rich estate owners like Shearer and them, reduced the wages of the labourers, almost to crab sauce – nothing," said he again, with his hands across his forehead.

"Ah telling you dey is parasites," interjected Terry.

"Well ah telling you," he narrated, "Uncle said dese parasites expected the labourers to accept the lower pay. Dey say if the labourers didn't accept the lower pay, dey will be fired and be evicted from the scrap of estate land that the owners give them to build dey little four posts on."

"So what did the labourers do? Tell us man, tell us," demanded Terry.

"They din take it," said the exhausted Team Leader.

The PDI stood looking on in utter amazement. The driver too, looked on as though he's seen a ghost. Then Terry took it up from the Team Leader and began enthusiastically:

"Dey organise themselves under their great Union Leader, Eric Matthew Gairy and dey protested. They even went in Town where some others joined. They matched up and down de place demanding better pay from the estate owners," said Terry, triumphantly.

The PDI by then began moving towards the Rover, believing everything had come to an end. However, Terry continued:

"They didn't get anything; the time wasn't ripe, their time didn't come yet. As their protest continued, Britain sent down a battleship, arrested Uncle and imprisoned him on the battle ship which was anchored far, far out in the sea in St. Georges. That was when things get hot."

"Maybe dey fraid," said Doc, "that the labourers woulda swim and rescue him from de ship if dey did anchor on the wharf."

Then the Team Leader said: "That was not the end of the story, for it was only a matter of time before the estates workers got what they wanted. After the strike about a year later - sometime in 1951 or '52, they got a raise of pay; they din have to work no long, long hours again, and women were not abused by the estate owners and their overseers as before. Tings began to improve for the labourers, not only for them but for all workers in Grenada," ended Wope proudly.

"Mischievous agitators," said Mr Shearer, who was listening attentively at a discreet distance. Both Terry and Doc made defiant gestures at him with their hands.

"UP shut," said Doc and shook his fist at him.

"Come on now boys, let's go, let's go; we can't stay here all night. I think you have made your point," said the PDI. Finally, before departing, they began to sing:

"We don't want to fight, to show our might,

but when we start we will fight, fight, fight,

In peacetime you will hear us sing,

God bless our leader, God bless Gairy for the ending of the strike,

the wage shall rise, we will never let our leader fall...

Never let our leader fall for we love him the best of all...."

Then they all moved towards the Rover, secured a comfortable place for Mano and drove off home.

But nothing goes on forever. The good times turn into bad times and vice versa, but the good people are always there, irrespective of the changing fortunes. The triumphant period experienced by our hero since he joined Plant Protection began to give way to less favourable circumstances. They had within them the seeds of change; they had some serious consequences; and at times consequences come without pity; and our actions, our deeds carry some difficulties, which are often not confined only to ourselves.

From the time he started work with Plant Protection, he had nothing but a constant series of successes to share with his mother. He had taken a great deal of command of his own life. He never forgot the Recitation with Sally Ann, especially those Shakespeare lines:

"*The fault, dear Brutus, is not within our stars,*

but within ourselves that we are underlings."

The work, spraying for many months, made him understand the strength and value of this statement, for changes once more were on the cards. But the intention of Cassius and Brutus was the planned assassination of their leader, Julius Caesar of whom they were very jealous because of his triumphs, both on the battlefield and with the populace in Rome, fearing that he would be given the crown and restore the monarchy. The reactions against Doc did not remotely resemble that of the Roman Emperor. The only common link was the one of fear and jealousy, which is to be found both in high, and low places, amongst rich and poor alike, and amongst all peoples whatever the Age.

The criticism of Doc began from within the gang; it was based on a combination of jealousy and fear. Jealously of the fact that he dared to talk up, questioning the working conditions and for better pay and for some safeguards for the boys. The fear was linked to possibly loss of work; for a number of them began to say, "half a loaf is better than none," and "eat little and live long" and other statements in like manner. Thus, months following the episode at Nianganfiox, there began a series of mutterings, and allegations about Doc by some members.

One afternoon, immediately after lunch, one said jokingly to another that, "Doc is playing a piece man," and how he has a lot of mouth; and that if he continued like that all of them will be out of work.

"I think," said the other, "that he coulda avoided the confrontation with Mr Shearer in Nianganfoix.

"Maybe, if he had gone to Mano's assistance in time, there would've been no need for Mano to burst out making that kinda noise."

Doc heard him and asked, "What you talking about man?"

"You coulda stop Mano if you de go to help him earlier."

"I went to his assistance almost at once," replied Doc hotly.

"I believe you took your own time because you wanted to run

up you big mouth and show off." Then he made other hurtful accusative remarks in similar manner.

As time went by, things did not improve. Then, one day the Team Leader, Terry and Joe tried to speak to the critics, pointing out that what Doc did, he did for everyone. But such conciliatory statements did not help, they fell on deaf ears. They paid no attention to them. Doc was openly rejected by a large number of the boys. At lunch-time the gang was now divided; there were two separate groups. There was no more of the *'make merry'* and *'make joy'* slogans. He was rejected and when his few friends were not around, he was effectively boycotted.

This, as expected, affected him gravely. He was disappointed and saddened by the fact that, what he spoke with the PDI about would be of benefit to all. And, as for Mr Shearer, he couldn't accept his forwardness, even if he was dead; he had to stand up to him. He couldn't allow anyone to speak to him the way Shearer did without affecting his manly, youthful pride. Even if the Queen of England talked so to him like that, he would answer back.

"Ah may be poor, but my mind is not poor," he said to himself. The dynamics in the gang became worse. He began missing days off work, two days this week, one the next, then the following week two, and so on. This went on for many weeks. Wope Sir tried to build bridges, but he failed. The others would not compromise. Wope Sir saw the cohesion of the team was disintegrating, and he knew also the attack on Doc was the main reason for his occasional absence from work. He knew though, that this situation must not be allowed to continue.

He watched and waited, hoping that the situation would work itself out without his unnecessary interference; but one month passed, then two. He was by then incapable or unable to bridge the gap through fear of antagonising friends, and perhaps family in the gang, so the situation remained in limbo, with Doc having to cope with isolation, insults and lies. He became depressed. He had to talk with someone. His mum sensed that something was not right when he began to stay home from work, but he said nothing to her, nor she to him. Now, however, he had to come out into the open with her. He must talk with her.

One afternoon after work, he approached his mother and told her everything, from his experience in Bagatelle, the attitude of the PDI, and the reaction from his friends. Then he told her about the incident in Nianganfoix, his confrontation with Mr Shearer, the way it was resolved, how everyone was jubilant; and about the speeches made and song sung in respect to Gairy, and how, not long after that, most of the members of the gang began to criticise him, saying how he was showing off, and playing a piece of man. How they then refused to sit with him and much more besides, how he was isolated and rejected and now he feels so much under pressure that he does not feel like returning to work. When he finished, he sat down. He felt like a broken man. He looked a pitiful sight. She looked at him sitting there with his head in his hands.

"Ah know something was not right, since you start missing work. Drink some juice. Let me tell you, you is man, you have to cope with dese failures, dese setbacks," she said taking up the empty glass he left on the step.

"I don't see what I've done..."

"You doh have to do nuttin. Sometimes life just hit you one cuff and knock you down."

"Just so?"

"Yes, just so, and let me tell you, if you smart you could gain something from it. You will have to learn to cope with failures, because dey go teach you a lot of good lessons that book can't teach you."

"Like what?" interjected Doc.

"Give me a chance. You say dey rejected you and all that, but it good. Yes, it good for you, because you will learn that rejection is not de end of the world. You go meet up with it again and again. You go have people hating you for nothing. You go meet up wid disappointments. Your life just start; you just take 18 years; you doh see nothing yet. And ah won't to be around all de time."

"What you mean?"

"Ah mean you will have to learn to cope. Stand up on your own two feet, you name man, wid an English tongue in you mouth. You must go on and continue to use it. Meet the failures, pass through de fire. You alone have to carry you cross. No one would do it for you; no cross, no crown." Then he got up, walked around and was about to go indoors when she asked him whether he was hungry, he said he wasn't.

"Well siddown, ah just want to tell you this, because ah know you is a good boy and you go make it. Yes, you go make it, but you have to toughen up, you have to be strong. Turn your failures into successes. You can do it."

Then this patient mother, this loving mother, this special gift of God, lowered her voice and spoke to her son quietly and calmly. She went and sat on the step next to him and her lesson was that: failures and successes, good and bad; disappointments and hopes, pleasure and pain, are all mixed up together like our weather, the sunshine and rain that God send us. That nothing in life comes easy and that he has a lot to learn, but he would learn.

"Have faith. Faith can move mountains. You must experience the pain of the rejection. That's how you go enjoy you achievements.

You have to have de nights before de days, the dark nights, then moonlights; if you doh have one, you can't get the other. You can't go through life without struggle. As you go through de struggle, de ups and downs, you learn tings about you. You get stronger. Trust in yourself son; doh be afraid of yourself; you go win, you must succeed in the end." She was exhausted and thirsty.

"Get me some water," she said to him.

She drank it, and her face became more relaxed.

"You awright?"

"Yes, ah okay. Ah just want to say dese last few words to you before we eat."

It was now his turn to look at her with sympathetic eyes, for a cloud of sadness came over her face.

"Son," she said in a pitiful voice, "wherever you are on the ladder of life, make the best use of it. You doh realise it yet, but that's what you're doing. You leave dat yard boy work, you learn a trade, for you is a good tailor, you spraying banana and you earning a living, you even planning to take a course. Keep moving on; failure and disappointments are only for a time. God knows you don't deserve it, but nothing doh come easy. Everything is for a time. Tings can't be tough and hard every day. Tings must change. Every day is not a rainy day!"

"Awright mum, ah understand."

"Before long........," she continued after blowing her nose.

"Before long, all de boys go come to understand that what you doing and what you saying are aright. Watch, you go see. Dey go come round. Whatever you do, stick to what you believe in. Doh give up. Have patience, doh give up, you go win. Even if ah dead, ants go bring news in me grave and tell me about your success," she said, tucking her handkerchief in the end of her sleeve.

Afterwards, they went in doors and had supper. During supper, he studied her with new interest and concern. The discussion with his mother uplifted Doc. As usual, she was a fathomless well of inspiration to him; and when he returned to work, he worked like a beast. Nothing bothered him. He was not concerned about the behaviour of anyone, yet he felt, and deep down he knew, that nothing could stand in his way. But they did not leave him alone. He was ostracised, ridiculed, made to feel small, and the snide remarks and the taunting: 'playing piece of man' 'playing big', were thrown at him. The Team Leader continued trying to mend the situation again, but to no avail.

- III -

One afternoon, the wily PDI, sensing the division in the gang, seized the opportunity to put extra pressure on Doc. Since after the situation on the Nianganfoix Estate, the PDI began visiting the gang much more regularly and was keeping a close eye on him. He too, thought that Doc was 'getting beside himself'.

That afternoon, after spraying and with his wet overalls, both from spray oil and from sweat, he was cleaning and wiping down his machine. The PDI called him in a not too kindly tone of voice. He asked him about his absenteeism from his work; and used the occasion to bring up his action and behaviour on the Nianganfoix Estate, especially Doc's response to Mr Shearer and for his final statements and his enthusiasm in joining with the singing of the Union's song: "we don't want to fight…", and his shouting out at Mr Shearer, 'United we stand!'

"Who is we?" shouted the PDI, and, "United against whom? Eh? – come on answer me!" said he in a military commanding tone.

Doc said nothing. He was alone with the PDI, wet and tired, actually exhausted after spraying almost the whole afternoon. He, (the PDI) sat under a grapefruit tree with a notebook in one hand and a large grapefruit in the other. He sat relaxed and cool, his hair well combed with a part, like a toe-path on the left hand side, wearing a white shirt and black shoes. He sat imposingly, but he spat out poison at Doc.

It was the opportunity he longed awaited: Doc on his own, division in the ranks. When Doc finished cleaning the machine, the PDI got up made a few steps towards him tossing the grapefruit from one hand to the other. He circled like a chicken hawk gauging his prey and then he sat down again playing with the grapefruit, with a sinister, spiteful scowl on his face, as if to say, "Ah get you alone by yourself and ah go make you see you nen-nen. Ah go squeeze you." And so he did.

"Answer me, answer me," he said testily. "What happen, you lose you tongue? Or you can't perform without your audience? You want me call your friends for you? How many friends you have in the gang now? Where is the 'United we stand' now? Eh? Call them, and you can put on a show for them," said the PDI, getting up. As he did so, he smashed the grapefruit against a tree. Then he attacked Doc once more:

"Come on man, tell me what you mean by 'united we stand'? PPB, MP is not enough for you? You know who Mr Shearer is? Speak up!" said Mr Roland venomously.

Doc was quiet. He was tired and indeed, he was not going to have an unnecessary argument with the PDI.

"Your attendance at work is another thing. Yes, ah notice you missing out work a lot now. You coming to work when you want. You is boss now, eh? You take over from me, eh? That's what you want, eh? You want to be the boss?"

"No sir," replied Doc weakly, "I was not feeling..."

"You was not feeling what? You know you suppose to come to work five days a week, not when you mind tell you to put in an appearance. Not when you feel like it. You realise who I am?" said the PDI beating his chest and moving closer to Doc.

"Ah could sack you. Yes, ah could take de damn bread outta you mouth – just so," shouted the PDI with a mischievous grin on his face. By this time Doc was fuming and couldn't care what happened.

"Ah say what ah say," said Doc, in a strong voice looking at Mr Roland straight in the eye.

"An if ah have to say it again, ah go say it," said he in the same tone, taking up the machine, moved forward.

"You go say it? Eh...?"

"Yes, Ah go say it, sir. Ah may be poor, but ah have me pride."

"Yes, Mr George Williams," replied the PDI, mirthfully. "Ah know you have you pride and a lot of speech too, but continue like that, and soon you go put your pride in your pot and cook it, and eat it," said he in a tone of disgust. "Go and put the machine away."

Sadly and slowly Doc went and secured the machine. When he re-joined the gang, some were grinning sheepishly. Sly remarks were heard, others looked at him obliquely without speaking to him, but they seemed quite pleased with themselves.

Wope Sir tried to mediate: "Ah man must live standing on his own two feet, not crawling on his belly like a snake. We can't sit down and let rich people walk all over us, and we should thank

Doc for his stand; he do it for us too, you know." They were quiet.

Then someone said, "Ah heard the PDI say he put in for an increase for the gang. We all know that was what Doc was saying for a long time now." That was Terry.

However, no notice was taken of the Team Leader and Terry. They continued their baying and snarling like vicious dogs.

Terry said, "Shut up,"

Joe said "They are jealous but jealousy is a disease. Doc is one of us."

"Go home and find something to read and improve your minds," said Terry as they headed towards the Rover.

Doc did not follow them. He went and sat down on a fallen cocoa tree some yards away. He held his head in both hands. His head was full, and sadly, the tears fell down his cheeks from the cutting blows. The behaviour of his friends pained him more than the attack from Mr Roland.

They boarded the Rover, and left him (or forgot he was there). No one seemed to miss him, until they were almost at the end of their journey, and then Joe asked, "Where is Doc?"

"In truth?" said Terry.

The Team Leader and the PDI exchanged looks, but they just carried on home. That afternoon, when he recovered from his depressive state, not seeing them he did not bat an eyelid. Somehow, it didn't matter, it was to be expected. He went to the nearby stream, washed his face and walked home. When he reached by Ghost, he gave him a weak brotherly whistle and Ghost returned it from indoors.

When he got home, he just dropped his tired self down on the step and gave an almighty groan like an animal. He felt hot, thirsty and tired. Doc was a very disappointed young man indeed. Then he gave his mother a detailed account of his confrontation with the PDI. Again, it was the rejection and isolation. And he mentioned how it was eating away at him and how very depressed and strenuous the situation made him feel. They seemed to be unending, and the disappointments just increased his depression.

"Mum," he ended with his tale of woe. "Ah thank you for standing up with me and ah glad you are there to always listen to me and give me advice and encouragement. Ah trying, you know mum and ah doh want to continue to burden you, but I find dis world real puzzling. Ah taught my trouble was over when I left my yard boy work in Paraclete. But now I see that it is just starting," said he in a subdued, melancholy voice.

"Can a mother's love grow cold?

Can she forget her boy?" asked the poet.

Mrs Williams was a woman of about fifty, medium built with taut looking limbs, and a bold concentrated looking face. A close look at her one could tell by her upright carriage and her big, warm bright eyes, that at one time in her youth she was full of life and love and that she was indeed a beautiful woman. But hard times, unfavourable economic conditions and untrustworthy men, all combined to sweep most of her beauty into oblivion, leaving her only with dregs, the residue of her one time beautiful self. But all was not completely gone. She still retained her self-affirming smile, which was as bright as an evening sunshine.

Moving as close as possible to her son, she smiled one of those sunshiny smiles which was the opposite of the look on her son's face. As usual, she gave ears to his catalogue of woes and when it was ended, her first words were:

"Cheer up son, you name man, it is always darkest before dawn, and a merry heart makes a cheerful countenance."

This woman of little formal education, this mother felt a deep affection for her son, and saw and felt too, that this child of hers, still a young man, needed some more inspiring and uplifting words, which would help him to brace himself, strengthen his resolve, and assist him to grasp the nettle of life with both hands.

Thus, from the scraps of her education, from the scattered pieced of knowledge; from these fragments of her experience gained through the dictated of circumstances, she began to weave a pattern of ideas and information that would help to buttress her son emotionally and strengthen his resolve to push his way through the world. She knew he needed a strong level of psychological cement for him to hold on to. This she tried to provide.

She knew that life is not a bed of roses, and that Doc will have to take some licks, that he would have to fall to rise, but she believed in her son. She never thought for a moment that he would fail. She knew that he would meet difficulties, but she believed too, that he would meet these difficulties and crush them. Thus, after he had a glass of juice and sometime had elapsed, and he became less morbid-less depressed, she said:

"Son, common sense make before book. Ah doh have plenty book sense. No, not much, because schooling in my days was a luxury and it was a luxury that my parents couldn't afford."

Doc, empty glass in hand pricked up his ears and began looking at his mother intently in the face.

"Look at me good boy, you must have courage, real courage to fail sometimes – a thousand times. You go lose a lot, a lot, but keep going on. Be steady as the Rock of Gibraltar son. Don't give up on life son; you go succeed. Your ancestors had to fight harder dan dat, and they din have the opportunities that you have. Most of dem don't know what school is, can't even sign dey names, dey just had to make d 'x'. You finish standard seven son, you is a man, doh fraid, just hold your head up and move forward." She paused to wipe her brow.

Then, "Have courage. Look de whole world in de face and laugh at it," said she in a firm and resolute tone.

"You remember the part you and Sally Ann use to say? Men is responsible for dey own fates…de fault is not in de stars…"

"Oh yes mum, ah din think you remember it. Ah like it," Said Doc, hopefully.

"Well use it son, use it. You have sense, use it."

And so once again that cloud of depression gradually moved. It got clearer. It gave way to a brighter ray of Hope. He stood up now with his hands in his pockets:

"Mum ah go use it. Ah see what you mean, but it go be hard. A lot of problems there you know, Mum, problems like bush."

"You have to solve them. You must have faith. Faith can move mountains. Dis is the fire you have to pass through. You go be stronger for it."

"Mum, even some of my friends reject me."

"Rejection is not de end of de world, ah tell you dat awready. And all I can say is you go make more friends."

"Mum, dey say ah showing off…"

Mrs Williams reflected for a while, then said in a quiet voice close to Doc:

"Ah believe you born for a purpose. Ah know life is hard. We from Africa started off with nuttin, not even a square foot of ground we could call we own. It's never been easy; but in dis world I believe some people are born to do unpleasant things. An you is one ah dem," then she reflected, paused and continued:

"Ah believe God give it to you because he know you can do it. De weight is heavy, but He know you have de shoulder to carry it, dats why he give you." She paused; he embraced her and not for the first time tears of hope and joy flowed.

Then she said, "Why don't you go and see Velma?"

"I will think about it," he said with a surprised look.

A week or more had passed and yet he did not go in search of Velma. It's not that he didn't care about her; he was longing to see her more than he would say. But Doc was pursuing the job with a level of dedication in order to consolidate and enhance his position in order to please the Plant Disease Inspector. He thought of a statement Velma made in Pearls: that sex is only a part of love and it's not the only way to prove their love for each other. This thinking had engulfed him from the day he passed his probation. He wanted and began aiming for things more fulfilling and enhancing and thought he could achieve some of these things from his job. Also, he wanted to be on top of his job and feel proud and satisfied in a way before meeting her again after such a long time.

He knew it was an uphill struggle but he pursued with the idea, the thought anyway. He was aware that the PDI had him under scrutiny and one wrong move and he will be done for. Despite the pressure, he opined too, that a secure situation will be good for both of them for it augured well for their future plans; and that his love for her was more than just sex. He wanted a love for life, a home and a family as well. Doc was maturing fast both physically and mentally. He was thinking and working towards a higher level of love. Not the one in Pearls only – he had moved on beyond that. He wanted a family, a lifelong love with Velma.

In his reflections, he also remembered that she said that he is the only one who's got the key to her locked up love, she was protecting. He wanted to bring something more to it, (their love) offer himself in a more – responsible way, so to speak, so that she can share her love with him, and he with her in a mutually complimentary manner.

Thinking thus, (and although he did not achieve all he wanted at work) he was, for now, satisfied that he could see her with a feeling of relative achievement. When he at last decided to go to her he did so with a certain amount of confidence.

Although Doc and Velma hadn't seen each other for months, he'd been receiving news about and from her through the grapevine; these came from Velma's friends. Nathlyne told him one afternoon in Grenville that Velma wished to see him soon.

"She pining away for you; if you don't go to see her soon, she go dead oui!"

Not long after Pearl, a confidant of Velma's said to him one day:

"Tell Doc to come and look for me soon. Ah miss him; ah need him."

Other similar messages came from Janet and Roslyn:

"Everyday she's asking for you; leave whatever you doing and run to her. Hurry!"

And they giggled as they left him standing outside Miss Chemi's shop on Salisbury Road.

- IV -

It had now been more than two weeks since the talk with his mother when amongst other things she told him that he should take a break from the pressures of work and go and see Velma. Saying this, the day after the news from Janet, he headed for Deblando. The place was easy to find and she was well known too when he arrived near her house, and when after these many months Velma saw him, and he saw her, the first thing they both observed about each other was how much they had changed physically. They reached out to each other with restrained enthusiasm, fixing their eyes now on the ground, now on each other, wavering and moving cautiously. Somehow, they seemed afraid, timid, even abashed.

Physically, she'd grown tall and slim. Her breasts were now fully formed and they jutted out of her thin bodice violently as though they wanted to bore a hole in it and jump out. Since pearls she'd matured into all the qualities of a young woman. Apart from her physical changes, she'd moved from La Fillette to Deblando. Her father had immigrated to England; also, her mother's illness caused her to be absent from school. Doc too was different in appearance and deportment from their last meeting in Pearls. His voice was deeper, he'd also grown taller. He now walked with a concentrated and deliberate style; in fact he'd assumed certain definitive characteristics of a mature young man. Velma too was in a similar situation.

All these personal observation took place in a very short time – a matter of minutes, although, standing there, it seemed a lifetime. Slowly, by degrees, they began moving closer towards each other and throwing shy, furtive glances at each other's arms. Then it seemed to her that her heart leaped out of her and into him. She felt a lifelessness in her knees and for a moment she had no strength to move.

He shouted: "Velma!"

"Doc!" And again words failed them. They stood face to face, as it were, without speaking. They remained still, immobile like the Palmist trees in La Digue Junction when there is no wind to stir them. Then as if a wind, a romantic breeze had aroused them, he rushed towards her shouting:

"How are you Velma, how are you? Ah glad…!"

"How are you Doc? My friend, my Doc!"

"I can see," he said, "dis is a love for life. Nothing can come between us!"

"Not even weevils," she said as their arms reached out towards each other and their lips met and his tongue was in her mouth.

They savoured each other for what seemed to be an eternity, languishing and fully satisfying their longings for embrace. When they finally released themselves, they eased back to have a better and longer look at each other.

"I'm so happy, so very happy to see you after all these months..."

"Yes ah know, ah know, so many things... I miss not having you around, Doc."

"Since I left the tailor shop we din see... I'm now in Plant Protection... How is you?"

"I'm alright in some ways, but I'm missing out on school. I'm missing you more than anything else. I have some little problems, Doc."

"Janet gave me a hint..."

"Much more than that, Doc," she said, cutting him short. "That's not all. Mum is not well, and dad gone to England... England is so far," she said pitifully. "And you move..."

"Yes I'm with agriculture now; well Plant Protection... Tailoring..."

"Yes, ah know."

"You know about Plant Protection? Okay. Ah leave home early to get the Rover and we travel from one place to another to spray."

He went on to explain the nature of his new job. He told her it was not like tailoring. It called for a lot of moving from place to place and some of these places could be very dangerous.

"It's risky, you could fall and hurt yourself," he said.

"Doc, I know something about the conditions of your work. One of the boys in the gang told me. The tall slim one dey call 'Jack Palance,' he lives in Walker," she said breathlessly as if she wanted to tell him everything at the same time.

He thought, 'Jack Palance'? "Oh Terry! Terry is okay."

"Ah thought you run away from me again, as you did in Paraclete. Ha!" They both laughed.

"An den ah say you don't want to be close to me. Ah say you was thinking about what happen in Pearls, or nearly happen?" She smiled and he gave a restrained laugh.

"Ah say you vex because of Pearls or something like dat. You said a lot of good tings in Pearls..."

"What did I say?" He did not elaborate.

"Well not Pearls, it's my new job I'm trying to hold down and work on something for..."

"One day ah saw your mother in the market. When I ask about you she told me all about your life with spraying an ting. The problems with the boys and the boss. But don't worry; you go make it, Doc. You go be alright."

Doc thought, 'that's easier said than done,' but it was good and considerate of her, despite her own problems to think about him and his problems.

"Ah know a lot more than you think, Doc. Ah have a pick-up in the gang. Ha!" She held his hand and squeezed it and he clasped his fingers, intertwining them between hers; as they exchanged meaningful affectionate glances.

Despite all her own problems, she shared his and for a while she was her old self once again with her honeyed smile and relaxed self-assurance which she seemed to pass on to Doc as she applied a little more pressure to his hand.

"Doc, take it easy. Ah dey here with you. Hug me up, put your arms around me again; close, close."

They embraced and shared their lips once more. They were out now in the large spacious yard surrounded by many trees. They walked towards the large spreading mango tree, looking like a gigantic umbrella. Under the tree was shady. It was in blossom, so the birds flitted from branch and the bees buzzed from flower to flower. In the process, small pieces of blossom covered their clothes and the scent wafted through their nostrils. They sat on a large protruding root, then she told him some more about why she was now living in Deblando.

"Just like you and your jobs," she quibbled.

"Moving out from your job in Paraclete, into tailoring, and now moving around even more with the Plant Protection."

"An you following me."

"Well, Paraclete, La Fillette and now here in Deblando. Where next?"

She smiled up at him and he kissed her forehead. To his surprise, she knew the Plant Protection Boys' Motto. She repeated: "Plant Protection Boys Must Prevail!"

"Ah told you I have me pickup in the gang. I like your motto though. It has a lot in it..." again she repeated: "Plant Protection Boys..."

Then she laughed at his surprise. They both did for he saw the funny side of it. Then she said with faraway look: "Plant Protection."

They both were moving around for different, but logical and necessary reasons. After a while she said reflectively and with some sadness in her voice:

"My father gone to England, ah miss him a lot you know, Doc. First he flew from Pearls airport. Pearls."

She paused and after a deep sigh, she repeated 'Pearls' again, "I almost lost my virginity in Pearls," she said, looking up at him.

"We won't go back there... not today. Leave it for our future memories."

"But you know I can't forget it."

"I know; but it's a new chapter now in we life; you said you father took the plane there."

"Yes. From there he flew to Barbados where he boarded a ship, 'Surriento' to England. I think of him up there in the cold, behind God's back and we doh know when he's coming back," she continued quietly in that sad, thoughtful voice.

She finally got up from the mango root, clasping both hands palm to palm. Afterwards, she pulled him up and hand in hand they strolled around the large mango tree, then further along the open grassy yard. A little further on, she said, still in that meditative voice:

"Not long after my father left, Mammie became ill, so aunt Celia, (that's the name of the aunt here) said we should come and stay with her. Is a big house and she wants to look after her sister because I have to go to school and I won't have enough time to look after Mam; you know, Doc? You see the reason for my moving, Doc?"

"Yes I could understand, and it's a good reason for moving."

They continued their lazy stroll along the yard, which looked like a garden. It had an abundance of citrus trees. Pawpaw and lots of Pumpkin vines running around the area.

As inquisitive neighbours began looking at them, she let go of his hand as they moved closer to the house. Standing in front of the house, she said, "Things are a little different now though."

"How and in what way?"

"Things are not exactly better yet. There isn't a great improvement in Mum's illness. Aunt Celia does a little work for the priest in Mt. St. Ervans, two or three days a week, so at times ah still have to stay home and care for Mum, You know what ah mean."

"You missing out on school," he said with some concern in his tone.

"But all is not yet lost. There is some hope along the way."

"You're not moving back nearer your cousins in La Fillette to get help..."

"No; thank God, another close member of the family – Aunt Cecilia's daughter is coming to take over everything and organise the place an ting."

"Who's that...?"

"Her name is Janelle, she's working in Town, and she will be taking time off from her job, in one of the Ministries, I think. It is all planned. They had a family meeting and all agreed, Janelle was there, so she should be here soon. Then I will be able to return to my education once again in earnest. Back to school! Ha!"

"You seem excited about her."

"Yes, she's very disciplined and quite good at organising things. But..."

"You behind?"

"Ah may have to stay down another year. I couldn't put in enough work last term so ah doh know about the exam."

"You did very well in your last one."

"Yes," she said modestly. "I feel a little saddened about the time I lost, but Mum comes first."

Knowing how conscientious she was about her studies, Doc could only offer a feeble:

"Doh worry, ah know you go catch up. You is a bright girl. Bright as the Northern Star. No one could outshine you."

She gave him a complimenting look of thanks. Then she said gleefully:

"Boy you have speech oui. Bright as the Northern star" she repeated and they both laughed, a happy, consoling and satisfying laugh. A bonding laugh. 'A Doc loves Velma and Velma loves Doc forever' laugh.

There was a workman on the roof of Aunt Celia's house. He was a tall, thin man with a long face, with prickly looking stubble of beard that looked like the spikes of a black sea egg. He was wearing a blue jersey and a large blue overall. One minute he was hammering nails through some shingles on the side of the house, in another minute he pushed the hammer down a pocket on the side of his overalls and started painting erratically. There were large smudges of paint on his clothes. It seemed that more paint was splattered on him than on the house. Feeling awkward as his eyes met with Doc's, he shouted to his young apprentice for the sponge.

"Pass me the sponge boy, and mind your own business."

The younger man, whose name was Jude, never took his eyes off Velma. Jude was a flabby looking boy with his wide eyes and an equally flabby looking stomach. He was wearing a grey torn up jersey over his equally paint-spattered blue pants. Jude spoke falteringly, lazily, as if reluctant to spare the words out of his mouth.

The painter shouted again, "Pass me the sponge and the two inch brush, and take your eyes off Miss Velma boy."

Jude went over to a much beaten up, dented bucket and took out the items that were in there, (the brush and the sponge) went up the ladder and handed them to his boss.

"He is always looking at me," said Velma.

"Doc, you must come and see Mammie. Ah go tell her you coming in to see her."

"Okay."

When his visit was announced he entered the room tentatively. As he did so, Aunt Celia sat up and greeted him. He held out his hand, which she shock feebly while looking at him with weak questioning eyes. She returned his greetings, "How are you?" "I am not feeling too bad today."

Aunt Celia was lying on a very large wooden bed, in an equally large spacious room. There was a sacred picture of Jesus and Mary on one side of the wooden partition. Above the head of the bed was another picture of Christ, with a sacred bleeding heart. In another corner there was a table which looked like a small alter with personal items at the bottom of the shelf.

There was the Holy Bible, a bottle of Holy water and a Rosary with a cross at the end of it, all placed on the bottom of the shelf. On the top of the table there were candles and a vase of fresh flowers. Further down, almost at the end of the room near a window there was an enamel basin and a wash stand for washing one's face. On the other side of the wash stand was a towel. Under the stand was a jug, or an enamel ewer filled with water. Still in the room, on another small wooden shelf, was a kerosene lamp with a large 'Home Sweet Home' lampshade and a box of safety matches.

Doc sat on the only chair that was in the bedroom, not too far from Aunt Celia's bed. All in all, the room was bright and cheerful. Doc turned to her and asked her for the how many times:

"How are you?" Because he did not know what else to say.

She said, "Same as yesterday, it does go and come, but the first few weeks was the worse."

Then she coughed a weak cough and wiped her month with a thin white cloth while trying to cover it with her other hand.

Doc felt a little conscious, and wanted to be out of the room. "Ex..cuse me" (more coughing again). Doc asked whether he should pour her some water. There was a glass and a jug of water close to her. She indicated with a nod, and he did. She sipped it and gradually the cough subsided. At this point, Velma entered the room and asked if she was alright.

"You want some water?" she enquired.

"Yes, but Doc poured some for me awready."

Saying this, she looked towards Doc and their eyes met. For a moment all three remained silent, and this silence prevailed in the room for what seemed to be an eternity.

Then Doc said, "I think I should go now; I hope you feel better."

He shook her hands again, and was almost out the of the bedroom door when she said in a weak voice:

"Thank you for coming to see me."

He went into the sitting room and waited for Velma. The sitting room was a large squarish room with a large wagonnette loaded with a fine selection of Chinaware, which glittered as the streak of sunlight came from the half open window. There were other items of sentimental value there on the wagonnette too. Things like chinaware, some made of porcelain, among them were two love birds looking like swans cast in a heart shaped mould and appeared to be smiling at each other, gliding down a pond.

Hanging on the wooden partition was a picture of Aunt Celia and her husband, then another picture showing a group of policemen looking smart and official in their Colonial uniforms. Another picture showed the whole of Aunt Celia's family: husband, with four children including Janelle. Aunt Celia was in a long dress reaching almost to her ankles. Her husband, Uncle Fred, was wearing a tight double-breasted jacket and a felt hat, leaning more to the right side of his head. Janelle had wide bright eyes and was wearing a white dress with a band or sash tied behind her back. She also wore long socks and an off-white hat, decorated with artificial flowers.

On the shelf of the same partition was an oblong shaped radio, with similarly shaped 'BEREC' battery near to it, and a hurricane lamp and a flashlight. Then there was that peculiarly shaped Demerara Shutter with an earthen goblet filled with water and a glass turned down in a saucer. The room, filled with domestic utilities, was quite interesting in its own peculiar way. Velma came out from her mother's bedroom with a slightly puzzled look on her face.

"I think she's looking better today," she said to Doc.

"Ah glad to hear that, Vel."

Then he got up from the chair and repeated his desire to leave.

"It was good to see your mother Vel, but I'm going now."

"I'm much better seeing you." She looked him over with a possessive air.

She followed him out into the large grassy yard where 'Desire me' was leaning up on the mango tree. Velma's Uncle Fred arrived from the mountain, just as he was leaving.

Uncle Fred was a broad, tough, hard-looking man, with a deeply lined face and a thick moustache. He was perspiring profusely, and his stained, torn shirt was stuck to his back from the sweat. As he pulled up his donkey-cart at one end of the yard, the hens began to cackle, the pigs grunted and the donkey began to bray. Doc waited for an opportunity to say good afternoon, but he was studiously ignored. Uncle Fred's attention was strictly concerned with unloading the bags of nutmeg, bunches of bananas, bags of yams, dasheen and callaloo, that he brought down from the mountain. Soon, however, his eye met with Docs, and he said:

"Good afternoon," in a odd manner.

Velma kept a respectable distance as Uncle Fred's sharp eyes gutted her from head to toe. He finally unloaded the animal, then he unharnessed it, and tied it on the mango tree, then he went inside the house, where he greeted his wife and refreshed himself.

"Ah leaving you now, but ah coming back soon; and we could meet outside the Convent gap – anyhow, we go see," said Doc, surveying her with sweeping glances.

"Okay, but one thing, Janelle is very strict, and with that she also taking on some financial responsibilities, she may not even want me to see you," said she in an unhurried, toneless voice.

"Doh mine," said Doc, "Dey say love will always find a way." Uncle Fred was standing in front of the door with his roving eyes.

"We go see," he said pushing his bicycle ahead of him.

"Okay," she said, "Not long eh?"

"But what about your cousin?"

"I agree with you - love must find a way." She said, now coming closer to him.

He held her hand, and with a boyish, charming smile, kissed it and was off. The day was quite an achievement for him. Seeing Velma gladdened his heart. When he got home, it was dusk. The birds did not sing, the fowls flew into the trees to roost for the night, the trees were motionless. In the west, there was the reflection of the sunset, for by now the sun had exhausted itself and gone to sleep.

After Doc left Deblando, Velma brought her mother her soup.

"He's getting to be a big man," she said to her daughter. Velma made no reply. Her mother finished the soup and sank back into bed.

"He's got some problems with his new job," said Velma while balancing the bowl in her hand.

"He change job again? He's a rolling stone. Be careful with rolling stones, you know, they just keep rolling along."

"Doc won't roll away from me, Mum."

"You sure de love is still strong?" she asked feebly.

"Yes, Mum and growing stronger. Ah tell you one day we go get married."

"Hm, hm, cough! Cough!" she had another sip of water.

After she was settled Velma kissed her on her forehead and went into the kitchen, then into her room, which she'd been rearranging for some time because of Janelle's visit.

The day after his meeting with Velma, Doc returned to his job with double resolve to 'work like a beast.' He go keep cool, keep his head down because he needed to make a future for he and his future wife. Yes, he knew that it was only a matter of time before they got married.

Unbeknown to anyone except his mother and young Samuel, Doc had been following a course of studies by correspondence with encouragement from Sam. He'd been pursuing a course in Blue Print Reading, part of building and construction, inspired, assisted and encouraged by young Samuel who was following closely on his father's heels as an experienced builder. Following his own intuition of not putting all his economic eggs in one basket, Doc applied a great deal of spare evenings in Blue Print reading with the assistance of the willing young Samuel.

A new and glorious feeling had come over him after his talk with his mother and his meeting with Velma. She is a nice girl, she is bright, one day, one day, he and Velma go marry. So he has to be strong for her, for both of them. He will return to work, work hard, as a beast, as he was accustomed, and he go continue his Correspondence course. Yes, he go improve his education. He could study to be a good builder, learn to read Plan and blueprint. Yes, he can do that. He must act with resolve. Then he thought of Sally Ann's reciting Shakespeare's Julius Caesar....

And so this young man, George Awosu Williams, popularly known as Doc, to our readers, decided again for the umpteenth time, to take his destiny into his own hands. Armed with a new injection of faith and courage, he felt fortified enough to take on the world.

"What the hell I have to be afraid of? Nobody can do anything to stop me. I'm going back to work tomorrow."

And so, back to work he went the next morning. They were spraying on an Estate in Grand Bras. It was a good place to spray. It was flat and the bananas were planted in rows which were very easy to walk through.

One morning Doc witnessed the death of one Grace Mitchell.

That morning, the labourers were engaged in picking cocoa. It was cocoa day. The men were the pickers. They carried the rod, a long bamboo rod known as the cocoa rod, with a sharp metal head. It had a hook which was sharp, for it was used for cutting the stem off the ripe cocoa from the tree. The women carried the cocoa baskets. When the men picked the cocoa, the women picked up the cocoa by sticking their cut lasses in them and filling up their baskets. Having filled up their baskets, they carried load after load and made them into strategic piles or heaps, which is then finally carried to the boucan.

Grace Mitchell was a weather beaten, dry looking scarecrow of a woman. On her way to the boucan with a basket of cocoa, she stumbled and fell from what seemed to be a combination off tiredness, hunger and exhaustion. Doc saw when she fell. He was spraying not far away and saw the wet basket of cocoa she was carrying sprawled all over her body while she was unable to move. She was lying there covered all over with the wet cocoa. Doc dropped the machine and rushed to her assistance. At close up he beheld the thin, emaciated, beaten up, prematurely old woman struggling for life. He took her head in his arms shouted for help while cleaning out the cocoa seeds from her face.

"Help! Help!" he shouted. "Grace fall down! She doh look well! Come quick!!!"

Jessica, one of Grace's closest friends was the first to come on the scene. Panic stricken, she tried to help her friend as best she could but irrespective of what she did there was no response from Grace.

"Oh God! Oh God! Ah hope she go be awright," she kept on wailing while cleaning the seeds off her friend's face and clothes. It was Friday morning, the last working day of the week. Jessica confirmed that Grace was hoping to complete the morning session (half day).

Normally, she would share her friend's lunch, which was not unusual. Someone would give her a piece of yam, another a grain of banana and still another, a dumpling and some salt fish and so she would get a proper lunch until she got paid in the afternoon, yes, the pittance of a pay! A pay that was spent long before it was received, so you could die for this pittance of a wage - the slave wage, because they earned just about enough to buy a morsel of food, very basic food to furnish them with sustenance to carry on their slaving tasks each week, week in and week out from sun up to sun down.

The state and condition of the labourers during this process was often very depressing. Men and women alike were pushed to the edge of endurance like some beast of burden; they were raggedly dressed. They looked haggard and emaciated from their strenuous, sun up to sun down work.

They trudged along drains; they often fell into hidden holes; knocked themselves against stones, broken stumps or whatever else lay in wait for them during their trips to and from the boucan.

These labourers worked like animals, and often were treated like animals, and apart from their physical exploitation, the women were often placed in compromising situations where sexual exploitation was not uncommon.

These hardened creatures protested in various ways, even appealing to the Almighty for improvement in their condition but very little came. They alone knew the hell they had to go through to earn a pittance from such slave labour, for that was slavery by any other name. They presented a pitiable and degrading sight to witness.

During the period of Trade Union progress in the 1950's, many Estate labourers and other workers like shop assistant and others had a substantial increase in wages. For people like Grace, however, with a thousand mouths to feed, the wage increase (which was very very low already) was a drop in the ocean. Therefore, many Estate labourers were not actually earning a 'living wage', and Grace with so many mouths to feed, including a husband who had been injured and had one of his legs amputated, and was unable to work, was in that group.

Compounded with the above problems, she had five children and an older mother to look after and she was the only bread winner, and that bread was a very small loaf indeed. Unlike the miracle of the increased loaves and fishes in the Bible in The Sermon on the Mount, she had no powers to increase that tiny loaf.

When she was finally dragged clear and they had a full view of her, she was foaming at the mouth. Long, thick, slimly, frothy substances just kept oozing out of her mouth, which was partly opened as she continued gasping for breath while holding her stomach with one hand. She looked stupefied, with her two big eyes rolling in their sockets, deep, deep down from her emancipated, prematurely aged and haggard-looking face. There she lay, helpless and stupid looking under the cocoa trees with her head in Jessica's lap, looking as though she had a one way ticket to Paradise.

Grace was dying from the hunger that knocked her down. When Jessica, her friend and confidant came, Doc stood back looking on. He did not move. He remained on the scene of the accident for some time after Jessica came. Sometime later the PDI, Wope Sir and some of the boys, followed by some of the labourers, came and crowded around.

The PDL looked on with an officious stare at the machine, the deep green painted "Dekker"' leaning upon a piece of stump on the ground. Then he looked up at Doc with that air of scorn, a contemptuous, hateful look. Doc looked at him, stared at him eyeball to eyeball if you like, without blinking. The driver looked casually at Doc. Then he shifted his focus from the machine to the half-dead woman lying in the arms of Jessica, and walked away from the scene with one hand in his pocket.

In the meantime, Terry, Mano, Joe and two other members of the Team came and stood silently next to Doc. The rest of the Team moved away from the scene of the accident. Not long afterwards, the overseer of the estate came bumbling and fumbling with a ramshackle walk, with a piece of Phoenix cigarette on the end of his lip as he approached the scene. Soon after, an old car was said to be waiting in the yard outside the boucan. The same yard where over two hundred years ago, hundreds, possibly thousands of slaves - ancestors of Grace and Doc, and the PDI and others -

must have assembled for their daily slave task, similar to Grace's and most probably sharing similar and even worst experiences than Grace's. And so, into the car she went. This car took her, Grace, accompanied by her special friend and confidant to the Princess Alice Hospital in Mirabeau.

And that night as the poet said:

...........somebody's mother bowed low her head,

In her home that night,

And the prayer she said was,

'God be kind to that Noble Boy,

who is somebody's son, and pride and joy.'

Three days later, Grace Mitchell, 49, looking more like 79, was dead. She died from gastro-enteritis. With death ended the struggle for living, that often futile struggle. She died of hunger, usually, the first course of death. The worthlessness of it all! Whatever the case, the struggle for living was over.

The night of her 'prayers' Doc was there with Ghost. After they sang: '*Rock of Ages cleft for me, let me hide myself in thee....*' They left, with the stars lighting their way home.

- V -

It was a dampish, drizzly Monday afternoon when Janelle, Aunt Iris's daughter and first cousin to Velma, came. The bus: 'In God We Trust', dropped her off just as the shower slackened and she walked the short distance home.

Janelle was a short young woman with a squarish jaw, shiny bright, marble, intellectual eyes, high forehead, small, too closely packed set of teeth - which made them appear as if they were overlapping - and a concentrated looking face. She looked like a no-nonsense person, and for some time (as Velma discovered) she acted like a no no-nsense person; for she was both bureaucratic and business-like in the organisation and running of the home. She said that's what she came for, and that's what she was going to do.

Everyone was glad that she came, taking time off her job in one of the Ministries to take on and sort out the running of the family affairs. After a short rest, and before supper, she took an inventory of the major tasks to be performed. It began with the responsibility for her Aunt's health. Then running of the home, her father's meals; washing and ironing; and keeping the house clean would necessitate a servant, for her cousin Velma, must be back to school, full-time.

After supper, she discussed her plans with her father, mother and Velma at the table, then went and talked with her Aunt Iris, whose eyes lighted up when Janelle explained her plans.

"You know what you doing, go ahead," said Aunt Iris, feebly. Janelle was in her mid-twenties and she and Velma generally got along very well together.

Velma always listened attentively to her cousin's superior experience and advice and that was what she expected in this tightly knitted family, where traditionally, the older ones take on the responsibility for the home and should be respected in every reasonable way. One evening after supper, however, as they were strolling around the yard and exchanging ideas, Janelle said:

"I hope you are not allowing boys to full up your head, you know."

"Nugh," replied Velma. "No boy is fulling up my head."

"Ah glad to hear that, because I won't like to know you wasting your time and my money playing around with those little force ripe men and them."

"Not at all, but ..."

"But what? Doh tell me you start taking boys seriously already. Are you?"

"Ah know a boy, well Doc and I ..."

"Oh dis Doc is still around. The same Doc who was at Aunt Muriel's wedding?"

"Yes," replied Velma.

"So dis Doc is still around, eh? He seems to take root. Ah go tell you now, keep you mind on you education and keep it off boys," said she in a calm, cold, schoolmistress-like voice.

There was a pause - a long silence ensued, then she continued: "After your education you have enough time to think of.......... well, getting married. So watch your step and don't go fooling around with this....... this Doc. Have nothing to say to him."

"But ah know Doc for nearly two years now; why shouldn't I talk with him?" asked Velma quietly.

"Talk with him, talk with him, talk about what? What do boys like Doc have to talk to girls about? What can they say to them?" asked her cousin, getting heated.

She went on to answer her own question; "They could talk about one thing, and one thing only. Yes, that is about how to get their hands under your dress and then down with your underwear. And you know what that can lead to?" Again she supplied her own answer:

"Pregnancy, yes, children, and as soon as you get pregnant, braps! They ups and gone. So forget this Doc."

"I could never forget about Doc," she said.

"What do you mean you can't forget about him? Doc is only a force-ripe little man. Ah tell you the sooner you forget about him, the better."

There was a longish silence again, then Velma explained to her that Doc is not a force-ripe man. That she and Doc are in love with each other, that Doc respects her.

"Doc is my boyfriend and we are going to get married one day," said Velma firmly.

"You must be living in cloud cuckoo land. You're out of your mind," replied her cousin in a sparring mood. Velma tried to reassure her that Doc will not force her to do anything she does not want to do, for they had their opportunity in Pearls after their Aunt Muriel's wedding to do 'something', but they never did anything.

"I am still a virgin," she said hotly. "Because Doc and I love each other. We are waiting to get married," she said with a definitive air.

"Married?" repeated her cousin heatedly, now with her hands on her hips and her neck craned towards Velma.

"Yes, Married. Doc is going to be my husband and we are going to have four children."

"Are you mad? Are you out of your little mind? You must be reading too much Jane Austen and Bronte's novels. You studying 'Wuthering Heights'? You think you're Catherine and Doc is Heathcliffe, running into each other's arms and shouting 'Cathy! Heathcliffe!' and falling down on the ground under Fenniston Craggs? That is only in storybooks!" she said, with hands stuck to her hips and pacing around.

"You can say what you want. We are only first cousins; you can't stop me."

"Wait until your mother hear about this. Wait until she gets well."

"Mammie met Doc at Aunt Muriel's wedding and he came to visit us here and he saw Mum, so she knows him."

"But I making the decision now."

"I don't care."

Janelle knew that she couldn't actually stop her cousin but that didn't matter; for she was now the main link in the family affairs; she also contributed to Velma's schooling at the Convent. She had to uphold and maintain the family tradition. She had a winning hand and she knew that she would be supported by all the other members of this family whose bond had never been broken. That's why she put her job on hold to be home at this crucial time.

"You better start using your senses. First cousin, or last cousin, I am in charge now and part of my responsibility is you –well, yes, you and your education, the stability and strength of this family; that comes first, and I'll see to that. I believe the only thing this Doc has to his name is the clothes on his back, and that funny named bicycle – what is it? 'Desire Me'?" she said again, laughing mirthfully.

"You don't know him, that's why you saying that. I love him, and I always will," Velma said weakly.

"You're being light headed and childish Velma. I can tell you – well, you mustn't put too much faith in love. Love is fickle and fragile and it is a burden too.

Love is blind dey say, but it does blind some people, especially school girls like you," she said, looking straight at her cousin.

"You read a lot about romantic love, but that's an ideal – it always end up with everyone getting married and living happily ever after. But that's the theme for romantic writers – like Byron, and those people who write love songs. They always build up a perfect picture about love. But be sensible and take it from me, this thing called love is really beyond us.

Love is beyond us, because it demands perfection, and we are human, and we can't be perfect. 'To err is human' and you....," she stepped away from her and took a long look at her cousin.

"You is just a girl, not even sixteen yet, you don't have experience. Being in love means falling short, yes, and failing each other more often than you think my dear cousin," said Janelle coming closer to Velma and extending her hands towards her, but Velma remained unmoved.

"Take it from me, no two people fail each other more than two people as young as you and Doc, pledging romantic and sentimental love, and loyalty. You can never be loyal to each other, you too young; your feelings can change," she emphasised in a sad tone of voice.

"Speaking from experience?" returned Velma, somewhat mischievously, for it stabbed Janelle. For a moment she wished she didn't use the 'speaking from experience' statement.

"Yes" replied her cousin shocked and surprised.

"Yes, speaking as one who gave her love, pledged loyalty and lost. And worst of all, I lost him to my best friend. The lice in your head..." said Janelle, in a quiet, sad voice.

Janelle lost her first love, schooldays sweet heart to her best friend. Velma knew the story of her cousin's love life, which left her a bitter teenager and very suspicious of men. She was only 18 at the time. Since then, she had kept away from men and more so, from best friends. Instead, she has committed herself to the love of labour and self up-lifting. So the statement 'speaking from experience' was cutting, it was a stroke below the belt and her cousin was flayed; she became quiet and sombre.

It had grown dark and a weak, watery-looking moon forced a pale light over the yard as a dull reflection came through the surrounding trees. A strong silence reigned between the cousins but neither wanted to leave and go to bed first. At last, Velma mumbled some incoherent words, left and went inside to their room, the one they shared together. She sat down on her table, pen in hand and looking into the empty darkness. When her cousin came into the house sometime later, she, Velma, was still sitting in the same position without stirring. It was frightfully quiet, especially with the lamps in the hall and in the sick room, where Aunt Iris was sleeping. Her father was down at the parlour having a 'little one', and a game of draughts.

When Janelle finally entered their room, Velma was enveloped in that melancholic 'I don't want to be disturbed' mood, still holding her pen and oblivious, (or pretending to be) of her cousin's entrance into the room. After a while she got up, went outside into the bathroom and had a shower. In her prayers before retiring, she prayed that God would soften her cousin's heart in relation to Doc and help her to understand. Then she said goodnight to her cousin in a low, soft voice. Janelle returned a 'good night' to Velma in a chastened, quiet voice.

As the weeks went by, the cousins continued to have their occasional verbal confrontation over Doc, but Velma stood her ground and with time her cousin Janelle, began to listen more to Velma and the story of herself and Doc. And a level of understanding developed between them.

As the months progressed, Velma's school work began its upward progress too. Her cousin began to see that she, Velma, was no flippant, giddy-headed schoolgirl. Velma too, somewhat penitent regarding the 'speaking from experience' speech, lest she might appear to be gloating in her cousin's misfortune, with love, looked and acted kindly and with genuine humility towards her.

Time, being a universal healer, both Janelle and Velma developed a more caring and sensitive relationship towards each other, and understanding began to prevail. This mutual sensitivity led to an undeclared truce. Nothing was said about being sorry or anything like that, but unspeakable demonstrative respect through action was in evidence.

They worked upon the saying that: 'the least said, the soonest mended.' They both decided in their own private manner to bury the hatchet. That being the case, a greater degree of love and trust grew between the cousins. Whenever Doc's name came up in conversation between them, Janelle offered a listening ear. She was less critical, less dogmatic; her response to Velma took on more of an inquiring nature.

"And why do you love him?" Velma was more than happy to supply the answers.

Velma continued her diligent studies, which resulted in the high quality of her work, which was outstanding. Education was all that mattered. Janelle, in the meantime, was hard at work reorganising and reconstructing the family affairs, while Uncle Fred spent long days in the mountain and for a time, Doc's name was never mentioned, and it began to fade away like the Grand Etang mist. But he was never forgotten. Velma knew that: Their patience and love for each other will lead to positive results. They loved each other and that's all that mattered. Janelle was anxious and Velma satisfied her anxiety.

"Doc and I are going to get married," she said one day when her cousin asked about him.

"You see him? You haven't mentioned his name for a long time."

"I see him passing on the Rover sometimes."

"Y'all don't meet up?"

"No, Doc know I have my studies to get on with. He understands. That's the way we want it. We understand each other. Everything is for a time and he has his problems at work too.

But everything is for a time," repeated Velma with proud satisfaction which left her cousin wondering, puzzled; but that was her cousin Velma, a girl characterised by earnestness, soberness, and conscious about what she wanted, she had nothing to fear about the certainty of Doc's love for her, and vice versa.

Janelle was an intelligent young woman, with great organising talent, so slowly, after taking on the responsibility for running her mother's home, she made some positive changes which resulted in some real improvement. The first was a remarkable improvement in her Aunt's health. It began by taking her to see another doctor to get a second opinion about her illness. When she told her Aunt Iris about it, it was done with a level of sensitivity and delicacy that her Aunt could not refuse.

"Dr. Mc Sween is good you know, Tanty, but what about trying a doctor from Town just to hear it from both sides?" she said while combing her Aunt's hair one morning.

"You think it's a good idea?" replied her Aunt quickly.

"Yes, I think so. You know its Town already, most good doctors, like many other things are in Town."

"Okay den, make the arrangements."

So Janelle went ahead and made an appointment to see a Dr Radix. The good doctor changed the medication after drastically reviewing it. Instead of the white, chalky peppermint tasting medicine, he recommended something, 'for the colon', said he. Together with the medication from the pharmacy, he also recommended some bush medicine.

"You must give her some Corilla every two weeks for about six weeks or so. After that, give her some Man-Betta-Man and Ven-Ven boiled together," said Dr Radix with a professional look in his eyes.

"She must move about some more. Let her do some more walking. She needs to take some physical exercise as often as possible. She should do it in small manageable proportions. Don't let her overdo it at first. Say about fifteen to twenty minutes each day; then as she gets stronger, increase it, up to forty minutes or more," he said, taking off his glasses and looking at Janelle with big, bright eyes.

To every suggestion, Janelle just nodded.

"Ah see you around one of the Ministries, you working in town?"

To which Janelle's only reply was, "Yes, Doctor."

On arriving back in Deblando, Janelle meticulously and scrupulously began to apply Dr Radix's instructions. She went around the garden and got some Corilla and boiled it the same evening for her Aunt. As the weeks went by, every part of the plan for her Aunt's recovery was implemented, and within the space of six weeks or so, she was on the road to recovery.

Her sickbed almost became redundant within the space of that time. She was walking for over a mile a day. Her protruding stomach, 'the growth' so called, was reduced to normality. She had lost weight, her limbs became firmer and she displayed a great amount of energy and vitality; so much so that she refused to lie down in bed during the day.

One day, Janelle had to say to her: "Aunt Iris, don't overdo it, please don't overdo it." But Aunt Iris was on the road to full recovery, and they both knew that...

Velma's Biology, Chemistry and Maths needed some extra attention as far as Janelle was concerned. When she put it to her cousin, Velma agreed, and Janelle organised extra private lessons for her, which Velma attended once during the week and on Saturday mornings.

Janelle thought her father worked too hard. He is getting old and he should have more time to rest. Five days a week spent in the mountains was too much. Up on Mondays, down on Fridays had been a way of life since she was child. But he was not young anymore, so she hired a labourer to help him, after a great deal of persuasion and strong opposition from the man of the house.

"I am de man here and you can't come and tell me what to do!" he remonstrated when the proposal was made.

But he yielded somewhat, after his wife gave support to the plan. A young man was employed to pick up the nutmegs two days a week. Her father would spend three days up in Clabony Mountains. Janelle wanted two days, but he was 'defiant and strong headed,' said his wife.

"I'm not ah old man as yet you know, and ah love me land," he put in. After the compromise, his wife took him by the hand and said:

"You go keep me bed warm now in the night." He smiled, then took his cutlass and went down to the garden with his packet of Phoenix cigarettes.

Janelle's mother, Celia, on her way to 'help' the priest the next morning, told Janelle how much she appreciated the things that she was doing for the family.

"You have always been a sensible girl. Is only one stupid mistake you make. Dis Tom. You was so full of Tom Jones. Everything was Tom Jones." She kept quiet, knowing what happened in the end.

Then Janelle said to her mother, "Is a long time we doh have all the family together. Before I go back to work, we should all meet up." Her mother agreed.

And so it was decided for the family to have a social gathering, a get- together. A date was set for the family meeting. It was not unusual. The Three sisters had always been close and held regular get-togethers, but it had been two or three years since they last had a good family social. It was also time for Uncle Johnson, Aunt Muriel's husband, to have the opportunity to meet with the family all together, with the exception of Velma's father, who was now in England.

The date was set for Sunday afternoon at 2 o'clock. After church, breakfast was prepared. While they ate breakfast, the peas was on the fire in the kitchen. Soon after breakfast, everyone (including the once ill Aunt Iris) put hearts and hands into preparing the meal. When Aunt Muriel and her husband, Uncle Johnson arrived hot and sweaty, lunch was ready. It was a sumptuous presentation: rice and peas, stewed chicken, pork and beef. Then there was fried plantain, bluggoe, yam and sweet potatoes. Finally, crab and callaloo was served.

After having a refreshing drink of lime squash, Uncle Johnson and his wife sat down to partake. Velma helped both with the preparation and the serving. She was dressed in a plaid dress, with white top and band or sash tied behind her back, with her hair plaited in cornrow. She quickly laid the large table and was at hand to serve as required. She appeared amiable, neat and well pleased to see all the family (except her father) together.

Janelle too, was in a happy state of deportment. She helped serve her Aunt Muriel and her husband, and she too was at hand to facilitate with the smooth running of the event. She was wearing pants and a jersey but remained demure throughout the conversation. After grace was said, they began to focus on Janelle. So while the big people were having their meal, she stood aside for some time. They spoke of her achievements towards the recovery of her Aunt, the role she played, "She was always thoughtful," said her mother.

"She is a blessed child with a good heart, and she have healing hands too," said her Aunt Iris.

"God sent her," echoed Uncle Johnson, wiping off the smudge from the corner of his mouth.

Then her mother once again stressed that, "She is a wonderful daughter. Uncle Fred now spend more time at home. Since dis child was small, she had a lot of sense..."

"Cept for her hard-headedness," said her father. "With this Tom!" he continued, slapping his thighs.

"That was when she was very young," defended her mother.

"But she should listen to her father."

"We is not perfect. Where is the ripe banana and the sweet bread?" enquired Aunt Iris diplomatically. "Ah feel ah could have something sweet."

Turning to Uncle Fred, Uncle Johnson said, "Well if dey go have sweet, we go have a little one."

So the men had their 'little one' - a glass of strong beverage, and the women their sweet and another glass of ginger beer, to which Velma efficiently attended. In the meantime, Janelle who had to bear the wrath of her father went into her room, for her case was not yet over. The table was cleared and everyone was taking chairs, stools draughtboard and portable small tables and heading outside under the large, spreading mango tree, on the side of the house where the family discussion continued.

The afternoon sun had just began its very slow descent, as they took their seats around the small table, where they rested their bottles and glasses. Then Uncle Fred said how pleased he was to see all the family together after a long break.

He added, "The only one missing is dis Wilson. What he want to go up in dis cold place for ah doh know; when he come back home, all you have is cold and not long after that, braps, you fall down and dead!"

"Well, is de house dat take up all the money we save up, and he doh getting work. Everybody going away and people doh building house now in Grenada. Everybody going in England, so will go too and see what he could do," pleaded Aunt Iris.

"Well ah man have to try something. He would soon be back ah hope," said Aunty Celia.

"He only gone for five years," supplied her sister.

"Well anyhow," said Uncle Johnson, "we hope he come back soon. For ah sure he missing his family, a man without family is like a fish outa water. We go try and keep the family circle strong, we shouldn't break it. Wilson will soon be back."

"Dats the way ah like to hear dis man talk," said his wife.

"Dis is a family dat went through many difficulties. Sometimes we feel we could eat up one another; ah fuss we use to quarrel. We can't agree on anything. We just hate one another, and what for? Eh, what for? And den we go home and siddown, and tink and when we tink so, we always come back again stronger dan ever," said Aunt Celia, breathlessly.

"You talk ah book," said Aunt Iris.

"If it was not for the help and support from this family ah woulda dead awready. Ah pray to God to keep us together."

"Good talk, good talk," echoed her husband.

"As a new comer to this family, I have nothing but praise for it. I'm happy to be a part of it. Long may we remain united and strong," said Uncle Johnson, pulling out a handkerchief from his seat pocket and wiping his brow, while his wife, Aunt Muriel, gave him a look of approval, and rested a loving hand on his shoulder.

Aunt Iris took up from where Uncle Johnson left off.

"I cannot help it," she said quietly, "but I have the greatest respect and love for her. Look at me," and she got up from her seat so that everyone could have a good look at her. "I am well again, thank God, and as happy as King George himself." Then she went up to Janelle, who as standing not too far off, and put her arms around her. Janelle became very self-conscious and was lost for words, as the tears welled up in her eyes.

Then she offered a shrill, "Thank you Aunt Iris, I did only what the family expects of me, my best."

"I owe a lot to Janelle," said Velma, speaking officially for the first time. "Although we had our own misunderstanding at first, I must thank her for what she's doing for me towards my education including the extra lessons in Maths, Biology and Chemistry."

But her father returned to her 'hard headedness,' and how she use to 'break stick in she ears' when he use to warn her about this Tom Jones.

Then Uncle Johnson said, "We all make mistakes," and he was sure that she had learnt her lesson for, "we must learn from past mistakes," he ended, with a kind, friendly look at Janelle, "so we will not make them again in the future."

It was difficult to quieten down her father. He took the whole thing very personally. She had failed to listen to him when he warned her about this Tom Jones and his womanising. He use to see and hear things. And as for her friend Alice, he never trusted her the way she looked at Tom when he and Janelle were together. She was always 'sticking up in Janelle's dress tail, especially when she and that boy...'

"Well awright," said his wife.

"Who can't hear must feel," returned her father.

"Come, come everyone, we must let bygones be bygones. I'm sure Janelle has learnt her lesson."

"I'm glad to be a part of this family and for the appreciation everyone has shown me. Janelle is a good girl, and she is performing wonders. Since she came here, she even get someone to go in the mountain two days a week, and a servant at home to wash and iron, once a week. She is a gem," said Uncle Johnson.

"Let us have a drink on that." But his opinion still differed from the others.

A light murmur emanated from her father, but everyone drank something in her name. Then Aunt Celia, her mother, embraced and kissed her on the cheeks and Uncle Johnson began singing, *"For she is jolly good fellow... And so say all of us..."*

Glasses were knocked together, and everybody praised everybody else, except for Uncle Wilson.

"Come," he said to Uncle Johnson. "Draughts."

He went into the kitchen and returned with the draughtboard and the knobs. They took their drinks and moved a little distance away from the group and started playing draughts.

By the time they left, all the serious issues had already been thrashed out. In a way, it was time for a little more relaxed form of discussion between the sisters, women-to-women like. Velma and Janelle loitered around for some time, with the latter wearing a humble mask and her cousin, one of modesty.

In the distant corner, the game of draughts was going well for Uncle Wilson. He was in a strong position. He started to whistle and sing and that was a good sign. There is nothing better to drive away the feeling of bitterness, sadness and frustration than music and the sounds of laughter, which was now evident, both from the draughtsmen and from the tete-a-tete among the women.

But everything comes to an end at some time, even the happiest times. Altogether, it was a constructive event. The unity of the family was reinforced and hopes and expectations were on the horizon. Janelle was given credit for the role she played in bringing it about.

Eventually, darkness fell like a heavy blanket, and stifled the crescent moon that was trying to force its weak light through the trees. Then it was time for Aunt Muriel and Uncle Johnson to leave, say good night and farewell, and this they did; after a great deal of some more hugging, kissing and endless handshakes, they made their way slowly down to their home in Cook Hill.

The day had been a constructive one, despite the occasional ruffles. Everyone was pleased. An inventory had taken place of the family's social situation. There was improvement with the sick. There was some home help, and help too, with the mountain. Velma's education was back to normal and she was doing very well. The family's Balance Sheet showed a healthy credit. Everyone had their say, whatever that was. It was a pleasant, democratic event, carried out with warmth and sensitivity, followed through with a delicious meal, and family loyalty was underscored. As always, such occasions were designed to be pleasant and constructive, and so it was, in the green, healthy surroundings of Aunt Iris home in Deblando.

The cousins wafted off to sleep, chatting or remarking about events of the day and the forthcoming Holy Innocents Harvest.

- VI -

As was customary, great preparations were made for the forthcoming Annual event: Holy Innocents' Harvest. Harvests, traditionally, are part of the social and cultural life of Grenadians. Generally, they are remarkable events. They bring people together in a relaxed social setting which provides the opportunity for young people to socialise with one another.

It was a time to wear new clothes, dresses with frills and lovely long ribbons; to display new handbags and nylon belts. For the young men to wear their 'bad' shirts, new 'hallow bottoms' trousers and two-toned shoes and much more. It was a time to fall in love, sometimes to get married. It was time too, for the farmers to display their produce – yams, potatoes, pumpkins, sugar canes, in fact, to display the gift of Nature tended by their skilful hands, and give thanks.

It was a bright Sunday afternoon when Doc arrived at the Holy Innocents Church. He had said to Velma that he would be there by 2 o'clock, but he got there earlier. The church looked formidable, made from granite and unplastered so that the stones kept staring grimly at you. It looked impregnable, like a miniature Medieval Castle. All it needed was to be built on a hill, with a moat and a drawbridge.

Velma was there before him. She and Janelle were casually walking in the church ground, some yards away from the church building. The ground was flat, with rich, well-trimmed grass looking like a small, green, carpeted football pitch. A hedge of buttercups and roses surrounded it on one side, and a host of wild flowers and plants on the other.

The church and the school (Holy Innocents' Anglican School) are located yards from each other. It is customary after the Harvest in the church, to hold a dance in the school to the end of the festivities of the day.

This school is shaded by a large spreading mahogany tree. Between both the church and the school there is a graveyard with many gravestones, some of them with quite legible inscriptions. One could see that close families were buried there from their markings. There was one of a Mr. Ross, who died in 1922, age 73 years. Next to him was his wife, Elizabeth Ross, who died a year later, age 70 years.

Still close to the school, another inscription tells us that Margaret Lane, wife of T. Williams, was buried there. And so it continued. People, especially school children, sat on the gravestones and ate, drank and rested on them. They provided play facilities for the school children in a most natural way. The living and the dead inseparable, if you like.

Velma was wearing a brightly coloured dress with a partly transparent nylon top. It was a two-piece kind of dress with two loops, and a thin belt. Doc went up to both of them as they were standing around, and greeted them warmly. Velma smiled her sweet, gracious smile at him. Janelle said 'Hi Doc,' as she formally held out her hand for the first time to Doc, then she excused herself and went over to some other friends not far off, where a handsome young man in his Sunday, Harvest best, was paying her close attention.

Velma and Doc walked around the stalls together while making small conversation. She talked about school, and he about plans to leave the job, his correspondence course and a range of general, informative subjects. They had ice cream and snowball. He brought a large packet of popcorn, which they shared, he running ahead of her, and she trying to catch him. Knots of people here and there were in the way and they stumbled aimlessly into them.

They finally drifted away from the crowd and were by themselves. They walked along until they came to the mahogany tree where he had left DESIRE ME. He took it, and they walked away from the harvest ground and down the La Digue Road, until they arrived at the La Digue Junction. Turning right, they strolled casually down the road, passing the Receiving Station of the Grenada Co-operative Nutmeg Association.

They finally reached Mt St Ervans Gap and followed the trail until they were a stone's throw from the Catholic priest's residence, with its commanding, majestic, panoramic view. Then finally trees, and a large growth of thick grass and wild flowers It was getting late by this time, and soon it would be dark, for the evening sun had disappeared behind the now orange looking horizon.

"You and Janelle are good friends now," said Doc. A squeaking flock of birds flew overhead.

"Well I would say we come to understand each other more better now than when she just came up," said Velma with cool assurance, looking up into his face and brushing off pieces of popcorn that were stuck to his lips.

"You all were having a serious talk when I came. What were you all talking about so?"

"Yes, we were talking about her, her love for Tom Jones, and how he left her for her best friend. And she told me how she felt. She told me private things, like how she had a crush on him since she was 13 years, and a lot more. I couldn't believe it," said Velma, after a pause.

"And she said to me, Doc, she said to me," said Velma, getting all excited and holding Doc's hand and squeezing it.

"She said to me, when you have a crush on a boy you can't think of anything else. You write his name on the big fat love leaf." Velma shook her head.

"And you put the leaf between the pages of your book. And if it makes root you know he loves you too, and the love is growing. Not only that, you write his name on everything and you walk around in a day dream and you act silly, until people start saying you love sick."

"True, true?" asked Doc, "Ah glad you all are better friends now, you know," he said shaking his head.

"I couldn't imagine that about Janelle. 'Lovesick?'" he said, quietly touching Velma's face.

It was now dark and the sun had disappeared completely behind the yellowish horizon. The orange sky looked like an artist's canvass. However, the colours of the day, the lovely bright evening were slowly being dominated by the dark grey skies of the night. A few evening stars had already sprinkled over the infinitely large, endless spread of canvass.

Doc moved his hand away from her face. He held her hands as they strolled under the stars; then he drew Velma off the track, or footpath, holding her carefully, and protectively, allowing his free hand to rest on her shoulder. They walked towards a large boulder, which jutted out from the side of the bank; the other half was hidden by the bushes that formed a short avenue, almost completely surrounding the boulder, and enclosing the footpath. They sat down and found each other's lips, as by now the dark night was fully apparent, for it had eclipsed the remnant of the day. And now, even now, in the darkness close together, very close, Doc could see that there was something in her smile yes, that the smile on her face was so angelically peaceful and compellingly beautiful – "My Velma," he thought. "Even in the dark your beauty is visible."

By this time, Doc was leaning up against the stone with his arm about her waist and she found herself almost sitting on him, with her right arm around his neck, caressing him. Then she suddenly released herself from the embrace. It seemed as if she was frightened of her own feelings. Velma loved being together with Doc right here and now in that position, that closeness. But…she thought of not going too far. Pearls…! They stood up and he kissed her again; she then gradually pulled him down once more on the boulder, they embraced each other, losing themselves in passionate kisses. Then his hand moved over her shoulders and down her hands, kissing each finger by turn. He rested his head against her bosom and groaned like a helpless child. She, while fondling his hair, closed her eyes and bathed in the cool passion that comforted them both.

"It's time for us to go," she said. "I'm feeling quite guilty. I don't know why I love you so much. I feel ashamed of myself." She placed herself at his feet, and his heart went out adoringly to her. He loved her! Oh how he loved her, this fine, African daughter!

"You must not feel guilty and ashamed, Velma," he said quietly. "We do love each other. We will be married someday. We must be honest with our feelings. We cannot feel guilty, ashamed, or anything like that for wanting each other." Crouching there in their embrace, his mind wandered back in Pearls.

"I'm finding it very difficult to keep our promise. I don't know why. Well I know why, but I'm a little confused right now. I'm thinking Doc, whether we shouldn't have let Pearls happen," said she in a deep, passionate voice.

"Pearls," he said, and repeated, "Pearls....."

"I want to be chaste. I want to maintain my virtue, Doc until our wedding night, as promised," she said in her sweet, earnest, but emotive voice. "I love you so much, but I'll have to be strong, Doc, and when am weak, I know you wouldn't take advantage of my weakness."

"I don't know," he said quietly. "I'll try and keep my part of the promise, too. Our promise is our bond, it ties us together. We must continue to trust each other, for without it, our love will be as empty as a lambie shell on the beach," he said this with an eloquence she was proud of.

"Hold me tight, tight," said she.

They embraced once more, stronger than before, and she pulled him down into her soft, youthful bosom, where they remained speechless for what seemed to be an eternity. By now, it was absolutely dark, apart from the twinkling lights from the silvery stars and the fleeting fireflies. The night was very quiet too, apart from the whistling wind through the palm trees, the chirping of the crickets, the croaking frogs from the drains at the lower end of the Priest's house, plus the combination of different sounds coming from the nocturnal insects. The last thing they remembered was the hooting of an owl in the far, far distance; then, as if awakened from a long slumber, they drifted off home a little dazed, he holding her with his left hand, while pushing DESIRE ME with the other.

- VII -

It was on an estate near Mirabeau; Mirabeau Estate was named after the Marquis of Mirabeau one of the leaders of the French revolution of 1789. He thought colonial agriculture was backward and degrading as a result of slave labour. It's ironical that, that place was the memorable point where that ominous meeting between Doc and the PDI took place early one Monday, when the Plant Disease Inspector informed the Team about the agreed increase of pay. In delivering the news, he strutted around like a Bantam Cock; hands in pockets, making short, deliberated strides, looking as pleased as Punch and smiling from ear to ear like Brer Anansi.

The estate was a large plantation, stretching all the way from L'Esterre, Lower Balthazar at one end, extending as far up as the cocoa Scheme, Plant Nursery at the other. This Nursery husbanded a large variety of plants, fruits and vegetables. It is one of the major nurseries which supply the farming communities in Grenada with a great deal of their plant needs.

The nursery is situated not far from the Princess Alice hospital in St. Andrews, about 3 or 4 miles from the town of Grenville. The land is partly flat, partly hilly, steep in gradient, where the hills are often difficult to manoeuvre. The outskirts are often indented by drains, and in the flatter areas, bananas are planted between long stretches of cocoa and a sprinkling of nutmegs and cinnamon, and underground root vegetables, such as yams, dasheen, tanias and so on.

On the side nearest to the yard where the boucan is situated, the field labourers, men and women, trooped in to receive their orders. Then some headed for a local shop, or parlour, to buy a loaf of bread, a tin of sardines, an ounce or two of cheese and some crackers, while others selected a piece of smoke herring, or salt fish, which helped to complete the breakfast that was started at home.

Time and hard work had hardened these labourers. They were tough and gritty, often ragged looking. Many were barefooted with large cracks on the sides of their insteps and under the soles of their feet. The women carried bamboo baskets hooked in the crock of their elbows, with a cutlass inside. The men often carried their cutlasses, and when it was cocoa picking time, they also had at hand a long bamboo rod, or cocoa knife. One particular man – the taskmaster, carried a 10 feet slim bamboo rod or pole for the measuring out of the task, which was often a 10 feet square piece of ground for cutlassing and clearing.

These workers trooped along in a single file or two abreast. They criss-crossed the Estate like so many ants, scuttling about the land, while still chewing on their half-eaten breakfast. The result of these frenetic actions was for the labourers to be at their post before the shell blew, for it was the warning signal: "Time to be at your post, and if you're late, it will be trouble for you. Hurry up." The workers also needed to make as early a start with their tasks as possible, for it was demanding and never ending. So they rushed along the loose stones, the occasional deep mud and the damp, sometimes coarse grass to make, "ah early start," before the fury of the blazing sun descended on them, or before the rain drenched them.

This was the situation on an Estate on an early morning, as the Plant Disease Inspector strolled amongst the luscious plantation amidst the den of human and animal commotion. As the sun got hotter, he found a shade under some banana trees, and sat down on a large piece of old mango stump to relax. He'd organise his staff with great efficiency and aided by a very disciplined Team leader, he was always on top of his job.

Doc was by now considered to be a model worker. He was diligent, industrious and a most expert operator, the best sprayer in the gang, officially and unofficially. The attempt to humiliate him by the PDI, and being shunned and sent to Coventry by the majority of the Team had no effect on him anymore. He pushed on stoically. There was pain but he never showed it. His mum was there. And Velma! As long as she was there nothing could hurt him. The thought of her eased all pain, physical or otherwise.

After leaving her that last time, he knew that their love was rock solid. At times though, he saw her love and future happiness as welcome interludes in the drama of life, played out within the Team, for he had become the moving target. So, in a manner of speaking, Velma was also a respite from the actual relation to the real overall drama but a welcome respite she was, and knowing that, no mountain was too high for him to scale, no valley too wide for him to jump, no ocean too large to swim; he knew and felt that anything and everything was possible.

He was in charge of his own life. He was the author of his own destiny; he could write and rewrite the script for the way he wanted his life too; he could always chart a new route, finding the road that suited him best. And if it didn't work, he could tear it up and start over again. He felt strong, positive and optimistic. Nothing could shock him now, nothing could stand in his way; he felt like a seasoned warrior, like Odysseus. As the poet says in The Village blacksmith:

'Toiling, Rejoicing, Sorrowing,

on-ward through life he goes...."

Doc suspected that something was ominous, for the PDI never came around that early if there wasn't something special to attend to. So, at 11:30, when he saw the Team leader speaking with the PDI, he knew something was up. After lunch, the PDI spoke with the whole Team:

"I want to tell you boys, that the Ministry has agreed to an increase in pay and this will be backdated to the last 12 months," he said, with an air of proud self-satisfaction, and of course he had reason to be proud, for the Team had done him full justice. He was not much without them.

By now he had joined the boys who were sitting under a large flamboyant tree. Their stomachs were filled. They were in a relaxing mood, yes, under the shady tree, with a full belly. What better news can you get? This news was, if you like, metaphorically speaking, music to their ears, and they danced to the engaging tunes. Everyone looked pleased and happy. Affable smiles and praise of adulation were showered on the Plant Disease Inspector.

"Well done sah, you is we man, you did well, you did well. That is why we go always stand by you." That was Fred a lackey's lackey.

"So when we go get this increase, Mr Roland?"

"Boy wait nugh boy. Wait.........., he go tell us in time. You always try to run ahead of everything...., wait," said Peter, in reply to Doc's question.

"Ah thought he'd finished what he was saying" replied Doc.

Then he said: "It is good to know that we will get this increase."

"But how he stop so. Still trying to show up yourself, eh Mr Lawyer," said Ken with some sarcasm.

And from amongst the team: "Still playing a piece ah man. Ah doh tink this work is for you, you too good for it, Mr. Englishman."

Terry thought he asked a good question, to which Mano also agreed. And the Team Leader thought, "It would be a good idea for us to know when the increase will start."

The PDI's complacent alligator's grin, turned into a very sarcastic smirk. Now, hands in pocket and moving closer to them, he stood within a hair's breath from Doc, and in a hard gritty voice said:

"Some of you boys are too impatient, too wanting... you must learn to wait. You mustn't try to bite the hands that feed you. I am in charge here. Doh follow no lawyers in your midst. Just wait and everything will be alright."

He wiped perspiration off his forehead with his blue handkerchief and returned it to seat pocket.

"But it was Doc who first said – well who first talked – well, thought we should get a raise of pay. I remember. Ah think all of us remember if we go be honest. So he and all of us have a right to find out when dis increase coming. One year, two years, five years from now, or when we turn old and grey?" said Steadman, one of the most quiet and loyal members of the team.

When he spoke, eyebrows were raised. What was left was a ghost of a smile on the face of the PDI, not looking at anyone in particular he said:

"I did my best. I sent up all names, so I hope ... well I hope," he said hesitatingly. "We just have to wait and see."

"So that means, some might get and others may not?" asked Doc searchingly, for his feeling of uncertainty was beginning to manifest itself. They became real now, and in fact, they were true. There was a long uncomfortable silence; they too felt there was something more than the mist from the spray.

"All of us should get it," said Terry.

"Yes, yes, regardless. We do the same work. We all carry Mr Wright's piece of tool in the boiling sun," agreed Mano.

"We will have to wait and see," repeated the inspector dubiously.

And again, the uneasy silence returned. The weak voice of a birdsong, singing a weak song, like a trite, both lifeless and dull, could be overheard repeatedly. The same trills, trills which must have been sung in the same place for centuries, when the slaves must have been in a not too dis-similar condition broke a forced and unwelcome silence, which was very pleasing indeed. At that point Doc resolved that it didn't matter; altogether everyone knew that it was only him who introduced the subject of increased pay, and the Team, whatever else they thought of him remembered it well, for they recalled the time when he spoke about it privately amongst themselves.

Come what may, he knew something had been gained from his contribution. Conditions of pay will be better for everyone even if he didn't get the increase himself, but the team will benefit. Even if he didn't get it, so what? By now he could deal with whatever hand life could deal him; rough or smooth, sweet or sour, good or bad, it's okay – this is his life! He could handle it. He had the freedom of spirit within him to stand up for what he believed was right. That's what he did when he joined the Team.

The work was hard, and rough and deserved more money and he said so! Something was done about it. His action paid off; in fact he knew all this stalling and prevarication by the PDI meant that he was not recommended for the pay rise. But the other members of the team would get it. Well done! He thought. Well done! The point was made! He could face up to his problems. They were only obstacles on his road to success, and although the way ahead will be piled high with much difficulties, he could overcome them as he had done it before. By now he was accustomed to difficulties and had accepted them as part of his life; he could take the hurt that they brought.

"Hope and despondency,

Pleasure and pain,

Are mingled together,

In sunshine and rain......." said the poet.

He was certain that neither the good times nor the bad times would last forever. Men rise and fall; slavery come and slavery go; kingdoms rise and kingdoms fall. The Roman Empire lasted for 1000 years or more, and where is it now? So what? Neither the good times nor the bad times were permanent. His bad times will continue to provide rich lessons for him.

Well, look at his mum, she could hardly read and write, but she is intelligent... if she was not there... well... so bad times provide lessons in life that you cannot learn in school, all you have to do is to persevere and have patience – nothing last forever. His good times will come. And when they do, he will savour them. Those who followed his ancestors from Africa have provided useful lessons, well learnt and must not be forgotten! The life on the plantation, without lands and money and after that ... Look at today – and Grace dying from gas... he knew his good times must come. They have to. He must succeed. He can't fail. Why should he fail? He banished failure from his vocabulary. His ancestors didn't fail. The fact that he is here today is testament of their indomitable spirit.

They succeeded, and he is here to tread in their footsteps, to carry on their proud tradition to succeed against the odds; and if he doesn't get an increase (although he was sure he wouldn't) he'll move on. Mr Samuel, the local architect wants him; he already started on his correspondence course. He can let go of Plant Protection, so that he can continue to grow, for a man cannot stand still in his world, as his mother said, "As long as there is life, there is hope." So let them keep their job, if he doesn't get a pay rise, he will be moving on. Where to? He doesn't know. But he will be going, toiling, rejoicing and sorrowing, onwards through life he goes...

Each morning sees some task begin

Each evening sees it close...

Something attempted, something done ...

So said the poet.

A heavy shower of rain made everyone scamper for shelter. It stopped almost as soon as it started. It was a 'passing cloud'.

The mechanic completed the repairs on the machine and wiped his greasy hands on his khaki trousers. He went into the Rover and took out a bag with some spare parts: plugs, fan belts, filters and so on, and gave them to the Team leader. By now it was time to depart, and so they did. Mirabeau would be completed by tomorrow. The air in the Rover was thick and he had a feeling of relief when he alighted.

The next morning he rode to work on Desire Me. After yesterday's meeting he was longing to see and talk with Velma. She was the person he wanted to see most of all, besides his mother. Yes, Velma, with that calming influence she had on him. He was thinking how little time they had shared together when they met up, although it is always happy times - enjoyable times, memorable times. Marriage? They will be married one day, two or three years from now; there is a lot more to learn about each other.

Velma is clever; her educational prospects are very high. She has that earnest face, a calm spirit and a deep, relaxing gaze, like looking into a pool of fresh, clear blue water. She is exactly the person he wants to see after yesterday's meeting. And as expected, he met her on his way, just by the Reservoir. There she was! She saw him coming towards her, they smiled, her friends nudged her and moved away from her. As he went up to her, she exchanged her bag from her right to her left hand.

"Hi," he said, "those stars on your face is shining."

"Boy how you have talk so? Where is the Rover?" she asked looking at him with calm expectancy.

"I wanted to ride to work today. Ah glad ah see you." He joined her, and they started walking back towards her school. He pushed the bicycle along with his right hand, as they walked side by side, she being on the inside of the road.

"You alright?"

"Yes. I wanted to tell you that we, well I don't know for myself, but the team will be getting an increase of pay; the PDI said so yesterday."

"Well, that's good. You have been talking about that months after you started. It got you into a lot of trouble. So you see it was not all for nothing. You glad?"

"Yes, but..."

"What?"

"Well, it's nothing."

"Tell me, Doc."

"Well, I don't think I will be getting it."

"Why?"

"Well you know..."

"Because you talk up a lot. Anyhow, don't worry; even if they want to be spiteful and don't give you, everyone knows that you were the first to stick your neck out for more pay. Don't worry."

"You are very sweet," he said, toying with the freckles around her cheek.

"Is that why you didn't take the Rover this morning?"

"The truth is, I didn't feel like going to work at all today."

"Ah glad ah see you to have this talk. We always seem so busy, we don't see much of each other. The last time we spent a good long time together was the evening of Holy Innocents Harvest."

"You have your studies."

"Ah finish now. I believe I did alright. I will soon know. Mother Superior wants me to teach at the Convent from next Term, until I decide what I'm going to do."

"Let me say I'm happy for you."

"For us." She corrected.

"Well, okay for us," he agreed.

Some friends passed them on the way, because by now they were just strolling along, sometimes just stopping anywhere along the road to chat.

"You reaching me by the gap?"

"Come on, let's walk." So they kept on.

And so they strolled lazily along the road passing the entrance to her school, they made their way down the small incline down Salisbury main road. They took a left turn and followed it until they reached the turning known as the Cemetery Deep, for the burial ground is on a rise, a mound, a small hill above. Agricultural lands, especially cocoa, surround the valley. The morning sunlight shone brightly through the trees, blinding their eyes as they stood facing each other.

"Ah know I'll be late, but ah doh want to go before you kiss me."

He parked Desire Me on the side of a large hog plum tree and she rested her bag near to it. Miss Johnson passed and said good morning to him. She is a short thin young lady with many spots on her legs, and always a permanent smile on her face.

"You know her?"

"Yes. Her brother and I were in the same class at school."

When she left Doc she hastened to school and entered her room. All eyes were on her, as she sat there daydreaming, thinking about those warm sunshine kisses. She was unable to concentrate on her lessons. For a while she was experiencing the feeling of a happy, sweet, emotional pain, as she sat there reliving her recent amorous episode with Doc.

The pay increase was official, and everyone except Doc received it. In fact, it was an open secret for a few days, until one afternoon after lunch the Team Leader said to him. "I have something to tell you," and he made slow, lazy strides towards him.

"Yes, Wope Sir, the increase came through. Mr Roland told me not to tell you, but I have to. When I was making up the books for this fortnight, ah see everybody get the pay rise except you."

"You serious?" replied Doc, not appearing to be surprised.

"Yes, is true. Ah can't hide it from you. If was not for you there would not have been anything as increase pay. Ah sorry," said Wope, with a genuine note of sadness in his voice.

"I can't believe it, although I am not surprised. Ah felt it in my bones since that day in Mirabeau. You sure, sure, sure?"

"You know ah make up the books. The PDI gave me all the papers about a week now. No doubt about it," said Wope with certainty. Doc sat down on a stone and pondered for some while, thinking hard.

"People are so unfair, so worthless. All ah dem except me, eh!"

Then he resolved that the tide of time was beckoning him unto a new shore. He must follow the flow.

"Thank you Wope," he said in a resolute tone. "Ah leaving Plant Protection."

"What for?"

"You can see for yourself, Wope. Life never been easy for me. It frightens me sometimes. It intimidates me. But ah doh fraid of it. I always take my life in my own hands."

"But still let me talk to Mr Roland about it for you."

"For me?"

"Well ah din mean it that way. I will tell him it's not right he did not recommend you for the increase, for in the first place you were the one who first said we should get more money for the work we're doing. You was the one. Ah go tell him that. He listens to me. He must change his mind."

"You can talk, Wope. Ah appreciate the effort. You are a good friend. A real pal; but on Friday I will give my notice. Ah go tell Mr Roland ah leaving, but ah telling you first," said Doc with an air of finality.

"Doc, trust me, ah go get him to change his mind, take it easy. Give it a little time."

"Wope, it's time for me to go. It's a sign. I'm here too long. Spraying is not a profession. He is doing me a good turn in a way. Wope, I took this job only for a time. Ah know ah din say for how long, but I can see it's time for me to move on. Wope, I cannot and must not allow people to humiliate me so. To try and put me down, to try and devalue me life. There is hope for my life, Wope Sir! All this is only temporary. Wope, I must not," and he stressed on the 'must.'

"I must not stay around people who want to put blight on my life, who want to make me feel like nothing. Where there is life, there is hope. Hope!" he repeated in that same air of completeness.

There was anger and resentment in his voice, for he spoke in a bitter tone. But by now Doc was master of his emotions. The same voice carried pride, dignity, optimism and courage. Leaving Wope standing there, he went over to his machine. Mano helped put it on his back and off he went through the bananas executing his work proudly. The PDI was standing up by the Rover near to the driver. Wope joined them, as they all admitted, and spoke about the high standard of his work.

"Not many could handle a machine like that," said the driver.

The afternoon session completed, it was time go. The driver went inside the Rover, and everyone (except the PDI) was scrambling to get in. Doc came forward with slow, resolute purposeful strides, and said to Mr Roland:

"I'll be leaving in two weeks' time sir. You have my notice from today."

It was like a bombshell. Everyone heard him. This was followed by an austere silence. No one spoke. Mr Roland's forehead became corrugated and his face as sour as vinegar. A grey, sombre cloud descended, and for a moment enveloped everyone and shaded out the evening sun. It seemed an age before the cloud was lifted. The Rover moved off slowly but the air was like a six-inch wall, for no one spoke until he unlighted half way through his destination.

He walked slowly with both hands in his pockets. He was hoping to meet Velma, but her friends told him she took the bus home. He told no one about his decision to quit Plant Protection.

He felt as if the chaos had come to an end. His spirit was lifted; he felt as though he wanted to fly. He felt fine. Pain is often twinned with pleasure.

He shouted to Ghost on his way home and after dinner he sat down on the step and gazed at that eternal blanket.

"Ah wonder what's up there; everything seems so peaceful," he murmured.

Two days passed before he told her what she now already knew, that he had given in his notice to quit Plant Protection. On their way home one afternoon before he opened his mouth, she cut him short.

"Ah know. Don't forget ah have me pick up in the gang," she said laughing at Doc's consternation, as she ran across the road to pick up a mango and a bicycle vooshed past close to her. The rider shouted out her name as he ziz-zagged to avoid hitting her.

"Doc," she said, "I know that you are a proud and sensitive man, and when you said that you did not get the increase, after all you did for the gang, I know – well I guessed you would leave. I believe it's a good idea."

"We are one," she said to her future husband, "Sink or float, we are in the same boat."

Doc was touched. He knew he could count on her but at this important time in their relationship, he thought she might have had some reservation, thinking perhaps that he is fickle and unstable. Paraclete, tailoring and now Plan Protection. Could she trust him? Is he an indecisive kind of person who does not know his own mind? Her support reassured him. He felt stronger, knowing that he had done the right thing.

"You have always been a special person to me, Vel. Now I have no doubt about it. I had that feeling from the second time we met up on the bridge in Paraclete. Although we never spoke a word to each other, I had the feeling that we had something special. I couldn't put my finger on it, but I just knew it. And to date, nothing in my whole heart has changed about you. My life's pledge is to serve you lovingly. That's the most important thing to me, Vel... to lovingly serve you," he repeated, with surprising eloquence, thought Velma.

"I'll complete my course in Blue Print reading."

"Yes," she assented.

"I know you would finish anything you put your mind to. I want to continue loving you too. No one else matters to me except you." She said, sidling closer to him.

"Let's break track and pass by the Villa. We have some lands there that I want to show you - piece of it could be ours, if we want it."

"I...I don't know..." he hesitated.

"Don't say anything. I know you. You would want us to buy our own lands. We could buy from mum. Dad said piece of this land is for me anyway."

"Anyhow, why don't we leave the visit to the Villa for another day? I promise mum I'll be home early. I have to help her with a few things. Not today."

"Tomorrow?" she asked quietly turning up her eyes at him.

"You won't be busy?"

"No. You know all schoolwork is over. Exam is over. I'm free! And Janelle is going back to Town," she said expressively.

"Mum is better, and things at home are back to normal. Well near normal because we are still living in Deblando but things coming on good, so Janelle is going back to work and I'm going with her to see her home and ting. If you're not busy you can come with me."

Doc agreed to accompany her to Town. Going to Town is like going to a different country, and he was very keen on the idea to go over to St George's.

The next day, Saturday, they, all three boarded the bus 'Why Worry', and travelled to St George's. The owner of 'Why Worry' was a tall, lanky man with a square jaw and a high forehead. He was wearing Khaki pants and shirt (American material, which was lighter than the British drill type). His name was Roy, but no one called him by his name. Everyone called him 'Why Worry'. He always replied, "Man must live."

Janelle paid the fare for all three of them, after some rocking and rolling, twisting and bumping, they reached the Capital. Janelle took them through what seemed to them a strange land. One Evans boy saw them and shouted, "Country bookie come to Town." Janelle was living on Green Street, near an alley not too far from the Methodist Church, which she attended.

"But you're Catholic," said her cousin.

"A church is a church, it's the same God."

They took the long way round, because she wanted to show them a few places, so they ambled around, spending sometime on the Carenage enjoying the view and the water lapping against the wall so close to the road; then they turned up some tiny, twisted, hilly roads, and after about an hour they were home, which was different from Deblando. They had cake and lemonade with lots of ice; they strolled around the house, meeting a number of different people. Then Janelle and Velma held a little conference in the bedroom.

Soon afterwards they left Town and returned home. When they got back to Grenville, they headed for The Villa, passing up Cook Hill. Arriving at the Village Junction, they turned left and walked along the road towards their destination.

They entered the plot which was a large rectangular piece of land, which she pointed out to him. It was full of fruits and vegetables, but a large part of it was almost empty, apart from the luxurious long grass that spread out covering a large plain of table land that jutted out over Harford Village. The Grenville Harbour appeared in a wide panoramic view, and the ocean seemed as though it was touching the horizon, offering a most picturesque view. It is the part Velma wanted them (to have) to build their home.

Doc thought it was a beautiful place. They wandered about for a while and then he picked two yellowish tangerines, and they sat down on the low branch of a guava tree and ate the fruit, he feeding her peg by peg. Afterwards, they sat down in a contemplative mood. Again, he told her how much he liked the place but he was taking time to absorb it. He knew he could live there, but how? Marriage means responsibility. He would like to take his full share of it, and he must begin by standing on his own two feet first.

"Now I know you are the most important person to me," he said in a faraway tone, as if he was speaking to himself.

"I'm glad you like it."

"We'll come back to see it again – earlier in the day some other time. I'd like to see it again."

"Okay," she said, holding him around his waist.

"At last," he said, "you are actually mine - we are one. I can see, in a few...well not long again, Velma my angel, we will sleep together in the same bed, in each other's arms. Think about that," he said with emotion.

"All your life will be mines, Doc, and all my life will be yours."

Sitting on the grass, or more exactly, leaning on their elbows, they were in their own heaven enjoying their own company and the view from the hill across the wide panoramic view of the harbour. By now the distant starlight twinkled on the ocean.

"My bounty is as boundless as the sea," she said. "My love is as deep, the more I give you, the more I have, for both are infinite," she quoted ecstatically.

And so their hearts sang as they lay down, enveloped amongst the long, smooth grass on the tableland in The Villa. Not long afterwards they made their way home.

Back to Plant Protection and by now everyone in The team knew about his decision to quit. Terry, Wope and Mano tried to persuade him to stay. He bluntly refused.

"No, I'm going," he said.

If he stayed, he knew that his spirit would be crushed by the boulder of injustice. Of course, he would earn his money and even get a back pay, but he couldn't live with what was not right for him. He was treated unjustly in the Team when all he did was help to improve conditions for all. They treated him most disgracefully and he couldn't live with that.

There was nothing more for him in Plant Protection anyhow. At the end of the day all you can do is spray bananas. Awright, but in a way he also wanted more out of life. Plant Protection won't afford him the opportunity to soar in the atmosphere of freedom while his soul was languishing for room to soar since leaving the Briggs. He will go.

The PDI, in a state of humility after his talk with The Team Leader, attempted to make it up to Doc, for the weight of the Team was thrown behind Doc, following from his decision to leave the job.

The PDI tried to make him change his mind, appeased him, if you like, for his prestige too was at stake. He is the boss, he can't go running after a worker who wants to move on from his employ.

On the other hand, his conscience was dogging him, for he knew that had it not been for his behaviour, Doc would not have left Plant Protection; well not yet anyway. His conscience was pricking him. He saw himself personally responsible, and the members of the Team (including the driver) did not fail to make it known openly to him or otherwise. He knew that Doc was that vanguard for the changes in the Team, both attitudinally and financially. They got their increase because of *his* initiative (the PDI too benefited financially).

There was also the personal prestige of PDI in the country. His salary notched up a point or two above the others. His Team was the most advanced spraying team too, and the best sprayer within his team was Doc, a man with ability and initiative. So the PDI, still wishing to persuade Doc to change his mind, approached him with an unusual level of humility, nibbling at a piece of humble pie.

He began by indirectly apologising to Doc for his 'oversight' for not advancing Doc's name for the increased pay, and promised to get Doc's increase back dated. He told him that Wope, the Team

Leader and he, the PDI, were now working on his papers so that it can go through before the end of the month, he would take it to Town at the office in Tanteen himself, personally.

"I don't want to lose you, George. I know I am partly responsible for your decision," he apologised.

"I'm sorry I've acted the way I did."

He was bending over backwards to have him stay. Doc sat down on a piece of nutmeg plank looking at him dispassionately.

"Listen George," he said on that final morning as he made an almost desperate last-ditch attack, using all his persuasive powers to encourage Doc to withdraw his resignation:

"Man, we expanding Plant Protection you know, because of the work of the Team, I'm given a new area down in Mama Cannes to run. Yes, we expanding. I will need more men and of course a Team Leader." Here he relaxed into a smile and pushed both hands into his pockets.

"I would like you to take up the Team leader's post in Mama Cannes, Doc. This should be coming up in about two or three months' time. All the boys think you are the best man for the post what do you say?"

"I thank you Sir, and the members of the Team for considering me so highly, but I'm leaving Sir," said Doc calmly.

"Why? You can forgive a mistake," said the boss flabbergasted.

"You see Sir, I cannot stand by and watch injustice and unfairness taking place and keep my mouth shut. Not me Sir. It is not right. If you keep your mouth shut against injustice, you're nobody and we all go end up as a race. If people don't talk up when something is wrong, the strong will continue to walk over the weak, and the rich over the poor. But strong or weak, rich or poor, we are all human beings and God made us all, Mr Roland."

"What you looking for? What you want, fame?" retorted the by now disappointed and somewhat shamed-faced Plant Disease Inspector.

Shamed faced because he had made concessions to try and persuade Doc to change his mind, concessions that he, the boss, the Plant Disease Inspector with a Team of working men under him, should not have made. And to be rejected, he felt humiliated. His mind ran back on what he thought of Doc in the first place, that he was ambitious, wanted fame and possibly wanted to step into his shoes.

"No Sir, ah doh want no fame. You won't understand." Then he paused, while the PDI stood staring him in the face with hate in his eyes.

Doc, on reflection then said: "You really want to know why I'm leaving? Ah leaving for meself. Yes Sir, for meself. Ah have to grow with life Sir. And life is about change and growth. Ah must leave, Sir, because ah have to grow with life."

"As Team leader you can grow."

"No Sir, too much has been done with PPD to try and beat me down already. Ah have to grow in new soil, and under different conditions, but thank you again Sah."

He continued looking at Doc with some interesting curiosity, thinking: "What is he looking for? What does he want?" He wondered, but was unable to figure out his motives.

In the end he said: "You are a strange young man who have a lot of courage and I respect you for that, although I believe you could be mistaken. How you go live? I could imagine it will be very difficult for you. Painful to say the least."

"Yes Sir, I know it will be painful. But life, the little I know of it, is that you don't get change and you can't grow without pains. Life begins with pain. You born in pain. Life is a constant struggle. All ah doing is trying to face up to it. Even when I leave here and ah don't know where exactly I'm going, I might come across other painful experiences for me.

Is better this way Sir; is when people doh face up to difficult problems and try to hide away from it instead, when dey want to cry but have to laugh, when they want to say yes instead of no, when dey want to shout and scream instead of keeping quiet and gritting their teeth; then that's a lot of pain they going through and dey have to live with dis pain. With me, when it comes to that, ah leggo. Ah quit. Ah look out for another opportunity as I am doing right now."

"But is there another way?"

"I don't know if there is. Ah sure there is for many people, but for me, is a different thing - a different kind of experience. Ah meet up a lot of difficulties and pain from my first real job to this one. I was often insulted and humiliated a few times too, but it was a job. Ah wanted food and clothes, and ah wanted to help my mother too, so ah stick it for a short time.

Ah gain knowledge and experience even as a yard boy, ah learn something. But then, like now, ah had to move on. Ah was growing, my mind was expanding – like now – growth and expansion. Ah leave, and went to learn tailoring. It was better than a yard boy's job. Ah learn to sew, ah learn something which I have up here," pointing to his head.

"Ah can't forget that. I can't unlearn being a Tailor. Although I didn't make a lot of money and ah wanted to move, you know?

And so I get this job with you, well, Plant Protection. Dey say ah make trouble, you say ah playing man. Ah have problems with some of the boys and with you. Ah can't continue dis way, so ah leaving. Ah must leave. I'm doing it for myself. For me, Sir. For me, Mr. Roland," with his right hand beating his chest. "For me," he repeated emphatically with a hard thud on his vital organ.

All that time Mr Roland stood still, almost at attention with an equally attentive ear, listening to this amazing young man. As if he, the PDI was a student and Doc the teacher.

After some time, he heaved a sigh of resignation, stamped his feet saying, "Doc you are a courageous young man. I don't agree with all what you say, but I respect you for your convictions, for you have the guts, courage and the determination too, to support your convictions. I don't know what your mission is, but I don't believe anyone can stand in your way to stop you."

Then he walked away with uncertain steps, and a puzzled, doubtful look on his face. Now he felt he was carrying the world on his back and not even feeling the weight, thus on and on he must go. During his forward movement, he summoned up support. Yes, the support of the sixty million or so men, women and children – his African ancestors whose souls are lying in the Atlantic, those who did not make it to the other side of the world. He conjured up their spirits to help him along. They drove off and left him sitting there, not for the first time and a definite silence followed throughout the journey.

"*Every bondsman*" said the poet, "*in his own hand bears the power to cancel his captivity*." He thought.

It was something very special he learned from Sally-Ann. He remained sitting there after they left, pondering, trying to find a meaning to express how he felt. There was no way of describing it. He racked his brains. It seemed comical: a man poor as a cockroach, spitting out, as it was his personal philosophy; one of pride and courage straight in the face of his boss. He felt he'd won but it was a pyrrhic victory – it was neither funny nor tragic. He neither laughed nor cried; there was joy and there was despair. For the umpteenth time in his life he ask himself:

"O Gwad, what ah go do?"

Then he answered his own question: "There is Hope. Ah going to see Mr Samuels tomorrow and ask him for a job in the building trade."

Yes, he had to substantiate his victory. He would devote his future working life to Construction and he and Velma would be man and wife. Yes! That's what he would do. He talked to his Mum and to his Father who was himself a Builder; and they both agreed that Mr Samuels was the best builder around. He's no stranger and he and young Samuels, although having an 18-year difference in age, were very good friends. A week later he and Velma met in Grenville by the jetty, not far from the Police Station. It was a cool evening and they sat down on some crates, where he held and squeezed her hand and broke the news of his new plans to her.

"Doc," she said, "Ah know we go make it. That's the time we've been waiting for. From now on our road will be paved with success." Then she kissed his forehead.

Following this, she said in a quiet voice: "I love teaching, Doc, and ah know building is in your blood, ah know. No more changing Doc."

"No, Vel. The next move we go make is to build we house and finally join our hands and hearts together." And so it was.

Two years later, Doc had consolidated his position with the Samuels – jobs, Contracts were plentiful both from public works and private individuals. Samuels junior was mainly working on projects in Town, Lance-Aux- Epines and True Blue. Leroy (that's his first name) asked his father if he would allow Doc to join him there; he wanted someone to help with some supervisory work.

"You must wear a good boots and doh go skylarking in Town; when you country boys go to town you all get so excited..."

"...No, sir," said Leroy, "remember ah know de place. Ah school dey."

"Anyhow, no risks. Good boots ah say again, and no jappa-jappa work. Be careful Doc, with some of the labourers in Town. Dey sometimes give you a six for a nine."

"Ah go be careful Sir. Ah go keep an observant eye open all the time."

This was another, wider scope on the business for Doc. The beginning of greater success was to follow. But life is tenuous and accidents happen; and one soggy afternoon after many heavy showers of rain Mr Samuels (Sr.) while examining piece of plastering work on a house in La Fortune, perched on a hill, the foot of the scaffolding moved and the whole thing fell on him. He died instantly.

It was tragic and it was a great loss to everyone. Leroy took it very hard as expected, and many sorrowful tears were shed for his loss. After a period of mourning, consultations and deliberations, young Samuels proposed a Partnership with Doc. Doc welcomed the offer and together they made the business one of the most successful in the country.

John Mc Kenzie Samuels and George Leroy Awosa Williams Construction Company etcetera, etcetera.

And so it was.

- VIII -

The day of the wedding was as bright and promising as the event that was to follow; and both Heaven and Earth had been kind to them. The ceremony was held in the church, which was a stone's throw from the Convent in Grenville, attended by Velma, and where she now taught.

The sky was a clear Caribbean blue, apart from wisps of cottony clouds floating feather-like way up in the distant sky, looking like miniature islands set in a sapphire sea. In this very beautiful warm tropical climate of Grenada, on that very momentous day, Mother Nature had adorned herself with an array of colourful Feminine garments.

There were the Bougainvillea displaying themselves in varied colours with grace and charm. The Hibiscus smiled and bowed as if in greetings to the party as the soft breeze blew through them. The Buttercups, in the middle of the garden in the Grotto, displayed their deep yellow flowers, between their thick green leaves, smiled too, but alluringly, and sensually commanding, or demanding attention. The Oleander stood tall with a mixture of bright colours like liveried decorated sentinels on the edge of the Grotto. Coconut palms swayed and bent like graceful Watusi dancers and bowed in obedience to Mother Nature's bidding. It was a combination of wedding ceremony and a carnival; with Nature in full array displaying itself on the earth's stage.

It came as no surprise to learn that Velma made the most charming bride. Her sunshine smile was like a rose in full bloom. Her bridal gown was made with professional elegance and it befitted the person who carried it with grace and charm. It trailed after her gracefully and the bride with her natural wholesomeness of person, did it justice.

Janelle was the chief bridesmaid (handmaiden) followed by Janet and others. They all wore little Coronets edged with green cocoa and nutmeg leaves with pieces of Bougainvillea on their heads making them look like Grecian Goddesses, yet they were only dimly lit stars surrounding and adorning Velma, the Moon.

Ghost had the Honour to be the Best man. He was now a responsible young man and he stood impressively close to Doc; somehow he looked a little uncomfortable, clad in his suit and tie. Nevertheless, he stood shoulder to shoulder with his Seasoned Comrade.

It was a solemn ceremony, but not dull. The congregation was reflecting the brightness of the sun, followed by a soft tropical breeze which blew lovingly through them. Everyone was happy, but none more so than Mr. and Mrs. Williams, the former in a well-tailored suit made my Mr. Gilbert of his tailoring days.

The wedding bells chimed loving harmonious notes and the organ played its melodious tune, while friends and relations sang lustily from their hearts, as the bride and groom strolled graciously - very slowly down the aisle to the tune of 'Here Comes the Bride'. Without a doubt, Heaven and Earth had united to bless the occasion, and so it was.

The wedding reception was held in Velma's mother's home in La Fillette, now that they had returned there. When the bride and groom came out of the car and entered the gap to the house, they passed through a specially constructed arch. It was made from coconut branches and had bamboo for the posts. They were greeted by showers of rose petals and various flowers. Also, showers of rice and corn were thrown at them by two children, a girl and boy, standing on each side of the arch. Emotions were unashamedly displayed amongst the frenzy of joviality where everyone hugged and kissed everyone else, and most of all everyone wanted to kiss the bride.

Slowly but surely the Master of ceremony (MC) made his entrance. He was a tall self-important looking lean man with a number of silver rings on his fingers. He wore a white long sleeved shirt, a flannel pants and a two-tone black and white shoes. After clearing his throat several times the enthusiasm subsided and he got the attention he wanted. Mr Milton Bowen, warmly introduced the bride and groom (as if he needed to) and said how many years he knew them. Since the bride was learning to walk and the groom was in shirt tails.

"At last," he said "love conquers all," and he quoted from Shakespeare's Romeo and Juliet to underscore his point.

"Brother and sisters, ladies and gentlemen," he continued, "we have before us a very beautiful young lady," looking at Velma, "and a most handsome young man," eyes in Doc's direction, "recently joined together in the union of holy matrimony. We hope and pray that this union shall never be broken, and we will do everything we possibly can to help and support these two young people. We plead with everyone here tonight to do whatever is possible to help them stay strong.

We must also call upon the assistance of our Ancestors to look kindly and lovingly and to rain down their blessings on Doc and Velma, their loving and dutiful children. Velma and Doc – Mr. and Mrs. Williams." He ended with a flourishing eloquence. Then he fished out a handkerchief from his back pocket, to stem the flow of perspiration coming down his face.

"Now ladies and gentlemen, let's drink a toast to this happy couple." And so they did. Then men outside poured a libation in each corner of the hall and rubbed their feet in it (the libation). Some shattered their glasses on the wall and others broke eggs saying:

"This is for the spirits and it will bring the bride and groom luck."

Then the Master of Ceremonies asked them to put their hands together. This they did in earnest and the hall resounded with deafening claps and shouts of:

"He's a jolly good fellow..."

Doc was congratulated by Mr. Gilbert, Ray and Congo, then the Team leader and Mano from the Plant Protection. The merriment followed in a frenzy of euphoria, where everyone kissed and hugged everyone else. This state of merriment dominated the event till late into the evening.

It was time for the happy couple to say farewell and this they did. It was dark when they arrived at their home in The Villa. The house was built on the table-land above Harford Village. It was called **"Nefertari's Villa"**, built by young Samuels. Doc opened the door but they did not enter at once.

They stood on the veranda looking up at the full moon, now rising and getting brighter, seen between Telescope and Marquis Rocks.

Then his mind returned to the words of the poet as if living a road to his success: *"Thanks, thanks, thanks to you my worthy friend for the lesson you have taught, thus on the flaming forge of life our fortune must be wrought. Thus on the sounding anvil shape each burning deed and thought"*.

They embraced, and tears of love and happiness flowed in equal measure, then they entered their home.

He led her into the bridal chambers and closed the door.

Nothing is ever finished......
Struggles are never truly concluded.
Sometimes we have to re-dream our lives
And life can always be used to create
More light.

BEN OKRI
SONGS OF ENCHANTMENT
WINNER OF THE 1991 BOOKER PRIZE

Acknowledgements

Many thanks to Mrs. Orvieto Williams for the typing of the text from a hand that is not often easy to read; also for her helpful suggestions for improvement and development of the story.

To Gail for advice on presentation and printing.

To **Alicia Amada** for her continued patience in the typing of the final draft of the book.

To **Mr. Thomas Chase MA,** Modern Literatures (Hons); Didactics French and Foreign Language (Hons); Philosophy in Culture of the Western World. He is a Poet, Researcher and Author of: Abridged Handbook of Grenadian Creole, English and French names. To him I am indebted, for his critical comments and assessment of this work.

Thanks to **Angie** for her help and assistance in various ways.

And of course to the memory of the **Grenadian Estate Labourers.**

And to **Matty, Faith, 'WOPE'** and the **PPB's,** for their inspiration.

To **Mr. Clyde Belfon,** Language Arts Lecturer, Writer, Teacher Education Department, T.A. Marryshow Community College, Grenada for his enthusiasm in reading and critically assessing the text and for his introduction to this work.